Greenwich Council
Library & Information Service

IN HOUSE
QUALITY
SYSTEMS

Coldharbour Library
William Barefoot Drive, SE9 3AY
020 8857 7346

Please return by the last date shown

– 7 MAY 2010

2 3 APR 2012

Thank
You!

To renew, please contact any Greenwich library

| Issue: 02 | Issue Date: 06.06.00 | Ref: RM.RBL.LIS |

A PHOTOHISTORY OF WORLD WAR ONE

PHILIP J. HAYTHORNTHWAITE

ARMS AND
ARMOUR

1. The standing armies of all nations were supplemented by the calling to the colours of reservists of various kinds, and by encouraging mass enlistment: this is a typical group of British recruits, probably to the Royal Engineers, photographed in September 1914 at Gillingham, Kent. A caption on the original photograph states 'having a fine time . . .'

Arms and Armour Press
A Cassell Imprint
Villiers House, 41-47 Strand, London WC2N 5JE.

Distributed in the USA by Sterling Publishing Co. Inc., 387 Park Avenue South, New York, NY 10016-8810.

Distributed in Australia by Capricorn Link (Australia) Pty. Ltd, P.O. Box 665, Lane Cove, New South Wales 2066.

Originally published 1989–90 as five individual volumes in the *fotofax* series.

British Library Cataloguing-in-Publication Data: a catalogue record for this book is available from the British Library

ISBN 1-85409-210-3

Designed and edited by DAG Publications Ltd. Typeset by Ronset Typesetters, Darwen, Lancashire; camerawork by M&E Reproductions, North Fambridge, Essex; printed and bound in Great Britain.

WORLD WAR ONE:
1914

▲2

2. Strangely, the commencement of hostilities was greeted with jubilation in certain quarters throughout Europe; here, Austrian officer-cadets salute their Emperor. All wear the standard soft peaked cap and greatcoat in pike-grey (*Hechtgrau*), though the officer taking the salute wears the stiff-sided version of the kepi which was restricted to staff and general officers.

3. Departing for the front: French infantry march out of Paris to the cheers of the population. Among the least modern of the uniforms of the combatant nations, the French infantry had a single-breasted blue tunic, but the rank-and-file wore a dark-blue double-breasted greatcoat, with red collar-patches bearing the regimental number in blue. The scarlet kepi had a blue band bearing the regimental number in red, but for active service the red was concealed by the 1912-pattern blue-grey fabric cap-cover. The red (*garance*) trousers even at this early stage of the war were sometimes covered by blue-grey overalls.

▼3

INTRODUCTION

When 'The Great War' broke out in the late summer of 1914, the concept of camouflaged uniform had not been accepted by some of the combatant nations, with the result that some troops sported styles of dress more attuned to the mid-19th century than to a 'modern' war. In matters of uniform, Britain was among the most advanced of all the European nations, having adopted a universl khaki serge 'service dress' as early as 1902, largely as a result of the lessons of the Boer War. Germany had introduced a uniform of field-grey in 1910, but retained the old spiked helmet (*Pickelhaube*), although with a camouflaged cover; other troops wore the shako, hussars the fur busby and the lancers the traditional *czapka*. From her experience in the Russo-Japanese War, Russia had evolved a light greenish-khaki service uniform by 1907; the Austrians introduced a pike-grey uniform in 1909, but their cavalry still retained their old coloured uniforms. Belgium was in course of a degree of uniform-modernization, but still retained the shako and cavalry uniforms which included *czapkas* and red trousers. Of all the major combatants in 1914, France's army wore the most out-dated uniform, for though one of the most powerful in the world and with considerable experience of colonial warfare, the military establishment had steadfastly resisted modernization. Experiments had been made to find a more practical service-dress, including a blue-beige uniform in 1906, a khaki uniform with felt helmet (*tenue réséda*) in 1910–12, and 'horizon blue' with leather or steel helmet in 1912, but none had been adopted and the army took the field in 1914 wearing blue coats with red kepi and trousers, and cuirassiers still wearing breastplates and maned helmets, uniforms more suited to the 1850s. The more minor combatant nations were influenced by the styles of one or other of the major powers, but in the Balkan states of Serbia and Montenegro the issue of uniforms was not comprehensive and many of the combatants wore only scraps of issue uniform, or even entirely civilian clothing.

The illustrations here were almost all taken on active service in 1914, during the opening campaigns of the war; a few exceptions are included only because they illustrate the uniform-style especially well. Numerous illustrated periodicals were published at the time, though care should be taken when referring to these, as contemporary captions can be misleading; many of the photographs published as ostensible 'war' pictures in 1914 actually depict pre-war manoeuvres, including a famous example reputedly showing French vedettes searching for Germans, but actually photographed in 1911 and showing the experimental *tenue réséda*!

▲4　▼5

▼6

4. French cuirassiers marching through Paris *en route* to the war; a British girl distributes packets of cigarettes. Amazingly archaic, these troopers wear the regulation dark-blue tunic (black for officers) with red facings, and red breeches with black stripes; they retain the iron cuirass with brass shoulder-scales and the maned helmet, though the latter was covered with fabric (of various shades) as a concession to active service.

5. The campaign uniform of the German Army in the first year of the war was the 1910-pattern field-grey (a lighter and less greenish shade than that worn later), with deep cuffs, coloured piping according to the branch of service and shoulder-straps bearing the regimental designation; greatcoat with coloured collar-patches, brown leather equipment and hide knapsack, and the spiked helmet or *Pickelhaube*. This is an infantry outpost in Belgium during the first advance.'

6. German infantry halted on the road near Brussels, with regimental transport in the background. The most distinctive item of German uniform, which became a symbol of German militarism, was the spiked helmet. Made of black leather, it had a brass spike and large brass plate (white-metal for some regiments) in the shape of the Imperial eagle, though regimental distinctions existed and some states displayed their own coats of arms. In the field the *Pickelhaube* had a field-grey cloth cover with regimental number on the front (originally red, green after August 1914), a number repeated in red on the field-grey shoulder-straps of the tunic. The unit illustrated is Regt. No. 36, 'von Blumenthal', from Magdeburg, part of IV Corps in 1914.

7. A German infantry band, apparently in the advance on Belgium, with army transport-wagons in the background. This is presumably a brigade or divisional band, assembled from the musicians of the component regiments, as a number of

7▲

different identities appear on the covers of the *Pickelhauben*. None wear the laced, projecting wings (*Waffenrock*) on the shoulders of the tunic which traditionally distinguished

musicians.

8. The German Army laid great importance upon the machine-gun, and in addition to the machine-gun sections in each infantry regiment, special machine-gun units were formed. This infantry company is dug-in in a shallow trench in Belgium, the men's equipment being placed at the rear of the firing-line. Note the dragging-harness worn by three of the machine-gun crew; mounted on a four-legged sledge and weighing 140lb, the gun was carried by two men, one at each end of the sledge.

8▼

9. German machine-gun post in a hastily constructed defensive position, believed to be in the vicinity of Antwerp. The shoulder-strap numerals identify the unit as the Grenadier Regiment No. 12, 'Prinz Carl von Preussen' (2nd Brandenburg), a unit whose home district was Frankfurt and which in 1914 formed part of III Corps of von Kluck's First Army.

10. German artillerymen manhandling a field-gun into position in Belgium. This illustrates the design of the flaps on the rear skirts of the 1910-pattern *Waffenrock* (tunic); the artillery had red piping on the skirts and tunic front, but black piping on the collar and cuffs. Artillery helmets had a ball finial instead of a spike, which was obvious even when helmet-covers were worn, as here; compare with the spiked infantry helmet at extreme right. The greatcoat worn bandolier-style was a common practice. The wicker basket upon the gun-trail was a carrier for half a dozen shells, to enable the gun to open fire immediately.

▲9   ▼10

11. German hussars in Brussels, a scene which more resembles an earlier age. The fur busby or *colback* was worn on active service without its decorative cloth 'bag' and with a field-grey cover, with an oval cockade on the front of the style also worn on the shako. The field-grey hussar tunic or *Atila* had five field-grey braid loops across the breast and braid 'Austrian knots' at the point of the cuffs; the shoulder-straps were formed of two-colour braid, the regimental button colour (yellow or white) and the colour of the full-dress *Atila*. The officers in the foreground wear the busby without a cover, with the chinstrap fastened around the fur. Note the regimental standard in the background, and the laced belt of its bearer.

12. The British Army wore a universal uniform of khaki serge, introduced in 1902, the tunic having a turndown collar and patch pockets, with khaki trousers and puttees. Buttons were brass (allowed to tarnish on active service) and brass regimental titles were worn upon the shoulder-straps. The head-dress was a khaki cloth cap (worn here with khaki cover), bearing the regimental badge on the front, in this case that of the Royal Army Medical Corps; note also the Red Cross sleeve-badge. The equipment was normally of khaki-green webbing, but old leather equipment was not uncommon.

11▲

12▲   13▼

13. British officers' uniform resembled that of the rank-and-file, except for the design of the collar, and the patches on the cuffs, edged with khaki braid, bearing the rank insignia, in this case the single star of a second lieutenant; the lines of braid around the top of the cuff increased with rank. The brown leather belt was of the pattern known as 'Sam Browne', and could be worn with two shoulder-braces instead of the more common single brace. The cap and collar-badges illustrated (bronzed for service dress) are those of the Loyal Regiment (North Lancashire).

▲16

▲14 ▼15

14. A defensive position near Antwerp: British Royal Marines, wearing the khaki uniform which replaced the blue tunic and trousers and German-style 'Brodrick' cap worn by the Marines who had landed at Ostend. The Maxim gun in the foreground was used until the adoption of the Vickers machine-gun in 1915; although it was the infantry's main support weapon it existed in very small numbers when compared with the German Army: initially each infantry unit had only two Maxims. The position here is typical of those utilized in the early stages of the war, when the mobile nature of the fighting precluded the construction of extensive earthworks.

15. British cavalrymen passing through Termonde, south-west of Antwerp. The cavalry wore the same khaki 1902-pattern tunic as the infantry, but retained the 1903-pattern leather bandolier equipment abandoned by the infantry in favour of the 1908 web pattern. Visible here is the 1908-pattern cavalry sabre, carried at the left of the saddle, and note also the canvas bucket slung over the scabbard by the horseman at left. The Lee-Enfield magazine rifle was carried in a leather 'scabbard' at the right of the saddle, behind the rider's leg.

16. British sailors manning the defences of Antwerp. The British 'naval brigade' sent to Antwerp to assist the Belgians included bluejackets as well as Royal Marines; the former wore their blue naval uniform, landing rig including leather equipment, which in this photograph appears to resemble items of the 1888-pattern valise equipment, known as the 'Slade-Wallace'. Like the army, they were armed with the Lee-Enfield magazine rifle capable of a rate of fire of 15 rounds per minute in expert hands.

17. Not all the members of the British forces who landed on the continent in 1914 were officially enlisted; photographed on their return from Antwerp with two khaki-clad members of the Royal Marine Light Infantry, this group of the Brierfield Ambulance Corps (Lancashire) represent the civilian medical personnel who supplemented those of the services. This unit apparently served in the battle wearing their blue civilian uniform; 'It was like hell let loose,' one of them commented!

N.B. 15, 16 + 17 *for captains pose!*

17▲

18. British cavalry watering their horses by a French river. In the modernization which followed the Boer War, from 1903 the lance was classified as a purely ceremonial weapon; but the 'lance lobby' was sufficiently influential to have it re-classified as a combatant weapon in 1909, and as such it was carried in 1914 (in common with the armies of many other European nations). Note the khaki neck-shades attached to the rear of the caps, worn in hot weather.

18▼

▲20

19. Many armies used bicycles for units of scouts. This British lance-corporal, receiving directions from a French civilian, wears the full 1908 web equipment (less the knapsack), with haversack and 1907-pattern bayonet at the left side; other equipment (including rifle and a chipped enamel mug) is lashed to the cycle. He wears the brass crossed-flags badge of a trained signaller on the left forearm, carries a binocular-case and has furled signal-flags tied to the cross-bar of the bicycle.

20. A British Maxim-gun section on the march, probably in the operations around Mons. Each British infantry unit had a Maxim section of two guns, served by an officer and twelve men, mostly expert marksmen. In addition to the Maxim itself, each gun was equipped with 3,500 rounds with a further 8,000 in reserve, necessitating the use of mule-transport. The men illustrated wear the 1908 web equipment, though the sergeant in command is also equipped with a pistol-holster, an item not normally carried by infantry NCOs.

▲19   ▼21

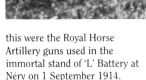

21. A British field-gun in action across a country lane, partly camouflaged by the hedgerows. The principal weapons of the mobile field artillery were the 13pdr and 18pdr guns, with ammunition carried in their limbers, one sited here to the right of the fieldpiece. The NCO at the rear is resting upon a swivelling bar which could be used as a seat. 13pdrs similar to this were the Royal Horse Artillery guns used in the immortal stand of 'L' Battery at Néry on 1 September 1914.

22. A British heavy gun at the moment of firing, showing the great recoil of the barrel. The moving barrel absorbed the recoil which otherwise would caused the gun to roll back many yards. The gunners in action here are in typical active-service dress, some wearing woollen cap-comforters, and all are protecting their ears from the blast.

23. The British Expeditionary Force was very rapidly in the front line; here a battalion breaks its march in a Belgian street, near Mons, rifles being stacked in the road and equipment piled alongside. This is apparently a unit of the Royal Welch Fusiliers (the shoulder-strap insignia consisting of a brass grenade over the letters 'R.W.F.'), both of whose regular battalions were in the BEF, the 1st Battalion in the 22nd Brigade (7th Division) and the 2nd Battalion in the 19th Brigade.

22 ▲

23 ▼

▲24

▲25

▲27

28▶

24. One of the most remarkable action photographs of the early stages of the war: transport-wagons of the 1st Battalion, The Middlesex Regiment under shrapnel-fire at Signy Signets, 8 September 1914, in which nine horses were killed and a water-cart riddled. As the infantrymen dive for cover, an officer (centre) is hit (there appears to be a gash on the right side of his head); he is probably a staff officer of the 19th Infantry Brigade, carrying binoculars and map-case and with automobile goggles around his cap. Remarkably, this photograph was published in 1914 despite its somewhat dispiriting content.

25. Scottish regiments wore similar equipment to the remainder of the British Army, but officially had tunics with rounded front skirts (as worn by the figure second left), and the kilt, hose, gaiters and glengarry cap of traditional Highland military dress. This group of lightly wounded prisoners (captured around Mons) wear the 'Government' (Black Watch) tartan kilt; the plain blue glengarry and red-and-black hose indicates the Black Watch, and the red-and-white hose and glengarry-band the Argyll and Sutherland Highlanders.

26 ▲

26. The first British Territorial unit to see action (at Messines on 31 October) was the London Scottish; this group was photographed at a French railway station a few days before. They wore the khaki 'Highland' tunic, kilts of 'Hodden grey', blue glengarry with white-metal badge, grey hose and khaki spats, and grey hair sporrans with two black tails. As a concession to active service the sporran-tails and glengarry-badges were removed on 29 October. The battalion's Mk I Lee-Enfields jammed easily, so at Messines they picked up Mark IIIs from casualties, and even used captured German rifles.

27. Belgian infantry on the march, wearing the 1913-pattern uniform unsuited for the war: a shako with oilskin cover and red pompom (green for light infantry), often with the regimental number painted on the front, a double-breasted, dark-blue greatcoat over or instead of the 1913-pattern tunic (*vareuse*) with nine brass buttons, blue-grey trousers and leather gaiters; the man fourth from the left is a corporal, distinguished by his single cuff-chevron. In the background is a civilian wagon commandeered as army transport.

29 ▲

28. Belgian infantry in the war-damaged streets of Termonde. This was the usual service uniform at the outset of the war; double-breasted dark-blue greatcoat, blue-grey trousers, leather gaiters and a German-style dark-blue cloth forage-cap with a red band, bearing the national Belgian cockade (black/yellow/red) on the front. The standard infantry weapon was the 1889-pattern Belgian 7.65 Mauser rifle.

29. A Belgian machine-gun post. The Belgian uniform being so unsuited for active service, it was quickly replaced by the 'Yser' uniform (named from its use by the troops fighting on the River Yser). The old shako was replaced by a blue or green soft kepi with arm-of-service piping (blue-grey for infantry), the 1913-pattern tunic by a single-breasted dark-blue or grey tunic with seven grey metal buttons and coloured piping on the cuffs, and the blue-grey trousers replaced by wine-red corduroy with blue puttees and ankle-boots, shortages being made up from French stocks.

▲30　▼31

30. A relic of a bygone age: a captured German officer (third from right) pays an old-style courtesy by saluting a Belgian colour-party on the roadside. The Belgian infantry (left) wear greatcoats and covered shakos; the man bearing the flag has a waterproof cape over his field equipment. The prisoners are escorted by a cavalryman wearing a caped greatcoat.

31. A Belgian Guide with a captured German cavalry horse. The two élite regiments of Guides cavalry wore the 1913-pattern double-breasted cavalry tunic in dark-green with crimson collar and piping, and crimson overalls with double yellow stripe; their green full-dress dolman with orange braid was rarely if every worn on active service. The Guides were the only ones to wear the black fur busby (*colback*), but like all other cavalry carried the lance; here, its pennon of red over yellow over black is furled.

32. Belgian Guides. The man in the foreground carries a wicker basket containing carrier-pigeons, which were used to communicate between Brussels and Antwerp. In addition to their sabres and lances, the troopers carry the 1889-pattern Belgian 7.65mm Mauser carbine.

33. A Belgian Guide surveys the rubble of Haelen, a bombarded town; he wears the 1913 cavalry tunic with light-coloured breeches and long gaiters. The goggles around the laced forage-cap suggest that he is crewing some form of motorized transport.

34. A Belgian *Chasseur à cheval* NCO reconnoitering, taking advantage of a convenient road-sign, the legend on which has been obscured to hinder the enemy. He wears the 1913-pattern, dark-blue cavalry tunic with red piping (yellow for the 1st Chasseurs), blue-grey trousers with red stripes (1st yellow), and the shako covered with oilskin. The 1889 Mauser carbine is suspended from a belt-clip; the sabre is carried on the saddle.

32▲ 33▼ 34▼

▲35

35. Belgian infantry with a dog-drawn machine-gun. Dog-carts were used extensively by the Belgian Army in 1914, though few were as heavy as this wooden version; some were merely machine-guns mounted on spoked wheels with

▼36

pneumatic tyres, with the dogs harnessed to the trail. The practice was a militarization of the dog-drawn milk-carts used in Belgian towns, but although the British Army experimented with the scheme it was not adopted by other nations.

36. Belgian field artillery in action, showing the recoil of the gun barrel. The crew wears a mixture of uniform, all with the dark-blue 1913-pattern tunic with scarlet piping, blue-grey trousers with scarlet stripe and black leather equipment; some

wear the field cap while the men at left retain the fur *talpack* (a squat busby) used by the field and horse artillery.

37. A Belgian fort outside Liège replying to the German bombardment; the guns are

protected by temporary field-works utilizing gabions (baskets filled with earth) and wicker hurdles, as would have been used two centuries before. The gunners wear dark-blue greatcoats with the skirts fastened back, and blue-grey trousers; their shakos with oilskin covers identify them as members of the Fortress Artillery.

38. King Albert (in the gateway) watches a detachment of Belgian cyclists. Cyclists of the two Carabinier regiments wore a peaked field cap, green 1913-pattern tunic with yellow piping and blue-grey trousers, but the men seen here wear a mixture of uniform, including shakos, the German-style field cap and the squat kepi of the 'Yser' uniform, with greatcoats and infantry equipment; the two NCOs nearest the camera wear the cavalry tunic, laced forage-cap and apparently puttees. Note how several men have turned back their greatcoat-cuffs to reveal the lining.

▲39

39. Belgian Civic Guardsmen at Antwerp. The *Gardes Civiques*, a 'home-guard'-style defence force, was not recognized by the Germans as part of the Belgian Army; thus, before the occupation of Brussels the Civic Guard was marched to the town hall and there surrendered their weapons, so as not to be treated as guerrillas. Their overcoat was like that of the army, but the black bowler hat was distinctive.

40. French infantry halted by the roadside at Amiens: the men wear their black leather waist-belts with 1877-pattern ammunition-pouches, but have removed the 1893-pattern knapsack which has the mess-tin strapped on top. The stacked rifles are the 1886/93 pattern 8mm Lebel. It is interesting to note that some of these men have their trousers worn outside their leather gaiters, and turned-up at the ankle.

41. French infantry defending a shell-damaged building which is apparently next to a cemetery; a picture probably posed for the photographer, but showing the large amount of equipment carried on the soldier's back, including a spare pair of boots, one on each side of the knapsack. Especially evident is the tan fabric 1892-pattern haversack over the right shoulder, and the unmistakable narrow metal scabbard of the Lebel rifle.

▼41

▼40

42. Peace and war: a dusty column of French infantry on the march past grape-harvesters in Champagne. The front skirts of the long dark-blue French greatcoat were commonly fastened back to free the legs, a fashion adopted by these men; all wear the 1912-pattern blue-grey kepi-cover with the possible exception of the man at the extreme right front, probably a non commissioned officer.

43. French infantry on the march, with transport-mules carrying the battalion's machine-guns and ammunition. From the numerals visible on the red collar-patches of the greatcoats, it is possible to identify this unit as the 8th Line Regiment, which in 1914 formed part of the 4th Brigade of the 2nd Infantry Division of I Army Corps in Lanrezac's Fifth Army.

ORDER OF BATTLE: BRITISH EXPEDITIONARY FORCE, 1914

(Organization was not totally constant during the period from August to November 1914)

Headquarters: Commander-in-Chief, Field Marshal Sir John D. P. French
Chief of Staff: Lt.Gen. Sir A. J. Murray

Cavalry Division: Maj.Gen. E. H. Allenby
1st Cavalry Bde: 2nd and 5th Dragoon Guards, 11th Hussars
2nd Cavalry Bde: 4th Dragoon Guards, 9th Lancers, 18th Hussars
3rd Cavalry Bde: 4th Hussars, 5th & 16th Lancers
4th Cavalry Bde: Composite Regt., Household Cavalry; 6th Dragoon Guards, 3rd Hussars
Artillery: 'D', 'E', 'I' & 'L' Btys. Royal Horse Artillery
5th (Independent) Cavalry Bde: 2nd Dragoons, 12th Lancers, 20th Hussars, 'J' Bty. R.H.A.

I Corps: Lt.Gen. Sir Douglas Haig
1st Division:
1st (Guards) Bde: 1/Coldstream Gds., 1/Scots Gds., 1/Black Watch, 1/Royal Munster Fusiliers
2nd Inf. Bde: 2/Royal Sussex, 1/Loyal North Lancashire, 1/Northamptonshire, 2/King's Royal Rifle Corps
3rd Inf. Bde: 1/Queen's West Surrey, 2/South Wales Borderers, 1/Gloucestershire, 2/Welsh
Cavalry: 'C' Sqdn. 15th Hussars
Artillery: 25, 26, 39 & 48 Bdes. Royal Field Artillery; '26' Heavy Bty. Royal Garrison Artillery

2nd Division:
4th (Guards) Bde: 2/Grenadier Gds., 2/ & 3/Coldstream Gds., 1/Irish Gds.
5th Inf. Bde: 2/Worcestershire, 2/Oxford & Bucks. Light Infantry, 2/Highland Light Infantry, 2/Connaught Rangers
6th Inf. Bde: 1/King's (Liverpool), 2/South Staffordshire, 1/Royal Berkshire, 1/King's Royal Rifle Corps
Cavalry: 'B' Sqdn. 15th Hussars
Artillery: 34, 36, 41 & 44 Bdes. R.F.A.; '35' Bty. R.G.A.

II Corps: Lt.Gen. Sir J.M. Grierson (died 17 Aug.); thereafter Gen. Sir Horace Smith-Dorrien
3rd Division:
7th Inf. Bde: 3/Worcestershire, 2/South Lancashire, 1/Wiltshire, 2/Royal Irish Rifles
8th Inf. Bde: 2/Royal Scots, 2/Royal Irish, 4/Middlesex, 1/Gordon Highlanders
9th Inf. Bde: 1/Northumberland Fusiliers, 4/Royal Fusiliers, 1/Lincolnshire, 1/Royal Scots Fusiliers
Cavalry: 'A' Sqdn. 15th Hussars
Artillery: 23, 30, 40 & 42 Bdes. R.F.A.; '48' Bty. R.G.A.

5th Division:
13th Inf. Bde: 2/King's Own Scottish Borderers, 2/Duke of Wellington's, 1/Royal West Kent, 2/King's Own Yorkshire Light Infantry
14th Inf. Bde: 2/Suffolk, 1/East Surrey, 1/Duke of Cornwall's Light Infantry, 2/Manchester
15th Inf. Bde: 1/Norfolk, 1/Bedfordshire, 1/Cheshire, 1/Dorset
Cavalry: 'A' Sqdn. 19th Hussars
Artillery: 8, 15, 27 & 28 Bdes. R.F.A.; '108' Bty. R.G.A.

19th Inf. Bde. (formed 22 August): 2/Royal Welch Fusiliers, 1/Cameronians, 1/Middlesex, 2/Argyll & Sutherland Highlanders
Line-of-communication Btn: 1/Devonshire (to 8th Inf. Bde. September)

III Corps: Maj.Gen. W. P. Pulteney
4th Division:
10th Inf. Bde: 1/Royal Warwickshire, 2/Seaforth Highlanders, 1/Royal Irish Fusiliers, 2/Royal Dublin Fusiliers
11th Inf. Bde: 1/Somerset Light Infantry, 1/East Lancashire, 1/Hampshire, 1/Rifle Brigade
12th Inf. Bde: 1/King's Own Lancaster, 2/Lancashire Fusiliers, 2/Royal Inniskilling Fusiliers, 2/Essex
Cavalry: 'B' Sqdn. 19th Hussars
Artillery: 14, 29, 32 & 36 Bdes. R.F.A.; '31' Bty. R.G.A.

6th Division:
16th Inf. Bde: 1/Buffs, 1/Leicestershire, 1/King's Shropshire Light Infantry, 1/York & Lancaster
17th Inf. Bde: 1/Royal Fusiliers, 1/North Staffordshire, 1/Leinster, 3/Rifle Brigade
18th Inf. Bde: 1/West Yorkshire, 1/East Yorkshire, 2/Sherwood Foresters, 2/Durham Light Infantry
Cavalry: 'C' Sqdn. 19th Hussars
Artillery: 12, 24 & 38 Bdes. R.F.A.; '24' Bty. R.G.A.

IV Corps: Maj.Gen. Sir H.S. Rawlinson, Bt.
7th Division:
20th Inf. Bde: 1/Grenadier Gds., 1/Scots Gds., 2/Border, 2/Gordon Highlanders
21st Inf. Bde: 2/Bedfordshire, 2/Green Howards, 2/Royal Scots Fusiliers, 2/Wiltshire
22nd Inf. Bde: 2/Queen's Royal West Surrey, 2/Royal Warwickshire, 1/Royal Welch Fusiliers, 1/South Staffordshire
Cavalry: Northumberland Hussars
Artillery: 'C', 'F' & 'T' Btys. R.H.A.; 22 & 35 Bdes. R.F.A.; 3 Bde. R.G.A.

3rd Cavalry Division:
6th Cavalry Bde: 3rd Dragoon Guards, 1st Dragoons, 10th Hussars
7th Cavalry Bde: 1st & 2nd Life Guards, Royal Horse Guards
Artillery: 'K' Bty. R.H.A.

Indian Corps: Lt.Gen. Sir J. Willcocks
Lahore Division: Ferozepore Bde: 1/Connaught Rangers, 57th Rifles, 129th Rifles, 9th Bhopal Regiment
Jullundur Bde: 1/Manchester, 15th & 47th Sikhs, 59th Rifles
Sirhind Bde: 1/Highland Light Infantry, 1/1st & 1/4th Gurkhas, 125th Rifles
Cavalry: 15th Lancers (Cureton's Multanis)
Artillery, etc: 5, 11 & 18 Bdes. R.F.A.; '109' Bty. R.G.A.; 34th Sikh Pioneers

Meerut Division:
Dehra Dun Bde: 1/Seaforth Highlanders, 2/2nd & 1/9th Gurkhas, 6th Jat Light Infantry
Garhwal Bde: 2/Leicestershire, 2/3rd Gurkhas, 1/ & 2/ Garhwal Rifles
Bareilly Bde: 2/Black Watch, 2/8th Gurkhas, 41st Dogras, 58th Rifles
Cavalry: 4th Cavalry
Artillery: 4, 9 & 13 Bdes. R.F.A.; '110' Bty. R.G.A.

Secunderabad Cavalry Brigade:
7th Dragoon Guards, 20th Deccan & 30th Poona Horse,
Jodhpore Lancers, 'N' Bty. R.H.A.

ORDER OF BATTLE:
GERMAN ARMY, WESTERN FRONT

Disposition of Corps at the start of the war was as follows:
First Army (von Kluck): II, III, IV, IX Corps; III, IV, IX Reserve
   Corps
Second Army (von Bülow): Guard, VII, X Corps; Guard, VII, X
   Reserve Corps
Third Army (von Hausen): XI, XII, XIX Saxon Corps; XII Saxon
   Reserve Corps
Fourth Army (Albrecht of Württemberg): VIII, XVIII Corps; VIII,
   XVIII Reserve Corps
Fifth Army (Crown Prince): V, VI, XIII, XXI Corps; V, VI Reserve
   Corps
Sixth Army (Rupert of Bavaria): I Bavarian, II Bavarian, III
   Bavarian Corps; I Bavarian Reserve Corps
Seventh Army (von Heeringen): XIV, XV Corps; XIV Reserve
   Corps

There is insufficient space for a complete German order of
battle for the outset of the war; but the typical organization of a
German Army corps is provided by the following composition of
II Corps of von Kluck's First Army, a corps based originally in
Pomerania with headquarters at Stettin.

II Corps
3rd Division:
5th Inf. Bde: 2nd Grenadiers (King Frederick William IV, 1st
   Pomeranian)
   9th Colberg Grenadiers (Graf Gneisenau, 2nd Pomeranian)
   54th Infantry (von der Goltz, 7th Pomeranian)
6th Inf. Bde: 34th Fusiliers (Queen Victoria of Sweden)
   42nd Infantry (Prince Moritz of Anhalt-Dessau, 5th
   Pomeranian)
3rd Cavalry Bde: 2nd Queen's Cuirassiers (Pomeranian)
   9th Uhlans (2nd Pomeranian)
   3rd Field Artillery Bde: 2nd Field Artillery (1st Pomeranian)
   38th Field Artillery (Upper Pomeranian)

4th Division:
7th Inf. Bde: 14th Infantry (Graf Schwerin, 3rd Pomeranian)
   149th Infantry (6th West Prussian)
8th Inf. Bde: 49th Infantry (6th Pomeranian)
   140th Infantry (4th West Prussian)
4th Cavalry Bde: 3rd Neumark Dragoons (von Derfflinger's
   Horse Grenadiers)
   12th Dragoons (von Arnim's, 2nd Brandenburg)
4th Field Artillery Bde: 17th Field Artillery (2nd Pomeranian)
   53rd Field Artillery (Lower Pomeranian)

Supporting Troops: 2nd Foot Artillery (von Hindersin's), 15th
   Foot Artillery (2nd West Prussian), 2nd (Pomeranian)
   Pioneers and 2nd Pomeranian Train Battalion.

CHRONOLOGY: 1914

Western Front
3–27 August: German offensive extending from Belgium south
   to Alsace, intent on rolling through Belgium, driving a wedge
between the Belgians and the newly arrived British Expeditionary Force in the north and the French in the south, then
wheeling south to capture Paris. Belgium largely overrun by
20 August, the B.E.F. forced to make a fighting retreat from
Mons (23 August), and at the Battle of Le Cateau (25–27
August). Initial French offensive plan was unrealistic and their
advances were repulsed by the Germans; French commanding
general, Joffre, forced to reorganize hurriedly.
5–10 September: Battle of the Marne. German attempt to
   capture Paris halted by French Army in desperate fighting;
   tactically indecisive, it was a huge strategic success for the
   Allies which prevented an almost immediate German victory.
15 September–24 November: 'The Race to the Sea'. Both sides
   attempted to outflank the other to the north, ever progressing
   towards the North Sea coastline. BEF almost annihilated in
   the First Battle of Ypres attempting to stop the German drive,
   but successfully prevented the German capture of the Channel
   ports.
14–24 December: Allied offensive repelled by German fixed
   positions; the era of fluid manoeuvre ended, and static trench
   warfare began. In the campaigning on the Western Front the
   Allies had suffered almost a million casualties, and the
   Germans almost as many.

Eastern Front
17 August–14 September: Russian invasion of East Prussia
   conducted incompetently, defeated by the Germans at Tannenberg (26–31 August) and First Battle of the Masurian
   Lakes (9–14 September), defeats from which Russia never
   fully recovered.
29 July–15 December: Austrian invasion of Serbia pushed on in
   face of severe resistance to capture Belgrade (2 December);
   Serbian counter-attack at Battle of Kolubra (3–9 December)
   repelled the Austrian advance and recaptured Belgrade (15
   December).
23 August–3 September: Austrian invasion of Russian Poland
   driven back by Russians, Austrians being defeated decisively
   at Rava Ruska (3–11 September).
17 September–2 November: German assistance to Austrians in
   Galicia halted Russian advance, ending in the Battle of Lódź
   (11–25 November), tactically a Russian victory but strategically an Austro-German success, preventing the Russians
   from renewing the offensive. Stalemate on the Eastern Front
   at the end of the year.

Turkish Front
29 October: Turkey joined the Central Powers by declaring war
   against the Allies; Turkish offensive against the Russian
   Caucasus halted at the Battle of Sarikamish (29 December).
   Britain declared a protectorate over Egypt (18 December) to
   defend the Suez Canal and began an invasion of Mesopotamia (23 October); Basra captured from Turks (23
   November).

Colonial Fronts
Operations against German bases in Africa, German East Africa
being defended stoutly. Several German island colonies captured, most notably Samoa, by British and Empire forces. Japan
entered the war on Allied side (23 August) and captured
Tsingtao, the German colony on the Chinese coast (7 November).

ORGANIZATIONAL TABLES: GERMAN ARMY, 1914

Although each army organized its forces in its own national methods, a number of similarities existed, in that it was usual for an Army Corps to be a completely self-contained entity with all necessary supporting services attached to the Corps, rather than to a central depot from which the necessary support units were drawn as required.

The following tables are typical, demonstrating the usual organization of the German Army in 1914, after mobilization. The most significant change between the pre-war and mobil-ization organization of a German Corps was that it was usual for the cavalry brigades to be withdrawn from the divisional organization and formed into independent Cavalry Divisions, leaving only a small cavalry contingent attached at infantry divisional level as a reconnaissance force. (The Order-of-Battle of II Corps above includes the pre-war disposition of cavalry with the infantry divisions).

A typical Army Corps upon mobilization was organized as follows:

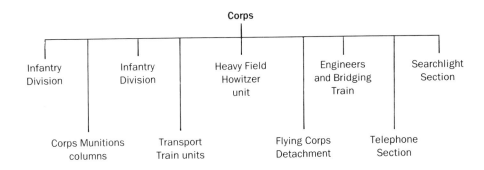

Divisional establishment in 1914 was:

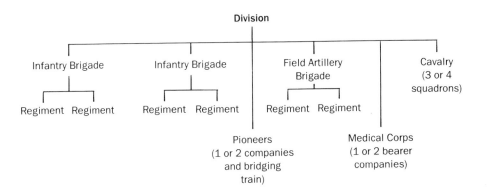

An infantry regiment in 1914 was organized in three battalions, with companies numbered consecutively from 1 to 12, with the separate machine-gun company (not attached to a battalion) numbered 13:

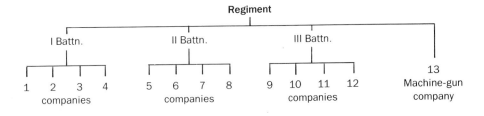

When the Cavalry Divisions were formed upon mobilization by withdrawing most of the divisional cavalry from their pre-war formations, the following was the typical cavalry organization:

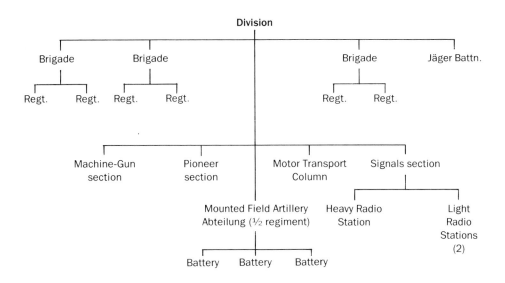

Artillery was divided into the Field Regiments, which manned the lighter guns attached at divisional level, and grouped in brigades; and the Foot Artillery Regiments, which manned the heavier guns attached at Corps level, normally allocated at one regiment per Army Corps. Field Regiments consisted of two *Abteilungen*, each of three batteries of six guns each, the batteries numbered consecutively throughout the regiment, from 1 to 6. The normal weapons of a regiment's 36 gun-crews were 7.7cm guns, but a number of IInd *Abteilungen* were armed with 10.5cm light field howitzers, so that two *Abteilungen* of howitzers were contained in each Army Corps. From October 1914 smaller batteries became common, each of four guns instead of six (thus increasing the number of batteries available while keeping the same total of guns), but 4-gun batteries did not become standard until 1915. Regimental organization of Field Artillery in 1914 was:

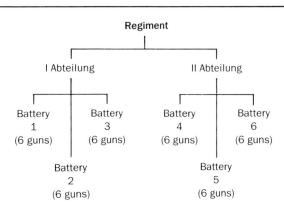

(For more extensive organizational details, see D. B. Nash's *Imperial German Army Handbook* as noted in bibliography).

DRESS DISTINCTIONS: BELGIAN ARMY, 1914

The following basic uniform-colours were worn by the Belgian Army at the outbreak of war:

Unit	Head-dress	Tunic	Trousers
Generals	kepi	dark-blue piped crimson	dark-blue, dark-blue stripe
Staff	kepi	green piped crimson	green piped-crimson
Infantry	shako	dark-blue piped blue-grey on 1913 uniform; otherwise piped red	blue-grey piped black
Grenadiers	bearskin cap	dark-blue piped scarlet	dark-blue, scarlet stripe
Chasseurs à Pied	shako	green piped yellow	blue-grey piped green
Carabiniers	Tyrolean hat	green piped yellow	blue-grey piped yellow
Carabinier Cyclists	kepi	green piped yellow	blue-grey piped yellow
Guides	colback (busby)	green piped crimson	crimson piped green
1st Lancers	czapka	dark-blue piped crimson	blue-grey piped crimson
2nd Lancers	czapka	dark-blue piped crimson	blue-grey piped crimson
3rd/5th Lancers	czapka	dark-blue piped white	blue-grey piped white

GERMAN CUFF PATTERNS

Designs of German cuff used
on the *Waffenrock*:
A: 'Brandenburg'
B: 'Swedish'
C: 'Saxon' or 'German'
D: 'French', with the *Litzen*
(lace loops) which
distinguished Guard units.

B

D

A

C

GERMAN HEADDRESS

Below: The *Pickelhaube*, worn here without its customary fabric cover, revealing the standard 'eagle' plate, metal fittings and cockades behind the chinscale-boss. Reputedly the first German to cross the Marne, this infantryman wears the greatcoat collar-patches, which were later discontinued.

Below: The German lancer *czapka* worn here with its service-dress field-grey cloth cover. This trooper — reputedly the German who approached England most nearly during the operations around Ostend — wears the dress tunic (*Uhlanka*) with epaulettes, though on campaign a field-grey version with pointed cuffs was worn. Excluding the Bavarian *Uhlans*, all cavalry wore standing collars.

Unit	Head-dress	Tunic	Trousers
4th Lancers	czapka	dark-blue piped blue	blue-grey piped blue
1st Chasseurs à Cheval	shako	dark-blue piped yellow	blue-grey piped yellow
2nd Chasseurs à Cheval	shako	dark-blue piped scarlet	blue-grey piped scarlet
4th Chasseurs à Cheval	shako	dark-blue piped scarlet	blue-grey piped scarlet
Field/Horse Artillery	talpack	dark-blue piped scarlet	blue-grey, scarlet stripes
Fortress Artillery	shako	dark-blue piped scarlet	blue-grey, scarlet stripes
Engineers	shako	dark-blue piped scarlet	blue-grey, scarlet stripes
Train	shako	dark-blue piped light-blue	blue-grey piped light-blue
Administration	kepi	dark-blue piped light-blue	blue-grey piped light-blue
Gendarmerie	bearskin cap	dark-blue piped scarlet	blue-grey
Medical Corps	kepi	dark-blue piped crimson	black, crimson stripe

DRESS DISTINCTIONS: FRENCH ARMY, 1914

The following basic uniform-distinctions were worn by the French Army at the outbreak of war:

Unit	Head-dress	Tunic	Buttons	Collar-patch	Trousers
Generals	kepi	black	yellow	–	scarlet, black stripe
Infantry	kepi, regtl. number	blue, faced red	yellow	red with blue regtl. number (white for territorials)	red, black stripe
Alpine Infantry	beret with grenade badge	blue, faced red	yellow	red with blue regtl. number	red, black stripe
Chasseurs à Pied	kepi with battn. number	blue	white	blue with yellow battn. number	blue-grey. yellow stripe
Alpine Chasseurs	beret with horn badge	blue	white	blue with yellow battn. number	blue-grey, yellow stripe
Cuirassiers	helmet	blue, faced red	yellow	blue with regtl. number	red, black stripe
Dragoons	helmet	blue, faced white	white	blue with red regtl. number	red, light-blue stripe
Chasseurs à Cheval	shako with horn badge	light-blue, faced crimson	white	crimson with light-blue regtl. number	red, light-blue stripe
Hussars	shako with knot-decoration (or helmet with horn badge)	light-blue	white	light-blue with red regtl. number	red, light-blue stripe
Artillery	kepi with regtl. number	blue, faced scarlet	yellow	scarlet with regtl. number	blue, scarlet stripe
Alpine Artillery	beret with grenade badge	blue, faced scarlet	yellow	scarlet with regtl. number	blue, scarlet stripe
Engineers	kepi with helmet-and-cuirass badge	blue, faced black	yellow	black with scarlet number	blue, scarlet stripe
Train	kepi with Corps number	light-blue, faced crimson	white	crimson with grey-blue number	crimson with grey-blue stripe

DRESS DISTINCTIONS: GERMAN ARMY, 1914

The following were the uniform-distinctions of the German Army, according to the 1910 regulations (worn until the introduction of the 1915 uniform). There is insufficient space to detail the considerable number of regimental variations and badge-designs; in the following table, 'R' indicates the use of a regimental distinctive- or facing-colour. All wore the standard tunic (*Waffenrock*) with stand-and-fall collar, with the exceptions that the Hussars wore the braided *Atila* and the *Uhlans* (lancers) the *Ulanka* tunic; all cavalry had standing collars save the Bavarian *Uhlans* and *Chevaux-légers*. Cuff-designs are indicated below by the letters 'S' (Swedish), 'B' (Brandenburg), 'Sx' (Saxon or 'German'), 'F' (French) and 'P' (pointed), in accordance with the line illustrations. Tunic-colour is abbreviated as 'F/G' (*Feldgrau* or 'field-grey') or 'G/G' (grey-green). The term *Pickelhaube* is used for artillery helmets below, even though they had a ball-top instead of a spike.

Unit	Head-dress	Cap-band & piping	Tunic
Generals	pickelhaube	red, piped red	F/G, S
General staff	pickelhaube	crimson, piped crimson	F/G, S
Staff officers	pickelhaube	crimson, piped crimson	F/G, S
Foot Guard regts. 1–4	pickelhaube	red, piped red	F/G, S
Foot Guard regt. 5	pickelhaube	red, piped red	F/G, B
Guard Grenadiers	pickelhaube	red, piped red	F/G, B
Infantry	pickelhaube	red, piped red	F/G, B
Infantry Leib. Regt.	pickelhaube	red, piped red	F/G, B
Guard Rifles	shako	black, piped light-green	G/G, F
Jägers	shako	light-green, piped light-green	G/G, S

Unit	Head-dress	Cap-band & piping	Tunic
Machine-Gun Btns.	shako	red, piped red	G/G, S
2nd Guard Machine-Gun Btn.	shako	black, piped red	G/G, F
Field Artillery	pickelhaube	black, piped red	F/G, S
Foot Artillery	pickelhaube	black, piped red	F/G, B
Cuirassiers	metal helmet	R, piped R	F/G, S
Dragoons	pickelhaube	R, piped R	F/G, S
Hussars	colback	R, piped R	F/G, S
Uhlans	czapka	R, piped R	F/G, P
Mounted Jäger regts. 1–7	metal helmet	light-green, piped light-green	G/G, S
Mounted Jäger regts. 8–13	pickelhaube (officers, metal helmet)	light-green, piped light-green	G/G, S
Pioneers	pickelhaube	black, piped red	F/G, S
Railway Battns.	pickelhaube	black, piped red	F/G, S
Airship Battns.	shako	black, piped red	F/G, S
Signal Battns.	shako	black, piped red	F/G, S
Aviation Battns.	shako	black, piped red	F/G, S
Motor Transport Battns.	peaked cap	black, piped red	F/G, S
Train	peaked cap	light-blue, piped light-blue	F/G, S
Medical Corps	peaked cap	blue, piped red	F/G, S
Veterinary Corps	peaked cap	black, piped crimson	F/G, S
Ordnance Corps	peaked cap	black, piped red	F/G, B
Fortification personnel	peaked cap	black, piped red	F/G, S
Military officials	peaked cap	blue, piped white	F/G, S
Bavarian infantry	pickelhaube	red, piped red	F/G, B
Bavarian Jägers	shako	light-green, piped light-green	F/G, S
Bavarian Machine-Gun Btns.	shako	light-green, piped light-green	F/G, S
Bavarian heavy cavalry	pickelhaube	red, piped red	F/G, S
Bavarian Chevaux-légers	pickelhaube	R, piped R	F/G, S
Saxon infantry	pickelhaube	red, piped red	F/G, Sx
100th/101st Grenadiers	pickelhaube	red, piped red	F/G, S
108th Saxon Rifles	shako	black, piped light-green	G/G, Sx
Saxon heavy cavalry	metal helmet	R, piped R	F/G, S
Saxon Foot Artillery	pickelhaube	black, piped red	F/G, Sx
Saxon Train	peaked cap	—	F/G, Sx
Württemberg infantry	pickelhaube	red, piped red	F/G, B
119th/123rd Grenadiers	pickelhaube	red, piped red	F/G, S
Hessian infantry	pickelhaube	red, piped red	F/G, B
109th Grenadiers	pickelhaube	red, piped red	F/G, S
Mecklenburg infantry	pickelhaube	red, piped red	F/G, B
Mecklenburg-Schwerin military officials	peaked cap	blue, piped white	F/G, B

Shoulder-straps were different for each regiment; of the uniform-colour, they bore the regimental number or distinctive badge, and coloured piping. The piping was arranged in the following scheme:

Guard regiments: colours white, red, yellow, light-blue and white for 1st–5th regiments respectively. Others had piping according to the Army Corps:

white:	Corps I, II, IX, X, XII, I Bavarian
red:	III, IV, XI, XIII, XV, XIX, II Bavarian
yellow:	V, VI, XVI, XVII, III Bavarian
light-blue:	VII, VIII, XVIII, XX
light-green:	XXI

XIV Corps had variously coloured distinctions. Other colours were:

Jäger and Rifles:	light-green piping
Cavalry:	regimental colouring
Foot Artillery:	white piping
Railway, Airship, Aviation and Motor Transport Battns.:	light-grey piping
Pioneers, Signals:	black shoulder-straps piped red
Train:	light-blue straps piped light-blue
Medical officers:	red piping
Medical orderlies:	dark-blue straps piped light-blue
Stretcher-bearers:	crimson straps
Veterinary personnel and military officials:	crimson piping
Fortification officers:	red/black piping

(For more extensive uniform details, see A. Mollo's *Army Uniforms of World War I* as noted in bibliography).

SOURCES AND BIBLIOGRAPHY

Among the enormous amount of literature concerning the First World War, the following are among the most useful for the events and armies of the first months of the war:

Ascoli, D. *The Mons Star: The British Expeditionary Force, 1914* (London, 1981).

Brown, M., and Seaton, S. *The Christmas Truce* (London, 1984).

Carew, T. *The Vanished Army* (London, 1964).

Craster, J.M. *Fifteen Rounds a Minute* (London, 1976).

French of Ypres, Viscount. *1914* (London, 1919).

Hammerton, Sir J. (ed.) *The Great War: 'I Was There'* vol. I (London, n.d.)

Hicks, J.E. *French Military Weapons* (New Milford, Connecticut, 1964).

_____. *German Weapons, Uniforms, Insignia* (Le Canada, California, 4th ed. 1963).

Macdonald, L. *1914* (London, 1987).

Mollo, A. *Army Uniforms of World War I* (Poole, 1977).

Nash, D.B. *German Infantry 1914–18* (London, 1971).

_____. *Imperial German Army Handbook 1914–18* (London, 1980).

Owen, E. *1914, Glory Departing* (London, 1986).

Tuchman, B.W. *August 1914* (London, 1962).

A wide range of photographs can be found in many contemporary periodicals: for example, *The Graphic*; *The Great War* (ed. H.W. Wilson and J.A. Hammerton, London 1914); *Illustrated London News*; *Illustrated War News*; *Navy & Army Illustrated*; *The Times History of the War*; *The War Budget*, etc.

GERMAN STATE COCKADES

German state colours were worn on the left cockade on the helmet (behind the chinscale-boss), with the national (*Reich*) red/white/black cockade on the right side. On the field cap, the state cockade was carried below the *Reich* cockade. Units wearing shakos (except Saxon), colbacks and czapkas had oval cockades which might vary from the ordinary pattern. Colours were as follows.

Prussia:	black/white/black; oval cockade, white/black
Bavaria:	white/light-blue/white; oval cockade, white/light-blue
Saxony:	green/white/green; oval cockade, white/green
Württemberg:	black/red/black; oval cockade, black/red
Hessen:	white/red/white
Mecklenburg:	blue/yellow/red; oval cockade, white/blue/red, trimmed with yellow braid
Baden:	yellow/red/yellow; oval cockade, yellow/red
Oldenburg:	blue/red/blue
Brunswick:	blue/yellow/blue
Anhalt:	green
Saxe-Weimar:	green/yellow/black
Saxe-Coburg, Meiningen and Altenburg:	green/white/green
Schwarzburg-Rudolstadt:	blue/white/blue
Schwarzburg-Sonderhausen:	white/blue/white
Waldeck-Reuss:	yellow/black/red
Lippe:	yellow/red
Schaumburg-Lippe:	white/red/blue
Bremen:	white/red/white
Hamburg:	white with red Iron Cross
Lübeck:	white with red Maltese Cross

44. The French Army's principal machine-guns in the early 20th century were variations on the Hotchkiss gun, the 1900- and 1914-patterns of Hotchkiss and the 1907-pattern St-Etienne; all had spindly legs and a seat for the gunner, and all except the 1914 Hotchkiss had a wheel at the left side for elevation.

▲45

▲46

45. A French infantryman samples English Christmas pudding in December 1914. He wears the grey-blue kepi-cover, and his greatcoat bears diagonal rank-bars, probably in the metallic lace which indicated a sergeant. The 1893-pattern black leather knapsack has the ▼47

1852-pattern mess-tin strapped on top.

46. French dragoons wore the crested helmet with fabric cover, dark-blue tunic with white facings and red trousers with sky-blue stripes. Here a dragoon officer (on foot)

converses with a light cavalryman whose sky-blue tunic appears to bear the crimson collar-patches and white trefoil epaulettes of the *chasseurs à cheval*. Light regiments wore a sky-blue shako bearing a brass horn badge for chasseurs and a

Hungarian knot for hussars, but (as here) some regiments wore instead the 1913-pattern white-metal helmet with brass comb, worn with a fabric cover on service.

47. French artillery firing at the Steinbach heights. These 120mm guns of the 1877 'Système de Bange' were too heavy for mobile field use, but were used for more static positions. The names painted on the barrels include '*Kultur*', the Allies' ironic term for the uncivilized German behaviour as protrayed in Allied propaganda. The gunners here wear grimy fatigue uniform; the artillery kepi was blue with red piping and numeral, and the trousers blue with red stripe.

48. The *Chasseurs Alpins* (Alpine Chasseurs), alias 'Blue Devils', were among the most renowned units of the French Army. Highly trained for operating in mountainous terrain, they carried infantry equipment plus an alpenstock, and wore a dark-blue tunic and puttees, white trousers, and, most characteristically, a dark-blue beret which on campaign could have a white cover. These chasseurs are crewing a light mountain howitzer.

49. The Belgian defenders of Nieuport were supported by French units; here a French medical officer attends to a casualty in the trenches. The doctor wears the black tunic of French officers, and has the red top of his kepi concealed by a cover. The facing-colour of the medical personnel was crimson, and their ordinary *garance* trousers had a wide black stripe for officers.

50. The most colourful of the French infantry, the Zouaves were Frenchmen dressed in North African style. Their uniform was highly impractical: red cap (*chéchia*), blue waistcoat and bolero-style jacket with red braid, and voluminous red trousers. This was modified progressively in the first months of the war, the white service-dress trousers being replaced by khaki and the caps issued with a blue cover. Eventually these impractical garments were replaced by 'mustard'-coloured uniforms, but in the early part of the war the classic zouave uniform illustrated was retained.

48▲   49▼

50▼

51. Among the troops recruited by the French Army in North Africa were the Algerian *Tirailleurs*, commonly known as 'Turcos', who continued to wear their African uniform; this group was photographed during a halt on the march near Rheims. Their original sky-blue zouave uniform with voluminous white trousers was eventually replaced by a more practical sky-blue greatcoat and khaki trousers and tunic (*vareuse*) at about the turn of 1914/15, and the zouave caps equipped with a sky-blue cover; ultimately they adopted a uniform of 'mustard'-khaki.

52. The Senegalese *Tirailleurs* of the French Army wore zouave-style head-dress and blue tunic and trousers, but even before the outbreak of war were issued with a khaki uniform and cap-cover, the tunic (*paletot*) having extremely short skirts; this adumbrated the adoption of mustard-coloured uniforms by all French colonial units in 1915.

▲51　▼52

53. Senegalese *Tirailleurs* of the French Army man a defence-line at Pervyse, between Dixmude and Nieuport, wearing their *chéchia* head-dress and greatcoats of infantry pattern (issued for service in the European climate). It was stated in 1914 that the African complexion of the Senegalese assisted in camouflaging them!

54. French 'marines' (naval infantry) were deployed on land during the early months of the war, serving at Ypres and Dixmude, for example. They carried equipment like that of the infantry, with the greatcoat, but retained the blue cap with pompom which traditionally distinguished French 'bluejackets'. The boy scout at the head of column in this photograph is acting as a guide while the unit passes through his town.

55. This group of Austrian staff officers (with German attaché, right) illustrates the staff version of the Austrian uniform introduced in 1909, a pike-grey single-breasted tunic, breeches with red stripes (for generals) and black riding-boots or brown leather gaiters. The pike-grey kepi in this 'stiff' form was worn only by staff officers and thus was nicknamed the 'artificial brain'! General officers' rank was indicated by one to three silver stars on the scarlet collar-patch, which had gold zigzag lace edging. Leatherwork was brown.

53▲ 54▼

55▼

56. Austrian artillery in Brussels: Austrian heavy guns assisted the Germans in Belgium. This illustrates excellently the 1909-pattern pike-grey uniform worn by all except cavalry, a single-breasted tunic with patch pockets and facing-coloured collar-patches (scarlet for artillery) and pike-grey kepi with leather peak and circular badge bearing the imperial cipher (FJI) in the centre. Officers carried swords and automatic pistols.

57. Austrian dragoons on the march, wearing the 1905-pattern leather dragoon helmet with brass edging and eagle-plate; on active service they were more usually covered with grey linen or were painted grey. The cavalry tunic was light-blue with madder-red facings, worn with madder-red breeches and brown leather equipment; the fur-lined light-blue over-jacket (*Pelz*) is not visible. Arms were the 1869-pattern cavalry sabre with steel hilt, and the 1890 Steyer-Mannlicher 8mm carbine.

58. The Crown Prince visiting Austrian troops in Poland; the men wear the pike-grey greatcoat with pointed collar-patch (*Paroli*) in the facing-colour, and the soft pike-grey kepi and brown leather equipment; officers have fur collars. Of especial note is the continuing use of the *Feldzeichen*, the green sprig worn on the head-dress, a relic of the 'field-sign' of the 17th century, which continued to be worn by the Austrian Army into the mid-20th century.

59. An Austrian siege-howitzer in action in Galicia. For campaign in winter the gunners wear greatcoats and a variety of over-shoe gaiters, with the soft cloth kepi (which had a front flap fastening with two buttons) and goggles. Shorter coats with fur collars are also in evidence.

▲56 ▼57

▼58

60. Austrian prisoners with Serbian guards. The Austrians wear the pike-grey 1909-pattern tunic and trousers, the two nearest the camera with the three white stars on the collar which indicate sergeant's rank. The first of these has the leather gaiters worn by mountain troops; others wear the ordinary trousers with the integral gaiter which fastened around the ankle with two buttons.

▲61 ▼62

▼63

61. A purported 'combat' photograph showing Austrian infantry in action in Galicia, firing from hastily dug rifle-pits. Note the hide knapsack with the grey, rolled greatcoat strapped across the top and down each side; the standard infantry weapon was the 1895-pattern 8mm Mannlicher rifle. A variation on this equipment was used by the alpine (*Landesschützen*) units, who carried a rucksack instead of the ordinary knapsack, wore pantaloons and knee-length grey woollen stockings and carried the 1895 8mm carbine, shorter and more handy than the long infantry rifle.

62. An Austrian encampment in the Carpathians, showing typical winter dress; the central figure in the foreground wears the kepi with flap lowered to produce a Balaclava-style helmet, and the ordinary pike-grey trousers with integral gaiters fastened around the ankle with two buttons. Others have the light-grey knitted woollen cap worn in winter.

63. Serbian artillery entrained for the front line. The Serbian Army was issued with a greenish-grey service uniform from 1912, but only front-line troops received it; others wore old coloured uniforms or even civilian clothing. The uniform comprised a single-breasted tunic with breast- and side-pockets, loose trousers (tight on the lower leg), low boots and double-breasted greatcoat, with facing-coloured collar-patches (black for artillery, as here, crimson for infantry), and the head-dress was a plain cloth cap. Officers wore facing-coloured velvet collars, a peaked kepi, and riding-boots or leather gaiters and ankle-boots. The standard weapon was the 1893 7.65mm Mauser rifle.

64. A German transport-wagon stuck on the eastern front; as one dispatch stated, 'The mud of Poland is a national asset. . . . At the present moment it is fighting, silently but none the less effectively, on the side of the Allies.' The soldiers are members of the German 'train' corps, wearing the 1910 tunic with 'Swedish' cuffs, and the peaked cap worn by transport, medical and ordnance personnel, with a light-blue band and piping for train battalions (black band and red piping for motor-transport).

65. The shako was worn by the German *Jäger* and *Schützen* (rifle) units, the machine-gun battalions, signal units, the *Landwehr* (second-line infantry of which 96 regiments existed in 1914) and by the *Landsturm*, the home-defence units which frequently had outdated equipment. Like the *Pickelhaube*, the shako had a fabric cover for active service, usually grey-green, often with an Iron Cross badge, the distinctive insignia of the *Landwehr* from its inception in 1813; and an oval cockade. This *Landwehr* soldier is equipped for winter on the eastern front, with a rabbit-skin coat over his greatcoat.

64 ▲

66. German infantry on the eastern front, wearing white coats (with fur on the inside), which served for both warmth and camouflage. Both wear the field-grey field cap (*Mütze*) with two cockades, the imperial black/white/red at the top and the state cockade on the band. This band was red for most infantry, black for rifles and artillery, light-green for *Jäger* and Bavarian machine-gun battalions, blue for medical officers and officials and light-blue for transport units; on active service the coloured band was sometimes covered by a strip of field-grey cloth.

65 ▼

66 ▼

▲67

▲68

67. Russian Maxim gun screened by foliage. The crew wear summer service uniform, with the rolled greatcoat slung bandolier-fashion, with the aluminium mess-tin fitted on to the end of the roll. At the left side was carried a waterproof

canvas haversack containing the spare clothing and equipment, and from the rear of the waist-belt the 'Linneman tool', a small entrenching-spade.

68. The winter uniform of the Russian Army: a grey-brown

astrakhan cap with a flap which could be lowered to cover the ears and neck, and bearing a cockade as on the field-cap; and the grey-brown greatcoat (*Shinel*) with falling collar, which fastened with hooks and eyes. The bandolier is one-sixth

of a shelter-tent, folded with the greatcoat when the latter was rolled over the shoulder. The photograph shows Gabriel Elchain, a French volunteer who enrolled in a Siberian regiment, speaking to a member of a Petrograd city delegation.

▼69

69. Siberian infantry in the streets of Warsaw, wearing winter campaign uniform of astrakhan cap and greatcoat; by unfastening a half-belt at the rear of the coat, it could be used as a blanket or cloak. Over the haversacks can be seen the water-canteen (aluminium or the older, copper version); some wear the greatcoat-skirts turned back off the legs, in French fashion.

70. The Russian advance-guard in Galicia: infantry in the streets of Kielce, Poland. The second dismounted man from the left has a furled marker-flag attached to his bayonet: battalion flags had black, orange and white horizontal stripes with the battalion number on the central stripe. Company flags were red, blue, white or dark-green according to whether the regiment was the 1st, 2nd, 3rd or 4th of its division (colours matching the regimental greatcoat collar-patches), with horizontal and vertical stripes indicating the company or battalion. The duck is perhaps a regimental mascot.

71. A Russian field-battery in action, supposedly near Przemysl. The artillery wore the khaki shirt and trousers, with their red arm-of-service colour borne on the shoulder-straps and as piping to the black greatcoat-patches. The shoulder-straps bore a stencilled crossed cannon device and brigade number in Roman numerals. To the rear of the gun in the foreground are piled the crew's greatcoat-bandoliers.

70▲

71▼

▲72

72. Russian artillery in Poland, wearing winter campaign dress of greatcoat and astrakhan cap. The officer (with binoculars, second right) carries his sabre in the peculiarly Russian fashion, the hilt pointing towards the rear.

▼74

73. The most exotic Russian units were the Caucasian cossacks, who wore a grey astrakhan cap and kaftan, the Terek *voisko* (territorial division) having blue shoulder-straps and greatcoat collar-patches and the Kuban *voisko*

red. The largest cossack group, however, was the *Stepnoy* (Steppe) Cossacks, who wore ordinary uniform (as here), with the facing-colour of the *voisko* on their shoulder-straps, greatcoat-patches and as stripes on their blue trousers (khaki

▲73

trousers were introduced later). Exceptions were the Don cossacks (red distinctive, but blue shoulder-straps piped red), Amur (green distinctive, but yellow shoulder-strap piping and trouser-stripes) and Cossack artillery (red shoulder-straps, black collar-patch piped red). Shoulder-straps for all rank-and-file were khaki with light-blue numbers or badges, dark-blue for artillery.

74. The Indian Corps of the Meerut and Lahore Divisions began landing in France in late September 1914. Among the finest of these troops, the officers of the 1st Battalion, Garwhal Rifles are shown in this most significant photograph. Sailing immediately from India, they were not equipped for European service: the light colour of the khaki drill

uniform (with shorts!) contrasts greatly with the khaki serge of the second lieutenant at the extreme right, and a tropical helmet is even visible inside the tent! Seated right is the battalion's French interpreter, wearing the 'INT' brassard.

75. A Maxim-gun section of the Indian Corps advances at the double, apparently in the vicinity of Lille. The Maxim with tripod had to be carried in this manner; the men wear a roll at the rear in the manner of the British 1903-pattern bandolier equipment. The men at the rear carry boxes of ammunition.

76. Indian cavalry on the march near the Franco-Belgian border, armed with lances and wrapped-up in greatcoats, the weather being quite the opposite of that experienced on leaving India.

The Lahore Division's cavalry was the 15th Lancers (Cureton's Multanis) and the Meerut Division's the 4th Cavalry. The 20th Deccan Horse, 34th Prince Albert Victor's Own Poona Horse and the Jodhpur Imperial Service Lancers formed (with the 7th Dragoon Guards) the attached Secunderabad Cavalry Brigade.

76 ▼

▲79

77. The first trenches to be constructed were generally very different from the more sophisticated type which became familiar later in the war; this is a typical communication-trench filled with British 'Tommies', impossibly narrow and of very limited defensive value.

78. First Ypres: a corporal (rear), second lieutenant (right) and company sergeant-major, 1st Battalion Cameronians (Scottish Rifles) observing from a primitive trench. Officers of Scottish regiments had 'gauntlet' cuffs on their tunic, with the same system of rank-badges as the others: here, the single star of second lieutenants. The crown over three chevrons badge of the NCO indicated company sergeant-major and company quartermaster-sergeant until 1915. The officer retains the unique rifle-green regimental glengarry with black tape

▲77   ▼78

edging, tuft and ribbons; the others have knitted 'cap-comforters'.

79. A defensive trench on the front line along the Aisne, held by the Essex Regiment. Captain Maitland of the Essex faces the camera; the officer with binoculars is a FOO (Forward Observation Officer) of the Royal Artillery. Along the trench in the background can be seen the rifles of the defenders, lying in readiness across the parapet.

80. Mud was a universal problem from the earliest days of trench warfare. In this picture from late 1914, British troops are using an improvised ladle to scoop out mud from the bottom of their trench. They wear typical winter service dress, the khaki single-breasted greatcoat with deep folding collar, knitted mufflers and caps, with the ordinary web equipment worn over the greatcoat.

81. British infantry rifle-inspection in late 1914, showing a selection of typical campaign uniforms, the men having removed their equipment. Only the lance-corporal (left) appears to wear the correct uniform; others have no puttees but apparently long stockings pulled up to the knee. The second lieutenant, examining the barrel of the lance-corporal's Lee-Enfield, wears the usual cord breeches but a very unmilitary

pair of gum-boots, a common expedient in the trenches.

82. Cuisine in the trenches: British infantrymen cook a meal in late 1914. All wear the standard khaki greatcoat, knitted mufflers and Balaclava helmets. The kidney-shaped mess-tin could be used as a cooking-vessel as well as a plate. Note the knife tucked into the puttee of the man at the left.

80▲

81▼

82▼

▲83

83. In the winter of 1914 a most unusual garment was issued to the British Expeditionary Force: goatskin coats and jerkins to combat the

▼84

cold weather. Nicknamed 'Teddy Bears' by the British troops, the garments came in all colours and designs, which may be observed from this company

parade just behind the front line in late November or early December 1914.

84. Improvisation in the trenches: French troops prepare to launch a grenade by means of a crude catapult. Such items were used in considerable numbers: the 'firer' wears the kepi with blue-grey service cover, while the 'loader' has the 1897-pattern fore-and-aft *bonnet de police* (forage-cap) in blue-grey cloth.

85. Typical 'trench uniform': Lieutenant Bruce Bairnsfather, 1st Battalion Royal Warwickshire Regiment, at St-Yvon on Christmas Day 1914, on his way to join the 'Christmas truce' between British and German front-line troops. Later made famous by his brilliant cartoons, Bairnsfather wears a sheepskin coat, Balaclava helmet and gum-boots. Behind him is a flooded hole made by a 'Jack Johnson' shell.

86. German infantry at the firestep of a sandbagged trench. The officer (right) wears the ordinary tunic (with rank indicated by the design and number of stars on the laced shoulder-straps), and the NCOs and officers' version of the field cap, which had a peak; the side-pockets of the tunic are clearly visible. Suspended from the private's bayonet-scabbard is the *Troddel* or knot, the colouring of which identified the company and battalion. The basic infantry weapon was the 7.9mm Mauser *Gewehr* '98 with 5-round magazine; 20-round magazines were used to increase the rate of fire but made the weapon more cumbersome to use.

87. Civilian transport was commandeered by all armies, but this vehicle in German service is unusual: a London omnibus, originally used to transport British troops, but captured in Belgium by the Germans. The infantrymen in front are identified by their helmet-numerals as belonging to the 87th (1st Nassau) Regiment of XVIII Corps, of Albrecht of Württemberg's Fourth Army. They wear the 1910 *Waffenrock* and have the old (1895-pattern) ammunition-pouches on the waist-belt, worn with its usual shoulder-braces.

85 ▲

86 ▲ 87 ▼

▲88

88. Newly invented armoured cars were operated by British and Belgian crews and fought many skirmishing actions against the German advance patrols along the Belgian frontier, the terrain being ideally suited to fast-moving motorized units, though mechanization was met with resistance from the more entrenched traditionalists. This vehicle was operated by the Royal Naval Air Service under Flight-Commander Samson, RN, and was crewed by a

mixture of naval and Royal Marine personnel, under the aegis of the Royal Flying Corps. Its sides were protected by steel plates, and it had a Maxim gun mounted on the 'conning tower'.

89. Flying uniform was entirely at the discretion of the individual aviator, though that depicted here is typical, worn by Flight-Sergeant William H. Duckworth of the Royal Flying Corps: a waterproof raincoat with fur lining, fur-lined leather

helmet, and apparently boots with high leather gaiters.

90. Military aviation was in its infancy in 1914, but most of the combatant nations had some type of airborne reconnaissance facility. Here Belgian aviators sit by their machine; note the wing service cap; and ordinary trousers and puttees. The woven insignia on the left sleeve of the capless officer, whose laced kepi lies on the ground beside him.

91. British aviation personnel

▲89

wore a unique uniform; although officers often retained the uniform and insignia of their original regiments, enlisted members of the Royal Flying Corps wore a khaki lancer-style 'maternity jacket' with side pockets, and which fastened down the right breast, and the 'Austrian'-pattern field-cloth shoulder-title (white on dark-blue or black) read

▼90

▼91

'ROYAL/FLYING CORPS' or, as in this photograph of Private George Steer, the initials 'RFC'.

92. Although most military operations in 1914 occurred in Europe, minor expeditions were undertaken against German colonies. Operations against the German territory of Cameroon began as early as September 1914, from the British base at Freetown, Sierra Leone. This photograph shows a British West African contingent embarking at Freetown to attack the German port of Duala, the point of entry to Cameroon on the Bight of Biafra. Despite the workmanlike uniform of 'shirt-sleeves', shorts and topee, it is interesting to note that the officer at left retains a sword suspended from his Sam Browne belt.

93. Japanese participation in the war against the Central Powers was restricted to maritime operations and one military expedition, against the German Chinese colony of Tsingtau, the 'Gibraltar of the Far East', in late 1914. In collaboration with a British-Indian contingent, the Japanese Expeditionary Force captured

Tsingtau on 7 November 1914. These Japanese infantry are eating a hasty meal a short distance from the firing-line; they wear European-style uniform peaked cap and heavy greatcoats. Note the 'rising sun' banner in the centre.

94. A scene which was to be repeated countless times from 1914 onward: men of the Loyal Regiment (North Lancashire) pay brief homage to the temporary graves of their comrades, winter 1914. The Loyals formed part of the 2nd

Infantry Brigade of I Corps, and are shown here in greatcoats with the 1908 web equipment (less knapsack) worn over the top. Note the shaft of the entrenching-tool carried on the bayonet-scabbard.

Joseph Jacques Césaire Joffre (1852-1931)

Joseph Joffre was the dominant Allied military leader in the first year of the war, having been a somewhat surprising choice for the position of chief of the French general staff in July 1911.

The product of a comparatively humble background, Joffre was the son of a cooper. He began his military training at the Ecole Polytechnique, interrupting his studies to serve in the Franco-Prussian War, in which he received a temporary commission and served with the artillery during the defence of Paris. In September 1872 he was commissioned as an officer of engineers, rising to captain in 1876 and spending three years working on the defences of Paris. To gain active service experience he requested a posting to the colonial army, and participated in the expedition to Formosa in 1885 (for which he was awarded the *Légion d'Honneur*). Until 1888 he was employed as chief military engineer at Hanoi, working on the defences of Upper Tonkin. He was later sent to Africa to direct work on the Senegal–Niger railway, and led a famous march to Timbuktu in 1894. Promoted to general of brigade when serving in Madagascar, from 1900 Joffre was employed in a succession of posts in France; a general of division from March 1905, he rose to command II Corps, HQ Amiens.

Appointed to the *Conseil supérieur de la guerre*, Joffre was nominated as head of administration and lines of communication, but when disagreements arose regarding the planning for the event of war, he was appointed chief of general staff – most surprising in view of his lack of combat and staff experience and the fact that most of his career had been spent in the colonies. He was, however, devoid of political or religious connections or bias, factors which at the time complicated the appointment of the higher command in the French army.

To compensate for lack of staff experience, Joffre selected as his deputy Noel Joseph Edouard de Curiéres de Castelnau (1851-1944), an expert in staff matters. The appointment was criticised by the political Left, as Castelnau was an aristocrat from a devout Roman Catholic family, but he formed an ideal foil for Joffre, and together they were responsible for Plan XVII, the strategy to be used in the event of war with Germany, Castelnau

exerting considerable influence, although Joffre was in overall command.

Plan XVII determined the French response to German attack, not by defensive measures but by launching their own offensive in Lorraine. The German threat to advance through Belgium was recognised, but as any French move into Belgium was unacceptable politically, the counter to such an attack had to depend upon the diversion of elements from the main French offensive. In under-estimating the German capacity for the rapid deployment of reservists, and in failing to predict the size of the flanking movement through Belgium, the French plan was seriously flawed.

Consequently, Germany came near to success in the opening stage of the war. Joffre duly launched his offensive in Lorraine, entrusting the blunting of the German advance through Belgium to General Charles Lanrezac's French Fifth Army. When this was overwhelmed and the flaws in Plan XVII were revealed, Joffre had to reorganise his strategy completely. In this desperate period, his calm demeanour did much to reassure both military and public, although his role in the actions which followed has been the subject of debate, his detractors suggesting that it was the counter-attack launched by General Joseph Galliéni, military governor of Paris, which turned the tide on the Marne. Important though Galliéni's initiative was, Joffre's contribution should not be discounted, for it was he who managed the entire front at a time of the sternest pressure, and co-ordinated the counter-attack that first stopped the German advance and then established a sound defensive line.

The Marne was the pinnacle of Joffre's military career, and he was hailed as the saviour of his country. An equally vital contribution was his purge of ineptitude in the French command, which resulted in a huge improvement in the quality of French military leadership.

Thereafter, Joffre's military fortunes declined. His limited offensives in Artois and Champagne (May and September 1915) failed for lack of resources, and his political masters began to attempt to limit his powers. Castelnau, who at the outbreak of war had commanded Second Army and later the Central Army Group, was brought in

as Joffre's chief of staff – in reality to supervise him. Joffre's promotion to commander-in-chief of all French forces on all fronts in December 1915 was probably intended to remove him from immediate command on the western front, but he continued to fulfil this role in addition to his new responsibilities. The huge losses in 1916, especially at Verdun and on the Somme, further eroded his position, and by December 1916 not even his popularity with the French people could protect him. In an effort to save his government, the French prime minister Aristide Briand replaced Joffre by the diplomatic method of promotion to be the government's military adviser; on 16 December he was created Marshal of France, the first since 1870. For the remainder of the war his duties were largely ceremonial, as others assumed responsibility for the conduct of the war.

Joffre was not especially gifted as a general, but his presence was vital at a time of intense trial. His large, avuncular appearance and imperturbability, characterised by his nickname 'Papa Joffre', was of the greatest value in maintaining national and military morale, and for all his failings in the later stages of the war, 'Papa' deserved the plaudits he received for his efforts in halting the German offensive on the Marne.

References

Joffre, Marshal J.J.C. *The Memoirs of Marshal Joffre*, London 1932.
Herwig, H.H., & Heyman, N.M. *Biographical Dictionary of World War I*, Westport, Connecticut, 1982.
Liddell Hart, Sir Basil *Reputations*, London 1928.
Recouly, R. *Joffre*, New York 1931.

WORLD WAR ONE: 1915

1. The last vestige of colourful uniforms disappeared at the end of 1914 and beginning of 1915. These French light cavalrymen are typical: they wear the light blue tunic with crimson facings, and red breeches with light blue stripe, of the *Chasseurs à Cheval*; they even retain the white trefoil epaulettes. The kepi insignia appear to identify them as members of the 11th Regt; note the 'tent-hat'-style forage-caps of two of the seated figures. The man in the background wears a trophy *Pickelhaube*, which appears to bear the winged lion badge of Baden. The sign on this railway boxcar, 'Hommes 36-40, Chevaux 8' (36–40 men or 8 horses) was one remarked upon with disdain by countless Allied soldiers of all nations who served on the Western Front.

▼ **1**

WORLD WAR ONE:
1915

2. One of the first casualties of the war was the traditional French uniform of dark blue coat and red trousers, supplanted from late 1914 by the uniform illustrated, in a colour styled 'horizon blue' or 'tricolor grey', the latter description arising from its manufacture from interwoven strands of red, white and blue. The resulting lightish grey-blue shade proved to be an adequate camouflage and was retained throughout the war. The cut of the uniform remained basically the same (a tunic with standing collar and a double-breasted greatcoat for infantry), although a common variation was a single-breasted greatcoat for cavalry and a similar pattern for infantry but with breast-pockets. The red kepi had been equipped with grey-blue covers from the outbreak of war, and was now produced in 'horizon blue', retaining its black leather peak. Equipment remained of black leather.

INTRODUCTION

It might be argued that 1915 was the year in which the realities of World War became obvious. The experience on the two major fronts that had been opened in 1914 proved that the war would not be 'over by Christmas' as many had predicted; that neither France nor Russia would be defeated by rapid German advances; nor would Germany be overcome easily by the Allies.

1915 began in virtual stalemate on both Eastern and Western Fronts, and when the year ended, despite considerable German gains on the Eastern Front and a terrible effusion of blood and casualties on a scale undreamed of in earlier wars, this stalemate persisted. Moreover, the war had widened considerably with the entry of Turkey on the side of the Central Powers (she had become involved in 1914, but the real, full-scale combat began only in 1915) and the opening of a new front when Italy joined the Allies.

However, perhaps the most significant features of 1915 were those aspects of the war which raised the combat to a new level of 'frightfulness' (to use a word that featured large in the vocabulary of contemporary Press reports when describing the conduct of the enemy!) – the expedition to the Dardanelles and the use of gas. Although the former established the reputation of the ANZAC soldier for posterity, it produced conditions so terrible that the very geographical term 'Gallipoli' is sufficient to epitomise appalling privation, mismanagement and the most bitter combat. The use of poison gas – initially on the Eastern Front but most effectively in the West from April 1915 – introduced yet another level of horror into the war. Initially condemned by the Allies, toxic gas was ultimately adopted by them so that both armies were compelled to wear masks, which rendered them as unearthly in appearance as the nature of the war itself. In uniforms and equipment, 1915 saw the increasing use of camouflage, with the abandonment of the red and blue French uniform and its replacement by 'horizon blue' and, in a fashion at once archaic but necessary, the emergence of steel 'shrapnel helmets', pioneered by France.

Many thousands of photographs were published at the time in contemporary works and periodicals (for example, the *Illustrated War News, Navy & Army Illustrated, Sphere* and *Illustrated London News* in Britain, from which some of the images here have been taken), but contemporary captions should be viewed with circumspection. Trenches that are pristine, with immaculately-uniformed occupants, are almost certainly not scenes from the front no matter what the caption may say, while others purporting to be views of the war are not: in many cases these are obvious (such as that depicting 'Infantery laring cower' [sic] illustrated here), but in other cases it is difficult to determine the authenticity.

▲3

▲4

◀5

3. A French outpost in northern France, with a shallowly-excavated trench. This illustrates the combat uniform of the French infantry worn for a comparatively short period in 1915, from the adoption of 'horizon blue' as the uniform-colour but prior to the issue of the steel helmet. The uniform's cut is similar to that worn previously, but in this case the greatcoat is the single-breasted variety with breast-pockets. Unit-identification remained similar to that used on the blue uniform, with the regimental number on the collar-patches of the tunic and greatcoat, initially intended to be in a distinctive 'branch' colour – yellow with blue numeral for infantry – but soon the patch reverted to the shade of the garment with only the number in a contrasting colour.

In this case the number appears to be '38': in 1914 the 38th Regiment (based at St-Etienne) formed part of the 25th Infantry Division of XIII Corps in First Army.

4. French troops using a rudimentary trench-periscope. The officer's light blue tunic (right) apparently has light blue facings (which would indicate a hussar regiment) with red trousers striped light blue. The officer's rank is indicated by the metallic lace band around the upper edge of the cuff and the chevron on the front of the forage-cap. The extreme neatness of the trench and smartness of the uniforms indicate that this photograph depicts a demonstration trench rather than one in the front line; nevertheless, such images are of

great value in illustrating the minutiae of equipment and the theoretical construction of trenches. The rifle is the 1892-pattern carbine.

5. Contrasting with some immaculate 'trench' photographs taken behind the lines, this group of dishevelled French infantry has a greater air of authenticity. These *poilus* (also styled *piou-piou*!) enjoy a meal and a smoke under the 'protection' of a chicken-wire trench roof. This was intended to prevent the entry of grenades into the trench; if these were thrown they would not explode at the level of the trench floor but would still cause considerable damage. The men here appear to wear the new 'horizon blue', but at least two patterns of greatcoat are shown, double- and single-breasted.

6. Also in contrast to the muddy trenches usually associated with the Western Front were the lines in the hilly terrain of the Vosges, such as this defence-work manned by French *Chasseurs Alpins*. They exhibit the usual mixture of regulation and other dress, mufflers and leather jerkins being added to the dark blue tunic and floppy beret which characterized the French mountain troops (infantry and artillery) and from which they took their nickname of 'blue devils'. This trench is topped by a parapet of dry-stone walling with loopholes through which to fire, with the ubiquitous barbed wire entanglement in front.

7. The field uniform of the German Army began to be modified in 1915; the distinctive buttoned cuffs were replaced by a simple, turned-back cuff, and

the piping was removed from the rear vents. In September 1915 a new tunic was authorized, the *Bluse*, in which the breast-buttons were concealed by a fly-front, but the previous patterns were still worn for some considerable time. This uniform includes the 1910-pattern field-grey tunic with 'Saxon' cuffs and 1909-pattern leather equipment; the *Pickelhaube* has a detachable cover and the spike removed; and note the rolled-up shoulder-straps. The original of this photograph is captioned on the reverse by a British soldier, 'Not a bad looking lad for a Boche', and states that he had a number of photographs 'on him'; it was thus taken from the subject either as a prisoner or from his dead body.

▲ 8   ▼ 9

▼ 10

8. The German Army was a composite force of the troops of the various states, which to a degree retained their identity within the overall organization. In this photograph the King of Saxony inspects a detachment of Saxon troops; their identity is not completely clear from the picture, but the *Pickelhaube*-cover of one man appears to bear the number 104, which would indicate the 5th Saxon Regt. (Crown Prince's), which in 1914 was the senior infantry unit in the XIX (Saxon) Corps. It is interesting to observe the use of the 18th-century practice of troops following the reviewing dignitary with their eyes during the inspection, retained by some nations to the present day.

9. Among modifications to the German field uniform were those made to the *Pickelhaube*. It was made with a removable spike or ball, and cloth covers were produced with no accommodation for the spike; a number of cheaper (*Ersatz*) patterns were produced, helmets made of pressed steel (painted black or field-grey), pressed felt or even *papier mâché*, with mounts of thin, dull grey metal. Another variety rarely illustrated is that shown here, of field-grey felt with a small ventilation-knob on the top, without ornaments save in some cases a small plaque on the front bearing the unit-number. This headdress could be worn with a neck-curtain, and was worn thus in Serbia; similar neck-covers could be used in any hot climate, like Macedonia. The tunic here is similar to the amended 1915 pattern but with standing collar.

10. German troops marching-past in Lille. The mounted officer and at least one of the column appear to have the three-button 'Brandenburg' cuff, while others seem to have the modified 'turned back' cuff, the amendment of the original field-grey service uniform prior to the devising of the 1915 *Bluse*.

11. A German machine-gun mounted for use in an anti-aircraft role. The gun is the Model 1908 *Maschinengewehr*; the tube that leads from near the muzzle carried the water-coolant for the water-jacket or *Mantel*, which surrounded the barrel to prevent over-heating. This photograph shows how the 'sleigh' mounting could be adjusted to position the gun as required; also shown clearly is the erect rear sight. The regimental identity of the crew is not clear, but they wear the 1910-pattern tunic with 'Brandenburg' cuff; and note the coloured knot attached to the bayonet of the man at extreme right, which identified battalion and company.

12. A German machine-gun unit wearing the shako with cloth field cover used by the Jägers and machine-gun units. Their Maxim guns have the wheeled 'sleigh' mounting; the team in the foreground demonstrates how it could be fired from a prone position. Metal protective shields measuring 97 x 80cm, painted khaki, could be fitted to infantry Maxims, the gunner having to sight his target through a hole in the shield, restricting his field of vision though gaining protection from enemy fire. A further disadvantage was the fact that the shield disrupted camouflage, so that in Austrian service it was usual to throw a khaki-green or olive cloth over the shield to break up its hard edges.

12

▲13

13. Submachine-guns were not in common use during the war, but an automatic rifle was used by the German Army in small numbers. Three units styled *Musketen-Bataillone* were created in mid-1915, composed of four-man sections crewing one automatic rifle (30 rifles per company, 90 per battalion; company-establishment was 4 officers and 160 other ranks). The *Muskete* had a length of 44in

▼14

and a 25-round magazine; it was similar to the Danish Madsen automatic rifle and had a bipod mounting. It was used principally as a defensive weapon, its crews being positioned behind the front line to oppose any breakthrough.

14. A column of German infantry marching up to the front line on the Western Front. A number of interesting items are visible

here, notably the waterproof trousers (reasonably common by this date) and the bandoliers of extra ammunition hung around the neck. A further attempt to exclude the Flanders mud is the presence of extensive wrappings around the breeches and mechanisms of the rifles, clearly visible on the central man of the second rank. The use of the undress cap even in combat zones was widespread.

15. Men of the 1st Battalion Royal Scots Fusiliers manning a defensive position made from a ruined house and sandbags, at St-Eloi, south of Ypres, in about April or May 1915. The battalion landed in France in August 1914 as part of the 3rd Division; in early April it transferred from the 9th Brigade to the 8th, but remained in the 3rd Division throughout the war. The appearance of the men here is

15 ▲

16 ▲   17 ▼

absolutely typical of British infantry at this time, plus the regimental glengarry cap; note the covers around the mechanism of the Lee-Enfield rifle to exclude mud and dust.

16. The officers' uniform of the British Army is splendidly illustrated in this photograph of Major C. W. Hines of the 7th Battalion Durham Light Infantry. The khaki uniform has bronzed badges, the cap- and collar-insignia consisting of a crowned bugle-horn with 'DLI' in the centre, and on the collar the letter 'T' beneath, signifying 'Territorial'. The 7th Battalion was based at Sunderland, landed at Boulogne in April, and was in the Northumbrian Division (later 151st Brigade, 50th Dvision). The inscription on the original records that Major Hines survived barely five weeks after landing.

17. Britain had used the Maxim as its principal machine-gun, but the Vickers gun, which came into widespread use in 1915, became the standard weapon and was so efficient and reliable that (in successive modifications) it remained in use until well after the Second World War. Firing a .303in bullet at a rate of between 450 and 500 rounds per minute, it was a water-cooled weapon into which cartridges were fed on a fabric belt, into the slot clearly visible just to the rear of the water-jacket in this photograph. Its tripod mounting enabled it to be used in an anti-aircraft role, as here, without modification. The gunners appear to wear the grey kilts of the London Scottish.

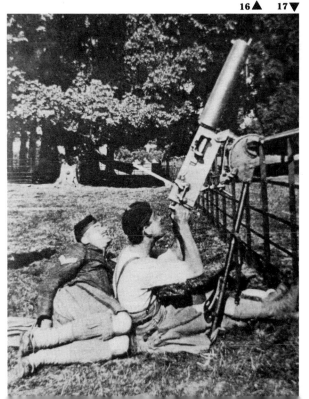

▲18

18. A private of the Black Watch in field equipment, illustrating the camouflaged khaki apron worn over the kilt, puttees over the hose, and the 1914-pattern equipment introduced from late 1914 or early 1915 to compensate for shortages of the 1908-pattern web equipment. It was intended that the 1914-pattern (which copied the 1908 but in brown leather, save for pouch-type cartridge-carriers) should be reserved for units training at home, but before long it was used on active service. An unusual feature here is the waterproof rain-hat; it is conceivable that the dark triangle on the front is some form of company- or battalion-identification.

19. In an attempt to overcome the effects of waterlogged trenches, various expedients were utilized ranging from 'gum-boots' to waders. Illustrated here

▲19

is a member of the 3/3rd Battalion City of London Regiment (Royal Fusiliers) wearing the 'wader-stockings' designed by F. B. Behr and pronounced a most effective method of remaining dry-shod even in freezing water. The waterproof waders were lined with wool and worn over the bare feet (i.e., without socks), inside the boots; damage could be repaired with a bicycle-tyre repair-kit. The battalion shown was raised in January 1915 and remained in Britain until late in the war, when it was absorbed by the 3rd Battalion. The 1914-pattern leather equipment is shown clearly; and the rank-insignia of a crown over three chevrons was that of company sergeant-major and company quartermaster-sergeant until 1915, and CQMS thereafter.

20. The different duties required by active service resulted in many variations in uniform. This private wears a costume unusual for his regiment, the Argyll and Sutherland Highlanders: riding-breeches and leather gaiters as worn by personnel of the regimental transport, instead of the usual kilt and hose. His tunic is the standard pattern, not the 'doublet' with cut-back skirts which distinguished Highland regiments; and the headdress is the balmoral-style bonnet introduced to replace the unfunctional glengarry in 1915. Known as a 'Tam O'Shanter', the bonnet was initially issued in blue cloth with khaki cover, and later made of khaki cloth; instead of the large cap-badges many units wore less-obtrusive tartan patches in the field.

21. Most of Belgium was overrun in 1914, and the remaining Belgian forces were dependent upon Britain and France for their uniforms and equipment. From early 1915 a khaki uniform was adopted, largely because the material was available from Britain; thus it resembled the British pattern but had leather gaiters instead of puttees. The new equipment was brown leather, and coloured collar-patches were worn on the tunic. Later the appearance became more French after the adoption of the Adrian helmet, painted khaki to match the uniform-colour.

20 ▲   21 ▼

▲22 ▼23 ▼24

25. Trench-warfare led to the reintroduction of the hand-grenade, a weapon that had enjoyed a considerable reputation in the late 17th century. Among the earliest grenades were simple iron spheres filled with combustible material ignited by tugging the fuze as they were thrown; this French infantryman demonstrates how a leather wrist-loop was utilized to ensure that ignition occurred as the grenade was thrown. Farther down the trench is a man who appears to be equipped with a rifle-grenade.

26. New types of artillery were devised for close support of the infantry in trench warfare; the trench-mortar was the principal development. In French service, weapons of great age were re-utilized to lob projectiles with high-angle fire into the enemy trenches, mortars as ancient as the 1830s being used until the development in 1915 of the first purpose-built weapon, the Mortar '58 cal. No 1', followed by other patterns. An odd development at this time was the 'aerial torpedo', a projectile resembling a conventional mortar-bomb with large fins to provide stability in flight. Recoil of the launch was absorbed by the large base-plate depicted here.

26 ▼

25 ▲

22. Contemporary captions should always be viewed with a degree of circumspection: views purporting to have been photographed on active service were sometimes staged for home consumption. This is included here as perhaps the most glaring example, published in France in 1915 supposedly depicting *Infanterie anglaise en ambuscade* and by implication at the front; actually it appears to depict a cadet unit on exercise at home. The 'English' caption which accompanied the French publication, "Infantery laring cower", did little to elucidate!

23. This photograph – remarkable if it is what it purports to be – was published in June 1915 and shows a German attack upon a position held by The King's (Liverpool) Regiment near Ypres. As the British wait with fixed bayonets, an officer crouches in mid-ground ready to direct his men. The caps worn here are the ordinary service variety with wire-stiffened crown; it was common on active service to wear a softer cap, without the stiffening, known as a 'trench cap'.

24. A French machine-gun post at Neuville St-Vaast, established in a shallow trench. The gun appears to be the Model 1907, known as the St-Etienne (from its being designed at the National Arms Factory there), a development of the Model 1905 (Puteaux, similarly named from the place of development). It was air-cooled and could achieve a rate of fire of up to 650 rounds per minute (normally 500). Ammunition was in the form of 'racks' of 25 rounds, the comb-like objects visible in the illustration, being handed from the ammunition-box at the foot of the trench. Two of the gunners have anti-gas goggles around their kepis.

▲27　▼28

▲29

31. From about July 1915 the French Army assumed the appearance it held for the remainder of the war, with the adoption of the 'casque Adrian', the steel shrapnel-helmet with medial ridge and front and rear peaks. Named after its designer, it was copied from the helmets of French firemen and was painted to match the uniform-colour. On the front it bore a stamped metal badge: a grenade for infantry and cavalry; grenade and crossed cannon-barrels for artillery; horn for light infantry; grenade and anchor for marines; helmet and corselet for engineers; and a crescent for Moroccans; all with the letters 'RF' (*République Française*). Stars were affixed to the front for general officers. These infantrymen wear typical service uniform with the helmet, and the 1915 single-breasted greatcoat with breast-pockets; the man on the right has in addition to his ordinary equipment a small automatic pistol tucked behind his shoulder-belt, and apparently a dagger, both of use in close-quarter fighting in the trenches.

31 ▼

30 ▲

27. A number of ancient armaments re-appeared in the First World War, most notably the steel helmet, but more bizarre was this contraption, a crossbow manufactured for the projection of hand-grenades. *L'Arbalète Lance-Grenade,* known colloquially as a 'grasshopper', was used by the French Army to hurl bombs a distance of between 20 and 80 metres. This particular example has a shaped stock like a rifle, the propulsion power arising from the steel and wire construction.

28. A popular method of manufacturing anti-aircraft protection was to affix a machine-gun to a wagon-wheel upon a post, the wheel parallel to the ground. This German construction takes the principle a stage further by mounting a field-gun upon a beehive-shaped wooden platform, which allowed it to traverse to follow the enemy aircraft. The gun appears to be the 1896-pattern 77mm *Feld Kanone.* The crew's protective dug-out is quite sophisticated and sturdily-built.

29. With sniping a common danger of trench-warfare, numerous patterns of periscope were devised to allow observation without danger, some sophisticated and others extremely rudimentary. One of the former is illustrated here, disguised with sacking and grass where it protrudes over the parapet. The viewer is apparently a German *Unteroffizier*, his rank indicated by the broad lace on the collar, but the identity of the unit is not evident from his shoulder-strap.

30. The first steel helmet of the war was a skull-cap without a brim used by the French Army, worn under the kepi or, as here, on top of it, giving the appearance of a peaked crash-helmet. It could be worn without the kepi (a very medieval appearance), and was painted light grey-blue to match the uniforms. The appearance of the classic 'casque Adrian' from mid-1915 replaced the skull-cap, though the earlier pattern was apparently quite effective: when the *Illustrated London News* published this photograph it reported an analysis of head-wounds on 42 men without the cap (23 severe or fatal) and on 13 who wore it, only 5 of whom suffered superficial injury. Note that one of the infantrymen here retains the earlier blue greatcoat.

▲ 32 ▼ 33

32. Armoured cars were common in many armies, the majority providing the crew with more protection than this French example. Cars mounted with machine-guns originated in the French Army with Captain Genty's *auto-mitrailleuse* of 1905–6, basically a Hotchkiss gun affixed to the back of his 1904 Panhard & Levassor automobile. Genty demonstrated the value of such vehicles in North African campaigning. According to its French identification, this photograph of a car firing over a street-barricade was taken in action; shortly after this a shell hit the ruined building to the left of the barricade, killing the NCO firing the gun and injuring the loader.

33. French casualty-evacuation in the Argonne. Supposedly a genuine photograph rather than one posed for the photographer, this shows French troops clearing casualties, a task never solely the responsibility of the official medical personnel. Stretchers are not used here: one casualty is being carried in a blanket. Note the anti-gas goggles worn around the kepi; the small pouch worn on a strap around the neck would contain the anti-gas face-mask.

34. A British casualty, with a bandaged lower right leg and liberally smeared with Flanders mud, is loaded into an ambulance by German medical personnel. This shows the peaked cap worn by transport and medical units of the German Army; in field-grey, it had a blue band piped red for medical staff. The rectangular box suspended from the second button of the tunic of the orderly immediately behind the bandaged leg is a battery-operated flashlight. Note the white brassards with red cross worn on the left upper arm, the universal symbol of medical personnel in many armies.

35. The introduction of distinctive battalion-insignia into the British Army occurred from early 1915; it only really proliferated in later years. A common location of this insignia was at the bottom of the collar at the rear, where they could be identified by following troops in action. The officer here is unidentified, but the badge appears to resemble the red felt Prince of Wales's plumes worn by the 1st Battalion The Welsh Regiment.

36. Family groups of this type are among the most common

images from the First World War (for all nations) yet can illustrate most interesting items of uniform and equipment. This member of the Lancashire Fusiliers wears the spurred boots and cavalry bandolier of the regimental transport, and the soft 'trench cap' with stiffening removed, colloquially termed a 'Gorblimey'. The sleeve-insignia is the white '8' on a red diamond worn by the 1/8th Battalion, a unit based in Salford and which served at Gallipoli.

▲37 ▼38

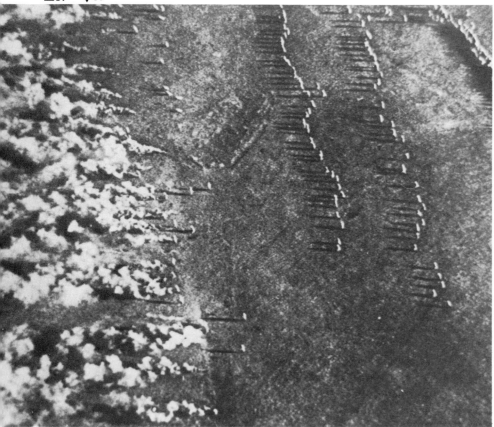

37. This bizarre photograph illustrates a group of German prisoners captured by the French near Bois le Prêtre, according to the original caption. The diminutive prisoner being questioned by the large, caped French officer measured 4ft 9in; but to illustrate such a 'Puny Hun' (sic) could be counter-productive for propaganda purposes, so the *Illustrated War News* accompanied the photograph with an account of how fit and strong the ordinary German prisoner was, thus explaining why the Allies were not immediately victorious over undersized recruits of this stature, wearing an over-large 1910-pattern tunic.

38. This photograph was published in 1915 as having been taken by a Russian aviator, showing a German advance on the Eastern Front preceded by a barrage of poison gas. Later in the war this terrible weapon was delivered by shells (especially effective when 'mustard gas' was used, as this dreadful concoction did not require employment in dense clouds to be fully effective); but initially the method of delivery utilized the strength of the wind to blow it towards the enemy. Cylinders of toxic gas might be buried with pipes leading out into no-man's-land, to be released in a cloud when the wind-direction was appropriate, as here. Infantry would second the attack, but unless equipped with respirators, they were vulnerable to a shift in wind direction.

39. Many varieties of protective masks were utilized in the period of the early use of poison gas, ranging from simple pads taped over the mouth to hoods covering the entire head. This French device is one devised in 1915 by Dr Detourbe: a wire grille worn over the nose and mouth with a similar grille attached by a hinge at the bridge of the nose, with a pad of impregnated cotton-wool fitted between the two. With such contraptions the French Army frequently wore goggles to protect the eyes.

39 ▲

40. At the date of this photograph only the Germans used poison gas, yet their troops were equally vulnerable if the gas-clouds blew towards them. Protection at this stage was no more sophisticated than a chemically impregnated pad worn over the mouth, but for resuscitation medical orderlies were equipped with oxygen-bottles carried on a breast-harness, with flexible tube and face-mask to treat the partially asphixiated. This is apparently Grenadier Regiment No. 12 (2nd Brandenburg, Prince Carl of Prussia), which in 1914 formed part of III Corps. The stretcher shown has a hinged end, which allowed the casualty's head to be raised.

41. A Highlander wearing an early variety of anti-gas protection, resembling a veil plus goggles; which, as one contemporary caption to this photograph remarked, resembled the Sphinx. The photograph also illustrates the khaki apron with pocket which could be worn over the kilt as an aid to camouflage; these were introduced as early as the Boer War but were not especially popular, and photographs also show the kilt worn without the apron. The puttees are worn over the hose.

40 ▼   41 ▲

CHRONOLOGY: 1915

1914 ended with action in four principal theatres. On the Western Front, the fluid manoeuvre of the first campaigns had ended with the establishment of trench-lines running from the North Sea to Switzerland; the virtual stalemate of the next four years was established. On the Eastern Front, stalemate also existed, with Russia and Serbia holding the Austro-Germans in check. Turkey's entry into the war on the side of the Central Powers put additional pressure upon Russia, which was already considerably dependent upon Anglo-French supplies. On the Turkish Front proper, the British invasion of Mesopotamia was just beginning; and in the fourth sphere of operations, the overseas colonies, minor actions were occurring against German colonial possessions.

The Western Front

January–March: Allied offensive in the Champagne and Artois area attempted to free French territory from German control, with limited effect as German counter-attacks stabilized the situation. British forces had a noted success at Neuve Chapelle (10 March), but bad coordination of support allowed the Germans to recover the lost ground.

6–15 April: French offensive at the Battle of the Woëvre beaten off.

22 April–25 May: Under cover of the first use in the West of poison gas, the German offensive of the 2nd Battle of Ypres temporarily broke the Allied line; but lack of support occasioned by the drain in manpower to the Eastern Front prevented a renewed drive, and after very heavy combat the British stabilized the line, having suffered enormous casualties.

May–June: Allied offensives made limited progress, the British drive being stopped near Festubert (May) and the French around Vimy Ridge (late May and June, also styled the 2nd Battle of Artois). After this both sides neared temporary exhaustion and merely held their positions.

September–November: Again the Allies took the offensive, having recouped their strength. A concerted attempt to break the German line had been planned by Joffre: in the 3rd Battle of Artois and 2nd Battle of Champagne the French made little progress; similarly the British at Loos (25 September–14 October). After further immense loss of life for little effect, the effort was abandoned, and in December Sir John French (taking the blame for lack of success) was replaced as British commander by Sir Douglas Haig, who held this command on the Western Front to the end of the war. Losses on the Western Front had been appalling beyond belief — almost 1.3 million French, over 600,000 Germans and 280,000 British — yet the battle lines on 31 December remained virtually as they had been on 1 January.

The Eastern Front

January: The efforts of the Central Powers were successful in the east, compared with the stalemate on the Western Front. The plan was to concert an attack on the Russian defenders of Poland from the Austrians in the south and the Germans in the north. On 31 January at Bolimov the Germans used poison gas for the first time, though with less success than later on the Western Front.

February: At the 2nd Battle of the Masurian Lakes, Hindenburg's Germans made considerable progress; but a Russian counter-attack (22 February) stabilized the position.

March: In Galicia the Russians successfully resisted Austrian attempts to relieve beleaguered Przemysl, which fell to the Russians on 22 March.

May–June: German resources were concentrated into reinforcing the Eastern Front, and an immense assault from 2 May burst through the Russian line, recapturing Przemysl (3 June).

June–December: As the Central Powers followed up their breakthrough, the Russians began a dogged retreat, only the skill of their commander, Grand Duke Nicholas, and the determination of the ordinary soldiers preventing a defeat of massive proportions. The onset of winter and the seasonal deterioration of the roads ended the 300-mile conquest, Vilna being captured by the Germans on 19 September. By then the Grand Duke had been removed (unfairly) and replaced by the Tsar in nominal command. The year ended with the Russians clinging to a front line virtually on the Russian frontier. The Central Powers had lost about a million men in the year's campaigning on the Eastern Front, and the Russians about the same, plus a further million captured.

The Caucasus

January: A Turkish attempt to advance north-east into the Russian Caucasus was repelled by a Russian victory at Sarikamish (3 January).

July: Russian failure to exploit Sarikamish allowed the Turks to resume their offensive, winning a victory near Van (16 July), but they retired upon the approach of Russian reinforcements.

August–December: Fighting continued without a decision; Grand Duke Nicholas was transferred from the Eastern Front from late September and began to prepare for a renewed offensive in 1916.

The Dardanelles

The Allied expedition to the Dardanelles was undertaken to relieve pressure on Russia and to remove Turkey from the war. The descent was an Anglo-French enterprise, initially a naval expedition, which was repelled by the Turkish defenders (18 March), and then by a military expedition under General Ian Hamilton, which was opposed by the German General Liman von Sanders.

25 April: Allied landings at Cape Helles and 15 miles farther north at Ari Burnu, the latter conducted by the ANZACs (Australian and New Zealand Army Corps). Neither landing was especially well-managed, and both met the stiffest opposition from Turkish forces in strong positions overlooking the landing beaches.

6–8 August: After a summer of bitter fighting around the landing areas, a strong British reinforcement landed at Suvla, north of Ari Burnu, to coincide with pushes from both the existing beachheads. Though Suvla successfully opened another field of operations, still little progress could be made against the resolute defenders.

August–December: Hamilton was replaced in mid-October, but the brutal fighting continued until the Allied commanders decided that the only practical move was to abandon the whole expedition; the evacuation was to be completed in January 1916. The Dardanelles expedition, though strategically valid, was one of the costliest failures of the war. Under the name 'Gallipoli' it became a synonym for extreme privation and untold feats of heroism on the part of both sides.

The Middle East

British efforts against the Turks were also made in the Middle East; in 1915 these were largely directed towards Mesopotamia. In January–February a Turkish attack against the Suez Canal was repelled by the British forces in Egypt; no further operations occurred on this front, but the threat was sufficient to prevent the British from releasing all the necessary resources to support the Dardanelles expedition.

January: British forces at Basra were built up to contemplate an advance on Baghdad, but initially Turkish probes had to be repelled. By midsummer about one-third of the distance to Baghdad had been covered by General Charles Townshend. In support, General G. F. Gorringe advanced up the Euphrates on Townshend's left and won a minor victory at Nasiriya (24 July).

September: Townshend continued to advance upon Kut-al-Amara, two-thirds of the way from Basra to Baghdad. The Turks were driven from Kut (27–28 September) and withdrew to Ctesiphon, midway from Kut to Baghdad; despite Townshend being in need of reinforcement, his superior, Sir John Nixon, ordered him to press on.

November: Townshend attacked Ctesiphon (22 November). After initial success, his lack of resources and Turkish reinforcements decided him to return to Kut (26 November), where he arrived on 3 December. Four days later he was besieged and in a parlous state.

In addition to the Anglo-Turkish conflict in Mesopotamia, sporadic fighting occurred throughout the year in Persia, which, though neutral itself, had been largely occupied by Russian forces. Russo–Turkish conflict there was subsidiary to the main spheres of operations in the Caucasus and Mesopotamia.

The Serbian Front

Serbia was important to the Central Powers if communication between Germany and Turkey were to be maintained; neutral Roumania closed the rail-link in June, which to a degree precipitated the main attack on Serbia, in which Germany and Austria were joined by Bulgaria. Bulgaria's entry into the war prompted Greece to mobilize in support of Serbia, and to aid the Greeks a Franco-British expedition was sent to Salonika (October); but immediately the pro-Allied Greek prime minister, Venizelos, was removed by the king, who declared Greek neutrality.

October: Serbia was overwhelmed by four enemy armies, one German, one Austrian and two Bulgarian. The Allies in Salonika were too weak to prevent the disaster.

November: With the Franco-British troops able only to defend Salonika, the Serbian Army retreated into Montenegro and Albania, from where the remnant was shipped to Corfu to be re-equipped and reorganized. The Allied intervention was uncoordinated and too weak to be of use, and was further embarrassed by being in possession of territory belonging to a neutral.

The Italian Front

A new front in Europe was opened when Italy joined the war on the side of the Allies (23 May) by a declaration of war on Austria (not Germany).

June–December: The Italians attempted to attack Austria on the Isonzo Front (north of Trieste). Four battles along the River Isonzo occurred (June/July, July/August, October/November and November/December), none of which actions enabled the Italians to make much progress against stout Austrian defence.

The situation at the end of 1915, despite the losses of immense numbers of men on both sides, was generally a stalemate. The Western Front remained static; Turkey had successfully repelled the Dardanelles expedition and limited British progress in Mesopotamia; while the Central Powers had achieved considerable success on the Eastern Front and in Serbia. Lack of Allied coordination had proved extremely costly and continued to inhibit the full utilization of their resources.

BRITISH ARMY SMALL ARMS (excluding machine-guns)

Until after the Boer War two varieties of personal firearm had been carried by the British Army: the infantry rifle and the cavalry carbine. The inefficiency of the latter having been proven in the Boer War, a universal rifle was intended for both dismounted and mounted troops (although a number of variants were actually carried). To accommodate both services, the existing infantry Lee-Enfield magazine rifle (approved in November 1895, although it did not immediately displace the variant of the first British magazine rifle, the Lee-Metford, currently in service) was reduced in length and styled the Short Magazine Lee-Enfield or SMLE (in several 'Marks'), 44½in overall (as against the 49½in of the earlier rifles, Lee-Enfield, Lee-Metford and Martini-Henry). It was introduced in 1902, and from 1905–7 a quantity of earlier Lee-Enfields and Lee-Metfords were converted to SMLE, and others modified to permit 'charger' loading of the magazine (by which five rounds could be inserted simultaneously, a system developed by Lee in 1892). The bolt-action rifle of .303in calibre weighed 8lb 10½oz without bayonet (1lb extra), and in the hands of a skilled infantryman (like those of the BEF of 1914) could discharge 15 rounds per minute and was capable of great accuracy. (Various Marks were in simultaneous use: for example, in their first action in 1914 the London Scottish found their Mark Is prone to jamming, so they exchanged them for improved Mark IIIs that were available on the battlefield).

In 1911–13 a new rifle of .276in calibre was developed, known as the 'Pattern 1913', of which a number were made for trial, but its adoption was prevented by the outbreak of war. Some of those produced were adapted to .303in and issued as snipers' rifles as they were capable of superior accuracy. The .303in calibre variant was styled 'Pattern 1914' (P.14) and from 1915 was manufactured for Britain in the United States by Winchester, Remington and Eddystone, and was used alongside the Lee-Enfield. From 1917, when the USA ran short of its own Springfield rifle, the P.14 was adapted to the US .300in calibre cartridge and issued to the US Army under the title 'Model 1917 (Enfield)'.

A number of older weapons were also used by British forces; even the single-shot Martini-Henry (developed in 1871–2 and originally issued in 1874, with improvements in 1876 and 1879) was used by some home-defence troops. The forces from the Dominions tended to use standard British weapons, though a distinctive pattern was used by the Canadian Army, the Mark III Ross rifle of 1910, also .303in and a development of the 1907 Mark II. It was an extremely accurate weapon but so prone to becoming fouled that by 1916 it was withdrawn and replaced by the Lee-Enfield, although some were retained for sniping.

The bayonet, long considered the British Army's 'traditional' weapon, remained important. The basic pattern in use was

bayonet in a hand-to-hand fight, was removed in 1913, although photographs of the First World War occasionally show it still in use. The P.14 was equipped with a bayonet not dissimilar, but the Ross had a shorter, sturdy blade akin to trench-knives, the privately-acquired weapons carried in considerable numbers especially in the later stages of the war (as were a variety of styled a 'sword bayonet' having a single-edged, knife-shaped blade with deep fullers, wooden grip and steel quillon. The 1903 Lee-Enfield bayonet had been almost 15in long; probably to compensate for the reduction in length of the SMLE, the 1907–pattern was increased to a blade-length of 17in. The hooked quillon, designed initially to catch or throw off the enemy's

ORGANIZATIONAL TABLES: THE BRITISH ARMY

(Organization naturally varied with circumstances, but the following is a basic outline of the principal formations):

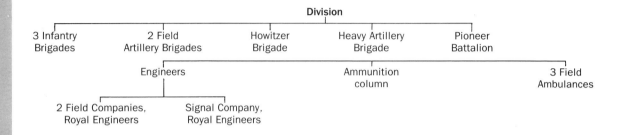

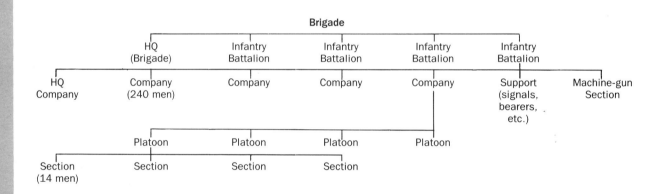

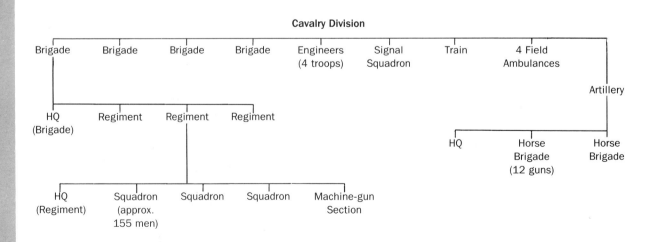

trench-clubs). The 1905-pattern Ross had a fine point, which was recognized as defective in action and was modified by grinding down the blade in 1907.

Swords were carried by officers and cavalry; the 1908-pattern cavalry sabre, which had a thin but strong blade designed for the thrust and a metal grip that provided an excellent hand-guard, was probably the finest cavalry weapon *ever* devised and compelled the user to execute the thrust, which the British Army had finally acknowledged as the most effective blow. Ironically, by the time this well-designed weapon was issued, the opportunities for its use in combat were virtually nil: in the only large-scale cavalry actions of the old style in the war, against the Turks, the sword had been virtually discarded and bayonets were used in its place. The swords of infantry officers existed in several patterns (officers of most Scottish regiments had the traditional Highland broadsword with basket hilt) but were rarely carried on active service.

Unlike the armies of some European nations, Britain preferred the revolver as a pistol rather than the automatic: the Webley Mark IV was typical: a 6-shot, .442in calibre weapon, double-action and self-extracting (the cartridges being ejected when the gun was 'broken' and the barrel depressed). The revolver was carried principally by officers and, like all pistols, was only of use at shorter ranges.

Hand-grenades were much neglected at the outbreak of war, only a few members of the Royal Engineers being trained to throw the 'No. 1' grenade, which consisted of a fragmentation-head mounted on a 16in cane with a 36in streamer to ensure that it landed nose-down, ignition being caused by the impact of landing. Patterns No. 2 (or 'Mexican', copied from an export order for that nation) and Nos. 3 (the Marten-Hale rifle-grenade) and similar 4 were all used prior to late 1915, but shortages led to the manufacture of grenades in the field, often from old tin cans (hence the colloquial name 'jam-tin bombs'). A wide variety of other patterns were devised, ranging from egg-shaped projectiles, some resembling the jam-tin, explosive devices on a wooden pallet resembling a hair-brush, archaic-looking cylindrical bombs resembling a Napoleonic howitzer-shell in miniature (No. 15), to a variety of rifle-grenades, some of dubious value and more dangerous to the thrower than the enemy. The best pattern was the No. 5, introduced in early 1915 and manufactured by the Mills Munition Company. It never completely replaced other patterns, but the 'Mills bomb' in its several guises became the commonest grenade in British service, and also existed in a rifle-grenade version, although variations on the Marten-Hale were also developed. The later patterns no longer relied upon percussion ignition (i.e., the impact of landing) but had an internal mechanism that exploded the charge by a plunger released by the extraction of a pin before throwing.

BRITISH ARMY RANK MARKINGS

Rank-insignia for NCOs took the form of chevrons on the upper arm: lance-corporal (or equivalent), one; corporal, two; sergeant, three; company quartermaster-sergeant (and company sergeant-major to 1915), three with crown above; CSM after 1915 (and regimental sergeant-major before) crown on lower sleeve; regimental QMS, star over four inverted chevrons (from 1915 crown in wreath on lower sleeve); RSM after 1915, royal coat of arms on lower sleeve.

Officers' insignia were in the form of stars and crown on the shoulder-strap of the greatcoat and foreign service tunic, and on the cuff for ordinary service dress, a 'gauntlet' cuff for Highland regiments and a flapped cuff for others. Badges and braid were in light drab: 2nd lieutenant, star, one line of braid; lieutenant, 2 stars, 1 line; captain, 3 stars, 2 lines; major, crown, three lines; lieutenant-colonel, crown and star, three lines; colonel, crown and two stars, four lines.

BRITISH ARMY BATTALION-IDENTIFICATION

The great increase in the number of battalions fielded by a regiment, and the anonymity of the khaki service uniform, caused the introduction of battalion-identity signs in cloth at the back of the collar or, on the sleeve below the shoulder. That these seldom bore many common regimental devices is illustrated by the battalion-insignia illustrated here, of the Lancashire Fusiliers.

A: 'Ordinary' cuff, left to right: lieutenant; 2nd lieutenant.
B: 'Highland' cuff, left to right: lieutenant-colonel; major; captain.

A

B

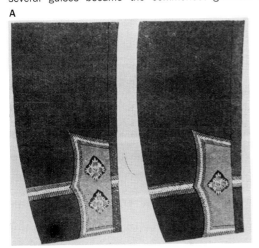

1st Bn: fig. 1, orange-yellow (left) and crimson.
2nd Bn: fig. 2, crimson with orange-yellow centre (sleeve).
1/5th Bn: fig. 3, red, bearing white '5' (sleeve).
2/5th Bn (formed Sept. 1914): fig. 4, red.
3/5th Bn (formed Oct. 1914): fig. 3, dark green (sleeve).
2/6th Bn (formed Sept. 1914): fig. 3, red (sleeve).
1/7th Bn: fig. 3, red, bearing white '7' (sleeve).
2/7th Bn (formed Aug. 1914): fig 3, yellow (sleeve).
1/8th Bn: fig. 3, red, bearing white '8' (sleeve).
2/8th Bn (formed Sept. 1914): fig. 3, black (sleeve).
9th Bn (formed Aug. 1914): fig. 5, yellow with black number
(indicating 2nd bn of 34th Inf. Bde., 11th Div., from 1915).
10th Bn (formed Sept. 1914): each company had different sign.
A Coy: fig. 6, crimson (left) and yellow; B Coy: fig 6, yellow (left)
and crimson; C Coy: fig. 7, crimson (left) and yellow; D Coy:
fig. 7, yellow (left) and crimson.
11th Bn (formed Sept. 1914): fig. 8, black bar over two red bars.
15th Bn (formed Sept. 1914): each company had different sign,
all of fig. 9 with upper red triangle: HQ Coy with black bars, A

Coy red bars, B Coy dark green bars, C Coy yellow bars, D Coy
blue bars.
16th Bn (formed Nov. 1914): each company had different sign,
all of fig. 10 with upper red triangle, HQ Coy with red triangle
alone; A–D Coys with three bars coloured as for 15th Bn.
17th Bn (formed Dec. 1914): fig 11, yellow (sleeve).
18th Bn (formed Jan. 1915): fig. 12, dark blue (sleeve). (On
back of collar, two vertical dark blue bars, one over the other.)
19th Bn (formed Jan. 1915): fig. 13, red. (From Dec. 1917 a
yellow rectangle upon crimson diamond worn at rear of
greatcoat collar.)
20th Bn (formed March 1915): fig. 14, purple.
  Such signs were normally worn only on active service; thus
battalions like the 3/, 4/Lancashire Fusiliers, etc., which
remained at home, had no such insignia. The 12th Bn. (65th
Bde, 22nd Div.) and 23rd Bn (176th Bde, 59th Div; 121st Bde,
40th Div. from June 1918) wore only the sign of their respective
divisions. A full table of this unit's signs is in *History of the
Lancashire Fusiliers 1914–18* (J. C. Latter, Aldershot, 1949).

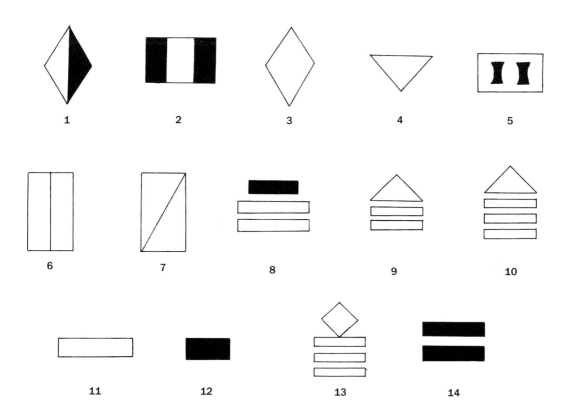

ORDER OF BATTLE: GALLIPOLI

The following skeleton order of battle lists the regiments
involved: there were in addition the usual artillery and
supporting services provided by New Zealand and Australia, and
by the British Army with Indian Mountain Artillery for the Royal
Naval Division; plus the Palestinian-Jewish Zion Mule Corps
attached to ANZAC Headquarters.

I ANZAC Corps
HQ and troops attached at Corps level:
2nd Lt. Horse Bde: 5th (Queensland), 6th and 7th (NSW) Lt
  Horse
3rd Lt. Horse Bde: 8th (Victoria), 9th (Victoria/S. Australia) and
  10th (W. Australia) Lt Horse
Ceylon Planters' Rifle Corps (attached to HQ)
1st Australian Div:

HQ etc: 4th (Victoria) Lt Horse
1st Australian Bde: 1st–4th NSW Btns
2nd Australian Bde: 5th–8th Victoria Btns
3rd Australian Bde: 9th Queensland, 10th S. Australia, 11th W.
 Australia, 12th S. Australia/W. Australia/Tasmania Btns
2nd Australian Div:
HQ etc: 13th (Victoria) Lt Horse
5th Australian Bde: 17th–20th NSW Btns
6th Australian Bde: 21st–24th Victoria Btns
7th Australian Bde: 25th Queensland, 26th Queensland/
 Tasmania, 27th S. Australia, 28th W. Australia Btns
New Zealand and Australian Div:
NZ Bde: Auckland, Canterbury, Otago and Wellington Btns
NZ Mounted Rifle Bde: Auckland, Canterbury and Wellington
 Mtd Rifles

4th Australian Bde: 13th NSW, 14th Victoria, 15th Queensland/
 Tasmania, 16th S. and W. Australia Btns
1st Australian Lt Horse Bde: 1st (NSW), 2nd (Queensland), 3rd
 (S. Australia/Tasmania) Lt Horse
29th Indian Bde: 14th Prince of Wales's Own Ferozepore Sikhs;
 1/5th, 1/6th and 2/10th Gurkha Rifles (Frontier Force)
Royal Naval Div:
Royal Marine Bde: Chatham and Portsmouth Btns, RM
1st Royal Naval Bde: Nelson Btn, RN, Deal Btn, RM

C and D: In 1915 the *Illustrated London News* captioned these
photographs of a sergeant of a fusilier regiment wearing the
1908 web equipment.

C

D

Original British contingent:

29th Division:

86th Inf. Bde: 2/R. Fusiliers, 1/Lancashire Fusiliers, 1/R. Munster Fusiliers, 1/R. Dublin Fusiliers

87th Inf. Bde: 2/S. Wales Borderers, 1/King's Own Scottish Borderers, 1/R. Inniskilling Fusiliers, 1/Border Regt

88th Inf. Bde: 4/Worcestershire Regt, 2/Hampshire Regt, 1/Essex Regt, 5/R. Scots

SOURCES AND BIBLIOGRAPHY

This lists some works applicable to the war as a whole, as presented in the earlier title *1914*, but emphasis is here given to the campaigns of 1915 and to the British Army, which features in the data section. The literature is immense, and the following are either some of the most significant or the most easily-accessible for further reading.

Anon *The Anzac Book* (London, 1916) a celebration of the Anzacs and their campaign in the Dardanelles.

Barker, A. J. *The Neglected War: Mesopotamia 1914–18* (London, 1967).

Barnes, R. M. *The British Army of 1914* (London, 1968).

Chappell, M. *British Battle Insignia 1914–18* (London, 1986).

Chappell, M. *British Infantry Equipments 1908–80* (London, 1980).

Chappell, M. *The British Soldier in the 20th Century: Service Dress 1902–40* (Hatherleigh, 1987).

Chappell M. *The British Soldier in the 20th Century: Field Service Head-Dress* (Hatherleigh, 1987).

Denton, K. *Gallipoli: One Long Grave* (Sydney, 1986).

Fosten, D. S. V., and R. J. Marrion *The British Army 1914–18* (London, 1978).

Fosten, D. S. V., and R. J. Marrion *The German Army 1914–18* (London, 1978).

James, E. A. *British Regiments 1914–18* (London, 1978), a register of units and the formations in which they served.

Laffin, J. *Damn the Dardanelles* (London, 1980).

Mollo, A. *Army Uniforms of World War I* (Poole, 1977), the most comprehensive and valuable modern work on the subject.

Moorhead, A. *Gallipoli* (London, 1956).

Nash, D. B. *Imperial German Army Handbook 1914–18* (London, 1980).

Nash, D. B. *German Infantry 1914–18* (Edgeware, 1971).

Walter, A. (ed.) *Guns of the First World War* (London, 1988), a reprint of the *Text Book of Small Arms*, 1909.

Wilson, H. W. (ed.) *The Great War* (London, 1915), contemporary work that includes many significant photographs.

▼42

42. The advent of poison gas produced some of the most unearthly-looking soldiers in history, as exemplified by these French *poilus* wearing anti-gas hoods (an appearance compared by the *Illustrated War News* with that of the staff of the Spanish Inquisition!). They also wear khaki overall-coats apparently over the equipment (presumably an attempt at camouflage prior to the issue of 'horizon blue'), and carry the 1886 Lebel rifle (modified 1893), at 8mm calibre the first small-bore military rifle officially adopted. Its metal-hilted bayonet of cross-shaped section, with hooked quillon, is well illustrated here.

43. A platoon of British soldiers wearing a variety of anti-gas helmets. The first protection was nothing more than a pad worn over the nose and mouth, often with goggles; but these men wear a number of more elaborate masks, some with rectangular viewing-slits and others with transparent patches for the eyes. The small pouches worn around the neck or over the shoulder were the means of carrying the mask in a place accessible for immediate use.

44. Following the rudimentary face-pads adopted as anti-gas protection early in the war, the next common British style was this hood-like helmet made of blue-grey or khaki cloth, with metal-edged eye-holes and a leather valve at the mouth, a voluminous garment, which had to be tucked inside the tunic-collar. The helmets were appallingly uncomfortable (a metal tube connected to the valve had to be held between the teeth) and produced an inhuman appearance.

45. A French infantryman in trench-fighting kit showing the 1915 uniform. He wears the new 'horizon blue' greatcoat with breast-pockets and blue regimental number on the collar, the Adrian steel helmet and apparently only rudimentary gas-protection, a muffler and goggles. The weapons shown were ideal for combat in the close confines of a trench: a privately-acquired dagger and a revolver, which appears to be the French Model 1892 8mm weapon.

43 ▲   44 ▼   45 ▼

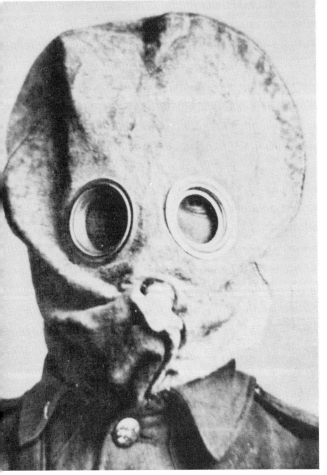

46. Only in late 1915 were the first British 'shrapnel helmets' issued to troops on active service. These were of the pressed-steel pattern known as a 'Brodie' (after its designer) and resembled a medieval *chapelle de fer* or a bowler hat, hence its nickname 'battle bowler'. (A more universal pseudonym was the ubiquitous 'tin hat'.) This group of officers, photographed in late 1915, wear winter trench equipment including the goatskin 'teddy bear' jerkins originally used in the winter of 1914–15. It was common at this period for officers to purchase helmets privately from their outfitters, some of which were slightly different from the regulation pattern.

▲46 ▼47

47. 'Over the top': a British charge in the Dardanelles. A number of photographs purporting to be action scenes from Gallipoli were in fact taken during training for the actual landings (French troops being also depicted in such photographs), but many genuine Gallipoli scenes were photographed *in situ*. The men depicted here are members of the Royal Naval Division that accompanied the ANZAC landings, wearing field equipment (less knapsack) and the tropical-service topee.

48. The Turkish Army adopted a khaki service dress from 1909, their equipment influenced by German styles, though unique was the khaki cloth 'Enver-Pasha' helmet shown here. Officers and mounted troops might wear instead a grey or black *kalpak* or lambskin busby. Equipment was brown leather, and officers wore knee-boots instead of the khaki puttees of the rank-and-file. Arm-of-service colours (worn on the collar) were khaki (infantry), olive-green (rifles or light infantry), dark blue (artillery), light grey (cavalry), light blue (engineers), red (train), scarlet (general officers) and crimson (staff officers). Turkey adopted the 7.65mm Mauser rifle in 1890; the national patterns of Mauser varied in detail, the Turkish version having the same calibre as the Belgian but with similarities to the Spanish pattern.

49. Turkey's army was re-modelled with German guidance shortly before the war and comprised two basic categories: 25 *Nizam* or regular divisions (each of 13 infantry battalions, 24 guns and a cavalry squadron) and a similar number of *Redif* or reserve divisions, one division of each combining to form a corps; but only the *Nizam* divisions were really effective, and benefitted much from German advice. Among the Turkish troops were those from the Arab territories; these infantrymen wear the Turkish service uniform but with native headdress and carry German drums. The drummers' shoulder-decorations are in Turkish style, but closely resemble the drummers' 'wings' used by the German Army.

48 ▲   49 ▼

50 ▼

50. 'Digger': an anonymous Australian representing the magnificent ANZAC troops who served with extreme heroism in the Dardanelles, Europe and the Middle East. Their equipment was basically of British style, the tunic (originally of khaki flannel which faded to grey/blue, and later of khaki serge) was of an individual style, with voluminous pockets and plain buttons. The badge worn on the upturned brim of the slouch hat and on the point of the collar comprised a crown upon a 'rising sun' device, supposedly inspired by a wall-decoration of a 'fan' of bayonets. The brass shoulder-title 'AUSTRALIA' was universal. The battalion-identification badge on the sleeve is the upright rectangle of the 5th Australian Division, perhaps the brown and red of the 55th Battalion.

51. Australian recruits about to embark for active service, Queenslanders according to the caption on the original: 'I am going to the Front with the Queensland . . . I Bade Chas. & Mrs. N. good bye . . . dont faint when you see this . . .'. Note the Australian tunic with its voluminous pockets; the web equipment is the British 1908 pattern. The oldest recruit at the extreme left appears to wear Boer War medal-ribbons.

52. A 'carrying party' at Gallipoli, exhibiting the first modifications of costume which soon multiplied until the ANZACS were nicknamed 'the naked Australians'. These men retain their ordinary service uniform, in some cases with the neck unfastened (as permitted officially for the march in Europe), and wear the 1908-pattern web equipment, the leading man having unfastened his waist-belt and removed his puttees. The caps are the variety with ear-flaps designed to protect from the cold, needed in the Dardanelles winter.

53. Australians at Gallipoli engaged in a most unpleasant task, which concerned the combatants of all nations: attempting to rid shirts and underclothing of lice. Attempts to eradicate vermin varied from fumigation (where possible) to the application of patent poisons or even to applying candle-wax to the internal seams of garments, but none was completely successful and often the only temporary relief was to crush the lice manually along the seams where they most commonly resided.

54. Probably no piece of military equipment of the war was as famous as the French '75', the 75mm field-gun introduced in 1894. The classic *Soixante-Quinze* was the Model 1897 gun, and it performed sterling service throughout the war. Its major development was in the first truly effective control of recoil. This example is part of a battery dug in at the Dardanelles and

protected by a rudimentary breastwork; immediately beside the gun is its limber, with harness-pole detached, and upturned so that its open top

faced the gunners, who were thus able to extract shells without having to reach up. The circular bases of the shells face the gunners in this illustration,

and a pile of empty shell-cases is stacked at the rear. Most of the gunners have the French tropical helmet worn in the Dardanelles campaign.

53 ▲

54 ▼

▲55 ▼56

▼57

55. Dispatch-riders of the Royal Engineers at Gallipoli, with transport-vessels in the background. This depicts a typical assortment of Gallipoli uniforms, ranging from shirt-sleeves to vest and singlets, caps with neck-curtains, topees and Australian slouch hats. Motorcycles were useful for carrying messages even in such comparatively confined spaces as the landing-grounds of the Dardanelles, but horses were also used.

56. 'Annie' in action at Gallipoli: a British heavy battery bombarding Turkish positions. ('Annie' is the name painted on the barrel of the gun.) The crew wear typical Gallipoli dress: shirt-sleeves, shorts and caps with neck-cloths. The rather casual attitude of the men working on the hazardous fuzed nosecaps of shells in the foreground recalls the caption to the Bairnsfather cartoon of advice given to a man attempting to remove a nosecap with a hammer and chisel: 'Give it a good hard 'un; you can generally hear them fizzing if they are going to explode!'

57. Manufacturing hand-grenades at Gallipoli. The dearth of proper grenades led to the utilization (both on the Western Front and in the Dardanelles) of home-made missiles constructed of empty food-containers and hence the name 'jam-tin bombs': tin cans filled with explosive and improvised shrapnel. These British or Australian troops (note the slouch hat worn by the figure at far right) are producing such grenades and cutting fragments of barbed wire to pack with the explosive to produce weapons capable of causing terrible injury. The two men at the right are chopping up strands of barbed wire upon an anvil.

58. Gallipoli: captured Turks are interrogated by British staff officers. The two British soldiers who guard the prisoners (left) apparently wear caps with ear-flaps fastened over the crown, and one at least wears shorts and puttees. The two officers questioning the Turks wear the

ordinary uniform with rank-marking on the sleeve; but the pipe-smoking officer at the right has his rank-insignia on the shoulder-straps of the tunic. The officer in the cap apparently has a white neck-curtain attached (khaki was the usual colour), and the other wears a staff brassard (commonly called an 'armlet') on the left arm, an item which came into considerable use during the war as a means of identifying the wearer's function or even the unit to which he was attached, when the formation's distinctive sign might be stitched to the brassard.

59. A wounded Turkish prisoner accepts a drink from the canteen of a member of the British landing force at Gallipoli. The British uniform includes the cap with ear-flaps fastened up over the crown, shorts (conceivably produced by cutting off the lower leg of the trousers, a common practice), and puttees over bare lower legs. The bayonet retains its curved quillon, generally removed in 1913 but still in evidence in a number of photographs dating from the earlier years of the war.

▲60

60. An unusual item of equipment deployed in a trench at 'Anzac' (the Gallipoli landing): a French spray designed to counteract the effect of poison gas. A contemporary recipe for

▼62

this liquid described its composition as 800 grammes of water to 200 grammes of carbonate of soda crystals, 1,000 grammes of hyposulphate of soda and 150 grammes of glycerine.

▲61

The man carrying the canister wears typical Gallipoli dress: a cap with neck-guard, vest and trousers. The officer in the background retains a more conventional uniform.

61. An ANZAC sniping-party at Gallipoli. These Australians wear typical Gallipoli uniform: shirt or vest, shorts and puttees or socks, and equipment reduced to a minimum. The sniper here operates a rifle sighted through a periscope, enabling him to fire over the sandbag parapet without showing himself; his 'observer' views through another periscope, while the other men – probably 'escorts' in case of a sudden raid by the Turks – sit with an air of resignation until something occurs. All wear the Australian slouch hat save for the sniper himself, who appears to wear an empty sandbag on his head, camouflage in case he should accidentally move into view over the top of the parapet.

62. The evolution of the ANZAC 'Gallipoli' uniform was a progressive degeneration from the regulation dress in an attempt to combat the appallingly arduous climate. From shirt-sleeves the 'uniform' in hot weather was reduced to vests, and then often only to shorts, boots, socks and slouch

hat – hence the sobriquet 'the naked Australians'. The 'shorts' were originally nothing more than the trousers hacked off at the knee or above, with no attempt to conceal or turn over the ragged edges of the cloth. These two ANZACs stand guard over a 'jack-in-the-green' figure, a captured Turkish sniper who still wears his foliage camouflage: 'sniping' was as great a hazard in the Dardanelles campaign as it became on the Western Front.

63. The increase in the use of the hand-grenade as a close-quarter weapon resulted in the devising of a number of new items of equipment, such as the bomb-carrying harness worn by this British fusilier at Salonika. It is difficult to determine which pattern of grenade is held here because of its concealment by the bomber's hand, but it *may* be the egg-shaped 'No 16' grenade. The single chevron visible on the left upper arm denotes the rank of lance-corporal.

64. In late 1915 the Serbian Army, having attempted to defend its country against overwhelming odds, was evacuated to Corfu for re-equipment in basically French style. These soldiers wear the native Serbian uniform of grey-green, which began to be introduced from 1912; however, it never reached the reserves and was worn only by the 'first Ban' or regulars. Arm-of-service was indicated by the facing-colour on the tunic and large patches on the greatcoat collar – crimson for the infantry illustrated here. Note the low boots of native style worn by the Serbian Army.

63▲   64▼

▲65

65. Much of Serbia's military and artillery transport was dragged by oxen (such unorthodox teams even being used by British gunners in Serbia), but these men have a better conveyance on the Salonika–Nish railway. The gunners wear the standard Serbian uniform with the black collar-patch of the artillery and the rather distinctively shaped grey-green cloth forage cap. Note that even in this theatre of operations the usual text is painted on the boxcar in the background: '40 men or 6 horses'.

66. The Bulgarian Army had begun to be re-equipped in grey-green Austrian-style uniform from 1908, but at her entry into the war this was not universal and older brown uniform and German stocks were pressed into service. The arm-of-service colour was carried on the collar-patch – here the infantry's crimson – and though the trousers were usually the same colour as the tunic, shortage of stocks probably resulted in a mixture of styles. The Russian-style cap was in the uniform-colour with black or grey-green leather peak; that illustrated lacks the usual oval cockade in the red/white/green national colours. Puttees or boots and gaiters were the prescribed wear, but this man demonstrates the usual shortages and wears civilian-style leggings and native hide sandals or *palanka*.

▼66

▼67

68▲

69▲

67. The Italian Army began the war in a mixture of the grey-green service uniform introduced in 1909 and older dark blue uniforms. The 1909 pattern illustrated included a loose tunic without pockets, with padded 'rolls' on the shoulders to hold the equipment in place, trousers and puttees, and boots with a high ankle. Regimental insignia was carried on the collar (patches of different colour and shape) and as a coloured (later black) embroidered or metal badge on the grey-green cloth kepi, which for other ranks was unstiffened until 1916. Equipment was black leather. The rifle was the 1891

Mannlicher Carcano, of 6.5mm calibre, and the older Vetterli rifle (of same calibre) was also used. The rifle had a knife-bayonet in a scabbard; the shorter Mannlicher Carcano carbine of 1891, however, had a triangularly-sectioned blade permanently attached, folding under the barrel when not in use.

68. This infantryman with an immense burden shows the rear of the Italian equipment, in this case not very symmetrically-arranged, including an untidily-folded grey-green greatcoat and spare boots carried atop the knapsack. The double-breasted

greatcoat had a deep falling collar; other garments included a fur-collared and cuffed grey-green knee-length winter coat; and a wrist-length cape of the same colour, with falling collar. Attached to the rear of the haversack below waist-level is the canteen; the mess-tin in its cover is strapped to the rear of the knapsack.

69. Italian officers wore a uniform similar to that of the other ranks, but with shoulder-straps and breast-pockets on the tunic. Being made of a lighter grey, these were easily distinguished by snipers; the other ranks' colour was generally

adopted where possible. The officers' kepi was stiffened and, unlike those of the rank and file, had a black leather peak instead of grey-green cloth. Rank-marking was borne upon the shoulder-straps (later transferred to the cuff) and kepi; the officer illustrated wears a single metal lace band around the kepi, which later in the war was replaced by less-obtrusive yellow or grey lace. He has the pointed-ended collar-patch of the line infantry, and puttees in place of the optional black knee-boots. Equipment was generally of grey-green leather, although brown was also used.

▲70 ▼71

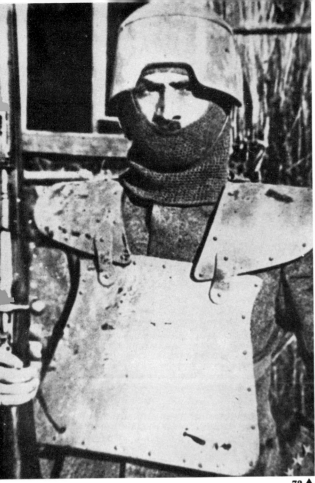

72 ▲

73 ▲

70. A sergeant of Italian artillery about to fire a small mountain fieldpiece. Such weapons were used in the Italian colonial campaigns (in North Africa) but were equally suited to mountain warfare in Europe. The sergeant wears his rank-chevrons (gold for artillery) on the forearm, two narrow bands above one broad; his black collar-patch (the artillery colour) was pointed at the end farthest from the opening of the collar. The tropical helmet (with badges worn even on active service) was a variation on the home-service uniform.

71. A considerable part of the Italian Army's campaigning was conducted in mountainous terrain; here is a front-line outpost of a shallow trench, overlooking Austrian-held territory. The troops are easily-recognizable by their distinctive headdress as *Bersaglieri* or rifle corps, whose black 'round hats' had grey covers on service. Their famous black cock-feather plumes were worn on the tropical helmet, and even on the steel helmet when Italy adopted the Adrian pattern. Their collar-patch was crimson. Other Italian troops with a distinctive headdress were the *Alpini* (mountain troops), who wore a 'Robin Hood'-style hat with feather.

72. In a war that saw the reintroduction of such medieval features as steel helmets, the most anachronistic equipment of all was that of the Italian 'Death Companies'. Before Italy entered the war, volunteer detachments were formed for hazardous duty such as wire-cutting, and these troops were issued with iron helmets, armoured cuirasses, shoulder- and abdominal-protection, gauntlets and 'pikes' with wire-cutting heads. These 'Death Volunteers' were later given the title *militare ardiot* ('bold soldier') and in 1917 were organized into assault units of *Arditi*. The man illustrated here wears the three cuff-stars of captain's rank and carries a rifle in place of the wire-cutting 'pike'.

73. The device illustrated here was described by its contemporary caption as an example of 'vitriolic warfare', a canister of acid which sprayed its lethal fluid from the Austrian lines into the Italian trenches on the Isonzo Front. The crew appear to wear the new Austrian field-grey uniform adopted in 1915, similar to that in use before but with a turndown collar, and with field-grey puttees instead of the earlier trousers with integral gaiters.

▲74 ▼75

▼76

74. British operations in Mesopotamia were organized by the Indian Army, a delegation of responsibility that led to lack of coordination in this theatre. Like British infantry regiments, each Indian unit possessed a machine-gun section, armed initially with Maxims; this section prepares to open fire on a Mesopotamian hillside. The British officer wears usual campaign costume including shorts, topee and a cravat at the open neck of his tunic. In the left background is one of the transport-mules used to convey both Maxim and ammunition.

75. German troops destroying a railway-line in South-West Africa. The troops formed for the German African colonies wore a uniform of similar style to that used in Europe, but in khaki-yellow drill known as 'sand grey', with Swedish cuffs and facing-colours of cornflower blue for South-West Africa, poppy-red for the Cameroons and Togoland and white for East Africa, worn with the ordinary arm-of-service piping. In 1913 the uniform-colour was officially changed to field-grey, but sand-grey remained in use for some time. The headdress was a low, grey felt slouch hat edged with the colony facing-colour, and bore the national cockade on the upturned right brim; weapons and equipment were as used in Europe.

76. The surrender of German forces in South-West Africa on 9 July 1915 on the railway between Otavi and Khorab; General Botha (right) represents the Anglo–South African forces. Next to Botha, the German governor of the province, Dr Seitz, signs the document of surrender; at the left is Lieutenant-Colonel Francke, commander of the German forces. This illustrates to good effect the tropical uniform of the German troops; especially evident is the red, white and black cockade worn upon the upturned brim of the grey slouch hat, edged with cornflower blue.

77. Among the Germans' most effective opponents in East Africa were the King's African Rifles, a force formed in 1902 by the amalgamation of the Central Africa, Uganda and East Africa

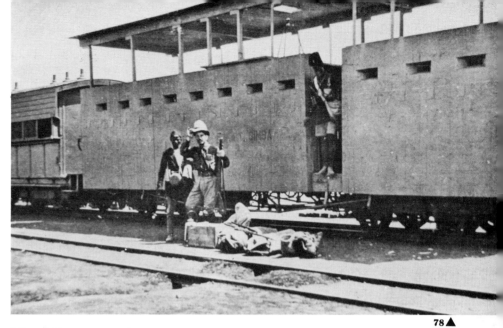

78 ▲

77 ▼

Rifles, which were recruited from the 'martial races' of central Africa and the Sudan, with officers seconded from the British Army. Full dress consisted of khaki drill and fez, but the khaki service dress with blue puttees is shown here, worn by members of the 3rd (East Africa) Battalion. The light straps across the breast are those of the haversack and canteen; at the right hip was carried a native machete, and two rolls on the back, a blanket over a greatcoat. The pillbox caps have a rolled-up neck-curtain and bear the battalion designation ('III') on the front; officers wore similar caps but peaked, like a kepi. Sandals are shown here, but the troops often preferred to go barefoot.

78. Although of comparatively minor significance, operations in East Africa absorbed considerable resources. The rail link between Nairobi and the coast was believed to be vulnerable to German raids, so the Uganda railway was provided with protection. Illustrated here is a 'mobile blockhouse': HMAT (His Majesty's Armoured Train) *Simba*, similar to the armoured, loopholed carriages used in South Africa during the great Boer War. A British officer with kit and bearer raises his topee to the photographer!

79. The Germans defended their African territory with considerable resolution, both sides using native units. This illustration shows a light fieldpiece in action at Jabassi in the Cameroons, directed by a British officer who appears to have a sun-shade draped over the front of his topee and secured under the upper vent. When this illustration was published in the *Illustrated War News* in September 1915, its caption made much of the heroism of the British West African Frontier Force, recounting an incident in which two natives had volunteered to act as the support for a machine-gun after its mounting had been shot away!

79 ▼

▲80

80. Co-operation between the component armies of the Central Powers was not always completely cordial, but this combined column of Austrian (left) and German infantry

(right) on the Eastern Front seems to comprise the 'brothers in arms' described by a contemporary caption. It is interesting to note the Austrian at the left front of his column,

who appears to wear the long woollen stockings of the mountain troops and *Landesschützen* in place of the ordinary Austrian legwear of trousers combined with anklet;

note also the prominent collar-patches on the Austrian greatcoats.

81. Austrian infantry crossing a river during the campaigning in

▼81

Galicia. As the Russians retired they destroyed many of the bridges, necessitating the use by the pursuing Central Powers of pontoons – in this case a 'flying bridge', a pontoon used as a punt, poled across the river. The infantry in the foreground wear the ordinary pike-grey field uniform (which in 1915 began to be replaced by a field-grey version, cut slightly looser), with the soft, pike-grey cap; but they appear to have a mixture of equipment. Some have the standard hide knapsack and brown leather belts, with the grey greatcoat rolled over the top of the knapsack; others appear to carry instead the rucksack of the *Landesschützen*.

82. Austrian cavalrymen captured in Galicia, with their Russian escort (extreme left and right). The Austrian uniforms represent one of the final uses of 'coloured' uniforms in action: a light blue tunic with red facings, red breeches, and a pelisse-like, fur-lined over-jacket styled a *Pelz*. Their head-dress varies from the black shako of the hussars, and the *czapka* of the *Uhlans* (lancers) with a grey or grey-blue cloth cover (figure

third from right), to the much more popular red cloth forage-cap bearing two buttons on the front and a cockade above. The Russians wear their standard grey-brown, voluminous greatcoats and peaked cloth cap.

83. The Austrian forces included their regular armies (Austrian and Hungarian) and the reserve army of *Landwehr*. These were not auxiliaries or militia but generally of a similar standard to the regulars; indeed, the *Landwehr* mountain troops (*Landesschützen*) were among the élite units of the army. From 1887 there was also a home-defence force of *Landsturm*, which, unlike the *Landwehr* which was generally uniformed like the regulars, wore less regulation items. Both the *Landsturm* of Austria and Germany made use of the peaked cap with black oilskin top, remarkably akin to the headdress worn by similar units in the 'War of Liberation' a century before. With their greatcoats and blanket-bandoliers, these *Landsturm* men manning a trench in Russian Poland uncannily resemble their forebears of 1814.

84. A German ski-borne patrol on the Eastern Front, showing the adaptation of the ordinary uniform according to conditions of climate and terrain. Four Bavarian ski battalions were formed in early 1915 and later grouped into the 3rd *Jägers*, serving in the Carpathians. They wore a hooded camouflage jacket and trousers of thin white fabric, over the ordinary uniform. This depicts the utilization of crossed ski-poles as a rest for the rifle. In addition to the ski battalions, others received white greatcoats and hoods for use in snowy conditions.

84

85. The Tsar's magnificent staff-car in Galicia. This group of Russian staff officers includes Tsar Nicholas II himself (third from left, with back to the open door of the car); the governor of Galicia (saluting him); Grand Duke Nicholas (far right), then commanding the Russian forces; and General Yanuchkevitch, chief of the general staff (standing in the car, second right). Later in the year, following Russian reverses on the Eastern Front, the capable Grand Duke Nicholas was transferred to the Caucasus theatre and the Tsar himself took over in nominal command of the Russian forces on the Eastern Front.

86. This photograph was published in the British magazine *The Sphere* as having been taken by their own special correspondent attached to the Russian Army in Poland, and it was stated that the gun was in action immediately before and after the photograph was taken. It presents a superb study of the 1910 Maxim gun used by the Russian Army, 7.62mm calibre, raised upon its bipod mounting, which folded back alongside the 'trail' upon which the gunner sits. The water-cooled gun was fed by a belt passing over the 'spool' at the right-hand edge of the shield, the gunner sighting through the small vertical slot in the shield.

▼85

87. The mode of transporting the Russian wheeled Maxim gun – dragged by ropes attached to towing bars – is illustrated in this view of Russian prisoners under German escort. The Russians wear typical service uniform, including the ubiquitous roll worn bandolier-fashion. When the British magazine *Illustrated War News* published this photograph in July 1915 it was accompanied by the caption 'An unsportsmanlike indignity inflicted on brave foes', i.e., being forced to drag their own guns. The concept that war should be 'sporting' would not have been recognized by those actually engaged in the fighting!

88. Despite its depressing view of the fate of an ally, this photograph was published in Britain as a genuine scene from the war, showing Russian infantry lying dead upon German barbed wire. Wire like this protected the trench-systems of all armies and added yet one more horror to the catalogue; it gave an awful truth to the British popular song that recounted the fate of a battalion hanging on the 'old barbed wire'.

86 ▼

88 ▼

Erich Ludendorff (1863-1937)

Erich Ludendorff has been described as perhaps the greatest of the leaders of the First World War, a general of considerable skill and reputation; yet he is often regarded as only a part (albeit the dominant one) in perhaps the greatest command partnership in history.

Born near Posen to a minor middle class family, Ludendorff entered the German Army in 1883, and in 1895 he joined the General Staff as a captain. From 1904 he served in the *Aufmarschabteilung*, the department which controlled logistics and planning, and was appointed its head in 1908. He drafted the 1913 Army Bill, most of his proposals being accepted, but his insistence over the need to form a further three corps (a plan rejected) was probably responsible for his transfer to command the 39th Fusiliers. In 1914 he was promoted to major-general, and shortly before the outbreak of war became chief of staff to General Karl von Bülow's Second Army. Leading the 14th Brigade after its commander fell, he established his reputation by his daring seizure of the Belgian fortress of Liège, for which he was awarded the coveted decoration *Pour le Mérite*.

Resulting from his new fame, and in response to German reverses at Russian hands, Ludendorff was appointed chief of staff to the Eighth Army on 22 August 1914 and sent immediately to the eastern front; at Hanover his train picked up his new superior, General Paul von Beneckendorf und von Hindenburg (1847-1934), who had been brought out of retirement in an attempt to reverse the situation in the east. This was the foundation of a memorable partnership, in which Hindenburg always maintained the superior position; but throughout, much of the energy and direction came from Ludendorff.

Their collaboration made an immediate impact upon the eastern front, although the plans adopted initially had already been prepared by Colonel Max Hoffman (1869-1927), senior staff officer of Eighth Army. The results were spectacular: the Russians were defeated massively at Tannenberg, and were driven from East Prussia by the First Battle of the Masurian Lakes. In November 1914, Hindenburg was appointed commander-in-chief over the eastern front; Ludendorff was promoted to lieutenant-general and remained his chief of staff. Despite further successes,

notably the Second Battle of the Masurian Lakes, their planning was undermined by the chief of the General Staff, Erich von Falkenhayn (1861-1922), who was somewhat antagonistic towards them and denied the resources to exploit their victories; being responsible for maintaining the war on both fronts, Falkenhayn favoured the western front at the expense of the east.

Lack of success throughout 1916 undermined Falkenhayn's position, and on 29 August 1916 he was replaced as Chief of General Staff by Hindenburg; Ludendorff was promoted to general and appointed as Quartermaster-General, actually to serve as Hindenburg's deputy. From this time, the worthy old Hindenburg acted mainly as a figurehead and rallying-point for German morale, his great popularity arising from the victories in the east. The real director of the German war effort was Ludendorff, whose influence extended beyond the military sphere: in July 1917 he was largely responsible for the dismissal of the Chancellor Theobald von Bethmann Hollweg, who was regarded as unwilling to prosecute the war to its ultimate. The appointment of an ineffectual successor, Georg Michaelis, left Ludendorff as the virtual dictator of German policy.

Undoubtedly, Ludendorff possessed a sharp intellect and very considerable military skill, augmented by the energy to put his plans into effect; but although his conduct of the war on the eastern front had displayed brilliance, in the wider sphere he failed to appreciate realities. His schemes for eastward expansion - the enduring *Drang nach Osten* which had so complicated German policies in the past - were incompatible with a decisive victory in the west, and consequently Ludendorff was as torn between two fires as Falkenhayn had been. His appearance, though, was sufficient to instil confidence: with heavy build, cropped hair, stern demeanour and monocle, he resembled the archetypal Prussian officer, yet was not devoid of personal vanity – for example, he later complained bitterly when the Ludendorff Fund for war invalids was re-named the People's Fund, claiming that his name alone had made it successful.

In spring 1918, Ludendorff organised the great offensive on the western front, codenamed 'Michael' but known

equally by the titles *Kaiserschlacht* ('the Kaiser's battle') or as the Ludendorff offensive, intended to smash the Allied armies before the American forces could arrive and overwhelm Germany. The offensive would have been sound had there been adequate resources to exploit successes fully; but Ludendorff appears not to have appreciated the level of the army's exhaustion. Consequently, although the repeated attacks made considerable progress, the necessary major breakthrough was not achieved. After the German offensive had become exhausted, the Allies counter-attacked and finally broke through the German front line, resulting in the collapse of some German formations; Ludendorff appropriately termed 8 August 1918 as 'the black day of the German Army'. The realisation that all was lost appears to have had a profound effect upon Ludendorff's clarity of thought, and he proved uncharacteristically vacillating, first counselling immediate surrender and then a continuation of hostilities to the end. His resignation was forced by the government on 26 October 1918, ending his military career.

Ludendorff's post-war reputation was overshadowed by his involvement in Nazi politics. He stood unsuccessfully as their candidate for the presidency of the Weimar Republic and, unlike Hindenburg (who became president and had the misfortune to be known as the one who appointed Hitler as chancellor), he remained a somewhat marginal political figure. His military reputation remained, however, as an organiser and strategist of great skill, albeit one who probably lacked the necessary grasp of political realities to enable him to succeed in the exalted position he reached.

References

Dupuy, T.N. *The Military Lives of Hindenburg and Ludendorff of Imperial Germany*, New York 1970.

Goodspeed, D.J. *Ludendorff*, London 1966.

Herwig, H.H., & Heyman, N.M. *Biographical Dictionary of World War I*, Westport, Connecticut, 1982.

Liddell Hart, Sir Basil *Reputations*, London 1928

Ludendorff, General E. *My War Memories 1914-1918*, London 1919.

1. A French soldier in trench equipment, including goggles and mask over the nose and mouth to protect against gas; waders; and a leather jerkin. The *casque Adrian*, the steel helmet named after its designer, was painted 'horizon blue' and bore an embossed metal badge on the front, for infantry and cavalry a bursting grenade with 'RF' on the ball.

◀**1**

WORLD WAR ONE:
1916

▲2 ▼3

▼4

2. A halt on the march: a French infantry company with full field equipment. The 'horizon blue' greatcoat was produced initially double-breasted for infantry and single-breasted with longer skirts for cavalry; almost immediately a second infantry version appeared, as here, single-breasted and with breast-pockets, here without the usual unit-numbers carried on the collar-patches. Note the spare boots tied to the sides of the knapsack. The smaller haversacks are probably containers for the gas mask.

3. The 'Blue Devils' in a new guise: a picket of French *Chasseurs Alpins* in the Vosges. These élite mountain troops were renowned for their dark blue berets, but although here some retain their dark blue tunics and perhaps white trousers, their head-dress is now the universal *casque Adrian*. Shown clearly on the man at the right is the 1886-pattern Lebel bayonet with white-metal hilt, narrow cruciform blade and downswept quillon, the latter being removed to produce the 1916 pattern.

4. A French trench mortar positioned in a sandbagged emplacement near a dug-out, typical of those in which the defenders of Verdun existed. Three basic types of mortar were employed at this time: the 1915 58mm and the later 240mm and 340mm varieties. The projectile about to be inserted into the barrel has tail-fins to provide stabilization in flight, leading to the nickname 'aerial torpedo'. Note the carpet of branches performing the same function as British duckboards.

INTRODUCTION

After the horrors of 1915, the abortive expedition to the Dardanelles and the advent of trench warfare and poison gas, the wretchedness multiplied in 1916. The war widened a stage further by the entry of Roumania into the conflict, and operations in the Middle East intensified with the Arab Revolt. Despite a successful Russian drive on the Eastern Front (the cost of which contributed to the upheaval of 1917) and a serious reverse in Mesopotamia, the Allies' main effort in 1916 was concentrated on the Western Front, centered around the French attempts to hold Verdun and the British Somme offensive initiated partly to relieve pressure on the beleaguered French. The attack of 1 July 1916 was the costliest day in the history of the British Army, yet the 60,000 casualties it sustained were only the beginning of an unbelievably sanguinary struggle which dragged on into early winter, causing about one and a quarter *million* casualties and destroying some of the best elements of the armies of both combatants. It also ushered in a new era of military tactics, that of the armoured fighting vehicle. Like the Dardanelles expedition, the development of the tank had been intended to break the deadlock of the war on the Western Front; against a less resolute enemy it might have done, but by the end of the year the terrible stalemate of trench warfare was once again in place.

In the development of military costume and equipment, 1916 witnessed fewer changes than the previous years apart from the advent of the tank, though by the end of the year steel helmets, virtually unknown at the outbreak of war, were almost universal, with the French Adrian pattern spreading to many of the Allied nations, the German 'coal-scuttle' being used by the Central Powers and the British 'tin hat' by the troops of the Empire. Light machine-guns came into greater prominence, providing immediate fire-support for each company, and with patterns such as the Lewis and Chauchat being immeasurably more mobile than the heavy machine-guns, the latter now took on the role almost of light artillery. In addition to the concentration of artillery fire providing bombardments of unimaginable intensity, 'trench artillery' was now more fully developed with the widespread use of the 'Tock-Emma' (T/M: trench mortar).

5. A French trench near Maurepas, the defenders of which wear the 'horizon blue' tunic in place of the greatcoat. Like most armies, the French used a number of patterns of hand-grenade, including spherical, racket (on a wooden handle like a table-tennis bat), egg-grenades with smooth casing such as the Modèle 1915, cylindrical incendiaries like the Modèle 1916, and these fragmentation grenades with short handle and segmented casing to explode into shrapnel. The narrow tin box worn on a shoulder-strap by the man in the foreground is the container for the 'Tissot' gas mask.

6. French infantry drawing drinking-water for their company from a 'dump' a short distance behind the lines. The availability of fresh water was often limited in the front line, and supplies often had to be carried manually from such central points. The water was sometimes carried in barrels on the shoulder, or in this case in tins; one man wears a rain-cape and the other a sleeveless jerkin over his greatcoat.

▲5   ▼6   ▲7

8▲ 9▼

7. French cooks and cook-wagon at Verdun. All wear the 'horizon blue' tunic in preference to the greatcoat (which at the start of the war was the almost universal upper garment) and the steel *casque Adrian*, one with a knitted balaklava helmet underneath. The filthy state of these men is typical for the campaign (even though they were responsible for preparing food), and the unshaven appearance makes the nickname *poilu* ('hairy one') more than usually appropriate!

8. Close-quarter trench fighting produced a number of bizarre and anachronistic uniforms, such as the improvised breastplate worn by this French infantryman at Verdun; others used steel bucklers (shields) in the hope of deflecting German bullets. Note the gong made from a shell-case hanging from the trench wall; when struck it acted as a warning of poison gas.

9. Under bombardment trench-systems could disappear into a series of half-filled gullies and hollows, as here: French troops shelter from the artillery fire which is doubtless the cause of the debris visible. Like that in the background, some shells exploded with a cloud of black smoke, hence the British nickname 'coal-box' for such projectiles.

10. The staff uniform of the French Army is illustrated in this portrait of 'Butcher' Mangin, who planned and directed the recapture of Forts Douaumont and Vaux at Verdun. Charles Marie Emmanuel Mangin (1866–1925) was one of the most capable, and certainly most fearless, of France's generals; trained in colonial warfare, he had the highest regard for the French African troops. Although he was prepared to sacrifice any number of men to attain his objectives, he was as careless of his own safety as that of his troops. He wears the 'horizon blue' tunic and breeches with black breeches-stripe, gilt stars above the cuff (indicative of general officers' rank, two to seven according to grade), the dress kepi with dark-blue band, scarlet top and gold embroidery, and brown leather belt and boots.

11. Verdun was supplied by a 40-mile minor road known as the *Voie Sacrée* (sacred way), supplies being brought up by convoys of lorries; but mule-trains were still used, like that halted here for refreshments. These mules carry machine-gun ammunition in 'racks'; French guns such as the Model 1905 'Puteaux' and Model 1907 'St-Etienne' used rigid metal bands holding 25 cartridges. Only one of the men illustrated wears the steel helmet; except when under fire, the kepi was often preferred for its greater comfort.

12. Crown Prince Wilhelm of Germany behind the wheel of his staff-car on the Verdun Front, where he was in nominal command. 'Little Willie's' uniform illustrates a practice, adopted by numerous German generals, of wearing regimental rather than staff uniform: though the motoring goggles conceal the lower black-and-white Prussian cockade on the cap, the upper badges identify the uniform as that of the 1st *Leib*-Hussars (of which he was colonel): a black cap with scarlet band, silver piping, and the national red/white/black cockade over a silver skull and crossed bones, the regimental badge.

▲10   ▼11

13. Until the issue of the steel helmet in mid-1916, the German Army continued to wear the *Pickelhaube* with field-grey cloth cover. This searchlight section (the light hung around the neck of one of the crew) wears the 1910-pattern field-grey tunic with 'Swedish' cuffs as used by the Guards, field artillery, most supporting services and a minority of infantry regiments. The *Unteroffizier* in the centre has rank indicated by the lace around the collar. The pouches on the waist-belts are the 1895-pattern, which continued in use despite the introduction of the 1909 multiple pouches, and jackboots are worn; though puttees were used from this period, they were never universal.

12▲   13▼

14. The German Army began to receive the steel helmet in the early summer of 1916, of the distinctive 'coal-scuttle' shape, with a frontal reinforcing plate for lookouts. The 1910-pattern field-grey tunic (*Waffenrock*) was amended in 1915 when a turned-back deep cuff was introduced and the piping on the rear skirts removed. A new garment, the *Bluse*, was authorized in September 1915, with simpler decorations and the breast-buttons concealed by a fly-front; but in practice all three patterns were worn simultaneously, so that the earlier tunics could still be encountered at the end of the war. The officer here wears the 1910-pattern tunic with 'Brandenburg'-style flapped cuffs; the others wear the amended version with plain cuffs.

15. A German water-cart at a village well. The purity of water in front-line areas could not always be guaranteed, hence the chalked notice on the cart, *Nur Trinkwasser*. The chimney affixed to the cart led to mobile stoves and cook-carts being nicknamed *Gulasch-Kanone* ('stew-guns'), for when stowed for movement the chimney resembled the barrel of a fieldpiece. The men here wear

the 1910-pattern *Waffenrock*; the coloured piping on the rear skirts shows clearly on that of the man operating the well-wheel, and the man to his left has 'Swedish' cuffs with *Garde-Litzen* (lace loops, normally white with a central red line), the insignia of the Foot Guards, grenadiers and certain other infantry units.

16. German infantry wearing the field cap and field-grey greatcoat. The man at the left retains the large collar-patches officially abolished in September 1915. The shoulder-strap identified the regiment (so that Allied raiding-parties were instructed to carry away any straps they encountered to identify the units opposing them); the straps were of the garment-colour with the regimental number usually in red, sometimes with piping (generally white for infantry); in this case it bears the scarlet '102' of the 3rd Saxon Regiment, *Infanterie-Regt. Nr. 102 (König Ludwig III von Bayern)*. The man at the right is from a regiment which bore a badge on its straps, in this case a crown, which, with the *Garde-Litzen* loops on the tunic collar, would seem to indicate the 1st Baden Grenadiers (*Badisches Leib-Grenadier Regt. Nr. 109*).

17. The ordinary German service dress: the 1910-pattern tunic, some at least with 'Brandenburg' cuff-patches, and the soft cloth field cap with coloured band and national (upper) and state (lower) cockades; a number of men have the coloured band concealed by a strip of field-grey cloth, common practice in the front line. The man in the immediate foreground wears the peaked field cap which could be worn by all ranks off-duty but was generally restricted to officers and senior NCOs.

▲14   ▼15

16 ▲

17 ▲

18. German infantrymen photographed in France, wearing the field cap and illustrating the simultaneous use of the 1910-pattern *Waffenrock* with 'Brandenburg' cuff-flaps and the 1915 amended pattern with deep, plain cuffs; the 1915 *Bluse* was similar to the latter but with the breast-buttons concealed by a fly-front. The field-grey cap (*Mütze*) had the band and upper piping in the arm-of-service colour (most infantry red, artillery black, *Jägers* light-green, train light-blue, etc.) with circular metal cockades, the national red/white/black at the top and the state cockade on the band, the latter often concealed by a strip of field-grey cloth. The tunic-buttons were produced either in matted metal or were painted field-grey.

18 ▼

Highlander (centre) and Lowlander (right) wear the khaki 'Tam-o'-Shanter' and the ordinary khaki tunic (the Highland 'doublet' pattern was rarely seen by this period), the Highlander with the 1914-pattern leather equipment; note the cover on his rifle, the others having the bolt-mechanism exposed. The flowers worn by all three were sold for charity on 'Alexandra Day' (named after Queen Alexandra), 21 June 1916.

20. A British infantry corporal on sentry duty on the Western Front. Although this shows the uniform and 1908-pattern equipment to good effect, it was probably posed for the photographer some distance from the front line: the rifle has a rag around it to exclude dirt, and at the 'front' the loophole would probably have had a sacking cover so as not to show light through and thus not attract a sniper.

21. War service was not restricted to the young; illustrated here in the uniform of the 8th (Ardwick) Battalion of the Manchester Regiment in 1916 is Corporal C. E. Madeley,

▲19 ▼20

19. Returning to the 'Front': British soldiers at Victoria Station, London, at the end of their leave (when weapons were carried). This illustrates the diversity of British uniform: the private of the Machine-Gun Corps (left) wears ordinary service uniform and 1908-pattern web equipment; the lanyard is a unit addition. The

▼21

an ecclesiastical stained-glass craftsman from Manchester. He was accepted for the 8th Manchesters in 1915 on account of his service with the Manchester Rifle Volunteers, which he joined in 1870, being aged 61 at the time of his enlistment; his son also served in the regiment.

22. The alteration of uniform which occurred during the war is demonstrated by the photograph here of Scottish Highlanders. This depicts the regulation uniform of a 2nd lieutenant, the tunic cut in 'doublet' shape, unique to kilted regiments, with rank-insignia borne upon 'gauntlet' cuffs; with kilt, hose, glengarry cap, drab spats and the sporran, the latter omitted on active service.

23. No greater contrast could be imagined than that of the regulation 'Highland' uniform and that illustrated here: only the head-dress is distinctive, the khaki serge Balmoral or 'Tam-o'-Shanter' bonnet which replaced the glengarry in 1916, here with the badge of the Seaforth Highlanders. The remainder of the uniform is entirely 'English': it is supposed that some units of the 51st (Highland) Division received ordinary trousers and puttees in 1916, in which Division the 4th–6th Battalions Seaforth Highlanders served in that year.

24. On 27 March 1917 the 1st Battalion Northumberland Fusiliers and 4th Battalion Royal Fusiliers (9 Brigade, 3rd Division) captured an enemy salient at St-Eloi. This shows the celebrations of victory, displaying German shakos (the one worn by the man seated at right apparently having a service dress fabric cover but with the plate affixed outside), a German gas mask and field-cap. The captain in the background wears the red cross brassard of medical personnel; the 7th, 8th and 142nd Field Ambulances were attached to the 3rd Division at this date.

22 ▲ 　 23 ▲ 24 ▼

25. A private of the London Scottish, wearing the regimental uniform as part of 168 Brigade, 56th Division (red triangle on upper sleeve). The tunic has the rounded skirts of 'doublet' pattern, and bears two wound-stripes on the lower sleeve. The khaki Tam-o'-Shanter was adopted by the unit (14th London Regiment) in spring 1915, with blue backing to the regimental badge and a blue 'tourie' (pompom). The kilt is of the regimental 'Hodden grey' colour, and the hose-tops similar, with blue 'flashes'; on active service puttees were preferred to the spats. The belt is from the 1908 web equipment; but for the removal of the sporran and the addition of a khaki kilt-apron, this is the uniform worn on active service.

26. The London Scottish on the march, wearing a mixture of ordinary tunics and 'doublets' with rounded skirts, khaki aprons and helmet covers. For a time after the issue of the steel helmet in March 1916 the regiment wore blue pompoms on the helmet covers, until it was realized that these were revealing the unit's identity to the enemy. Despite active service conditions, the officer in the foreground retains his sporran, and appears to have web equipment instead of the usual 'Sam Browne' belt; the medical party in the foreground carry a rolled stretcher, their white brassards on the left upper arm bearing the letters 'SB' (stretcher-bearer).

▲25 ▼26

27. No offensive could have been contemplated without an immense preliminary bombardment; the amount of artillery deployed by both sides on the Western Front was astonishing. This British howitzer is 'dug-in', such a pit being usable due to the breech-mechanism which absorbed recoil, without which the gun would have been driven backwards many yards by the discharge of each shell. The poles support camouflage-netting to conceal the position from German aerial observation.

28. Canadian infantry in a trench in which corrugated iron is used as wall-supports and dug-out roof; note also the slatted wooden 'duckboards' to provide firmness underfoot. One of the men uses a trench periscope, of which many varieties existed; the man at the extreme right wears gumboots instead of puttees, the corporal at the left has a raincoat, and the man next to him a sleeveless leather jerkin.

29. Lunch in the trenches: three Canadians in the front line. The uniform is like that of the British Army; note the leather jerkin and small pouch for the gas mask worn by the man at the right, and the 'C/5' regimental collar-insignia of the man at the left. Very prominent is a rum-jar, a common feature in the trenches as rum was issued regularly to combat the cold and dampness. The jars were made of buff earthenware with a dark-brown glazed neck, and bore the letters 'S R D' (Special Ration Department), which with their usual humour the troops said indicated 'Seldom Reaches Destination'!

27 ▲   28 ▼

29 ▼

▲32

▲30   ▼31

30. 'C' Company, 1st Battalion Lancashire Fusiliers fixes bayonets, supposedly immediately before the attack of 1 July 1916. The officer (second right) wears a less conspicuous ordinary tunic with rank badges on the shoulder-strap and the battalion crimson-and-yellow diamond insignia on his back below the collar. Yellow flashes on the left of each helmet represents the regiment's traditional yellow hackle; the shoulder-straps bear a brass grenade over 'LF', and the red triangle of the 29th Division is worn on each upper sleeve. Just visible on the pack of the corporal at the left, below the blade of his entrenching-tool, is a tin triangle, used as a recognition-symbol of rank for the men following. The man at the right has the crown insignia of company sergeant-major on the lower sleeve. This one attack cost the battalion a staggering 486 casualties.

33 ▲   34 ▼

31. 'Fix bayonets!': Canadian troops prepare to advance. Note that they are equipped with the British Lee-Enfield rifle instead of the Canadian Ross, the latter a weapon of great accuracy but so prone to becoming fouled that by 1916 most had been withdrawn, only a limited number being retained for sniping.

32. Roll-call of the 2nd Battalion Seaforth Highlanders at the end of the first day of the Somme attack. Note the khaki kilt-aprons and the large white letter 'C' stitched to the upper sleeve, a battalion-identification sign worn especially for the attack of 1 July. Less clearly visible is the triangle of Mackenzie tartan on the upper sleeve, and the coloured patches on the khaki helmet covers used by the 4th Division to identify the brigade: green, yellow and red respectively for the 10–12 Brigades, and horizontal bar, vertical bar, square and diamond for the 1st–4th battalions of each brigade. As the second battalion of 10 Brigade the 2nd Seaforths wore

a green vertical bar; a green diamond was the sign of the 2nd Royal Dublin Fusiliers (fourth battalion, 10 Brigade), and so on.

33. 'Over the top': British infantry leaving the trenches to support the attack on Morval. Visible in the far distance is a line of troops, illustrating the excellent target they presented to the Germans when attacking in this manner. Note the different methods of carrying equipment; the small pouches slung over the shoulder contain the cotton 'PH' (Phenate-Hexamine) gas helmet.

34. German prisoners under escort near Thiepval. This illustrates the variety of uniform encountered on the Western Front: the British escorts have a mixture of 1908 web equipment and the 'emergency' 1914-pattern leather equipment; the narrow strap over the shoulder supports the cotton pouch for the 'PH' gas helmet. The German with the bandaged head wears the ribbon of the Iron Cross at his neck.

▲37

▲35   ▼36

35. German prisoners at Contalmaison, July 1916. Several of the escorting British troops have additional cartridge-bandoliers slung over the shoulder (cotton bandoliers with 50 extra rounds were issued before the great attack of 1 July). The Germans – some of whom appear not unhappy at being captured – wear the field cap: the steel helmet was heavy and not as popular as the soft cap. All appear to wear the 1910 *Waffenrock* with 1915 modification, and have the white *Garde-Litzen* loops on the collar.

36. German casualties and prisoners await evacuation during the great British attacks of July 1916. Those in the foreground wear the 1910 tunic with 'Brandenburg' (flapped) cuffs, despite the 1915 modification and the introduction of the *Bluse* in that September. The shoulder-strap of the man seated right identifies the unit as the 38th Silesian Fusiliers (*Füsilier-Regt. Graf Moltke, Schlesisches, Nr. 38*). Both German and British medical personnel are shown, the former with a red cross

brassard and the latter with a red cross badge on the upper sleeve. The 'Tommy' in the foreground – resembling Bairnsfather's immortal 'Old Bill' – dispenses refreshment from what appears to be the regulation rum-jar.

37. The artillery bombardments on the Western Front exceeded anything that had occurred in the past: this is the main street of Guillemont, captured from the Germans on 3 September 1916. Much of the Somme battleground was reduced to this level of utter devastation.

38. Canadians returning from the front line in typically mud-plastered condition. The man on the left wears his helmet over a woollen 'cap comforter', and has a jerkin over his tunic; the other has a civilian-style cardigan under his tunic. Both have waterproof legwear, waders or gumboots.

39. A British Rolls-Royce armoured car stops at a dressing-station near Guillemont. Both horse-drawn and motor ambulances (that in the foreground a Daimler) are parked amid the barren, shell-

torn terrain; visible in the extreme background is apparently a stretcher-party bringing in another casualty. Note the padre to the right of the armoured car, wearing officers' service dress plus clerical collar.

38▲ 39▼

▲40 ▼41

40. A British 'CCS' (casualty clearing-station) behind the front line, the injured on stretchers awaiting evacuation; rudimentary treatment would have been given at advanced dressing-stations which went by a number of titles including 'RAP' (regimental aid post). The staff here are medical orderlies, doctors and chaplains. This is one of the better stations; many were situated within the range of enemy shelling and in appalling and muddy terrain.

41. Cynics remarked that 'walking wounded' have every reason to look cheerful, for a 'Blighty one' (an injury necessitating evacuation to Britain) removed them from the horrors of the firing-line. This group of injured Canadians includes a Japanese serving with the Canadian army, and a member of the 16th Battalion, Canadian Expeditionary Forces (British Columbia Scottish) whose glengarry bears the regimental badge of a crowned saltire with '16' over a scroll inscribed 'Deas Gu Cath'. Note the tunics with more than the usual British five buttons down the breast, and the labels giving details of initial treatment, identity, etc.

42. British infantry just returned from duty in the front line; the man at the right has brought back only half his rifle and has his equipment festooned around him (note the mess-tin). He wears his 'tin hat' on top of the service cap, and both men have improvised capes from what appear to be blankets as some protection from the rain which is evident from the muddy ground.

43. A 'wiring party' of British infantry. Stringing barbed wire was a hazardous operation, especially as it was often conducted within range of the enemy and often at night. The corkscrew-like implements carried by the man at the head of the party are stanchions upon which the wire was strung. In the foreground is a large coil of wire and what appears to be a water-pump.

44. Probably nothing changed the nature of war more than the advent of the tank, first deployed on 15 September 1916 at Flers-Courcelette. The British Mark I tank came in two varieties: 'male' with two naval 6pdr guns, and 'female' with Hotchkiss machine-guns mounted in sponsons bolted to each side. Crew comprised a commander, driver, two gearsmen and four gunners.

42 ▲

43 ▲   44 ▼

The large wheels at the rear were intended to facilitate minor changes of course (proper steering was by changing gear on the tracks, which operated independently) and were subsequently discarded. Despite a top speed of less that 4mph and limited range, the initial effect of these 28-ton monsters was devastating; though prone to become bogged down, they could have played a major role had they been deployed in sufficient numbers.

45. Each battalion maintained its transport section, crewing motor vehicles and mule- or horse-drawn wagons. This battalion transport cadre of the East Lancashire Regiment have the ordinary uniform with the addition in some cases of cavalry legwear; the lance-corporal (second right) wears riding-breeches and laced leather gaiters, but others have had to improvise, such as the man at the extreme right with socks pulled up over the trouser-leg.

45 ▼

GERMAN HELMET PLATES AND RANK INSIGNIA

▲ a. ▼ b.

▲ d. ▼ e.

▼ c.

▼ f.

Many different variations on the standard head-dress plate existed in the German Army, of which a representative selection is illustrated here, most obviously the 'state' plates of non-Prussian units, but many regimental patterns also existed:

a. The standard Prussian 'line eagle' *Pickelhaube*-plate with motto *'Mit Gott Fur Koenig und Vaterland'*.
b. The same basic plate with the addition of a *Landwehr* cross insignia, indicative of a reserve or *Landwehr* battalion.
c. The 'Guard eagle' with outstretched wings, without the 'Guard Star' on its breast (the star of the Order of the Black Eagle, which featured on most Guard badges): this version worn by the 2nd, 3rd and 8th Grenadiers and 1st and 3rd Dragoons.
d. Plate of the 13th and 14th *Uhlans* bearing the battle-honours 'Peninsula', 'Waterloo' and 'Garzia Hernandez' gained by the forebears of these units when part of the British King's German Legion.
e. The 'dragoon eagle' with upstretched wings, with the 'Waterloo' honour of the 16th (Hanoverian) Dragoons.
f. Busby (*Pelzmütze*) badge of the 7th Hussars, which bore the title 'King Wilhelm's', hence the 'WR I' cipher.

g. The Saxon state plate of the arms of the kingdom in silver on a brass or gilt 'sunburst'.

h. A similar plate with the *Landwehr* cross in silver behind the coat of arms, indicative of a reserve battalion.

i. A typical infantry shoulder-strap, the primary method of identifying the unit, red numerals on field-grey, in this case of the *Niederrheinisches Füsilier-Regt. Nr. 39*, from Düsseldorf.

j. Officers' shoulder-strap pattern, silver and black braid on branch-coloured backing (here scarlet) with gilt badges, the grenade and number indicating a *Leutnant* of the 66th (4th Baden) Field Artillery.

k. Officers' dress rank-insignia: gilt-crescented epaulettes with padded cloth centres in the branch-colour. Left: *Leutnant*, 66th (4th Baden) Field Artillery; right, *Hauptmann* (captain), Medical Corps.

l. Field officers' epaulettes had bullion fringes: with no rank-badge, major, here of *Infanterie-Regt. von Horn (3 Rheinisches) Nr. 29*, from Trier. Other rank-badges were: *Oberleutnant*, one star; field ranks with twisted braid straps or fringed epaulettes, *Oberstleutnant* (lieutenant-colonel) with one star and *Oberst* (colonel) with two.

g.▲

h.▲

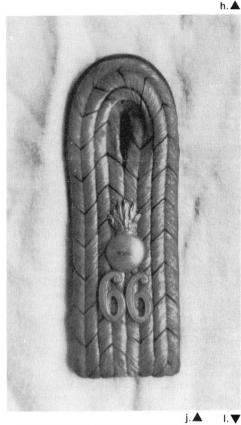

i.▲   k.▼

j.▲   l.▼

CHRONOLOGY: 1916

1915 had seen the extension of the theatre of war to include the Middle East, and a widening of the campaigning in Europe. The Western Front remained deadlocked, and would be the focus of the major Allied effort in 1916; the Caucasus and Italian Fronts similarly remained without decisive advantage, though on the Eastern Front the Central Powers were in the ascendant, the Serbian Front had virtually collapsed (the Allies clinging to Salonika), and the Allied expeditions to the Dardanelles and in Mesopotamia were in a parlous position. Thus far, the Allies had not enjoyed the success they envisaged when the war commenced almost a year and a half before.

The Dardanelles
8–9 January: After untold privation and immense casualties, the Allied expedition to the Dardanelles was withdrawn without the loss of a man, in sharp contrast to the mismanagement of the landings. The cessation of operations in the Gallipoli theatre enabled the Western Allies to concentrate their efforts on the Western Front.

The Western Front
Both sides determined to make a major effort along the Western Front. France was beginning to experience a serious drain on manpower, so that the Germans hoped that even if they were unable to break the Allied defences, they could reduce France to a situation of desperation. Masterminding the Allied strategy, Joffre attempted to overcome the lack of co-ordination which had bedevilled Allied plans in 1915 by organizing a concerted offensive in the West, East and Italy, intended to take place towards the middle of the year, by which time Russia would be prepared.

February-December: Verdun. The German assault was launched long before that planned by the Allies, directed towards the fortified French position around Verdun. From 21 February massive German attacks drove the French from part of their defences, including Fort Douaumont; Joffre appointed General Henri Philippe Pétain to hold Verdun at all costs. From the outset Pétain's policy was exemplified by his statement *Ils ne passeront pas* (they shall not pass) – a marked difference from the attitude he adopted in 1940 – and when the next German assault occupied more territory (6 March) he counter-attacked and recovered it. This was the pattern for the remainder of the battle, the French clinging on grimly, supplied only by the *Voie Sarée* (sacred way), a 40-mile minor road which was their only route for reinforcement. A third German drive was resisted in April/May, until in June/July the French were reduced almost to the point of defeat, with the loss of Fort Vaux on 9 June; yet they hung on until demands for reinforcement on the Eastern Front caused the Germans to transfer 15 divisions, and by early September the Germans realized that their resources were insufficient to break Verdun and switched to the defence. The French then counter-attacked and recaptured Forts Douaumont (24 October) and Vaux (2 November), so that by the end of the year almost all the captured territory had been regained. The horror of Verdun had accomplished little save the loss of more than 540,000 French and 430,000 German troops.

1 July–November: The Somme. Joffre's planned Anglo-French offensive was amended to a primarily British assault due to the immense pressure upon the French at Verdun. The main attack was launched on 1 July by General Henry Rawlinson's Fourth Army, with Edmund Allenby's Third Army farther north, against heavily-prepared German defences. The initial attack was the blackest day in the history of the British Army, which lost about 60,000 men on 1 July; it was especially terrible in the involvement of new battalions raised within a small locality — for example those units styled 'Pals' — so that some towns were devastated when their battalion was annihilated. It has even been argued that 1 July 1916 changed the face of British society more comprehensively than any other event in history.

Despite the losses, the British continued to launch smaller attacks; on 13 July the German second line was penetrated briefly, and on 15 September further ground was gained by the first attack of 'land-ships' (tanks), marking the beginning of armoured warfare, at Flers, but their use was premature and the attack was halted. By the end of November only about eight miles had been gained, at a cost of about 420,000 British and almost 200,000 French casualties; yet though the losses were manifestly not worth the result, it had relieved pressure on Verdun which might otherwise have fallen, and the continuous German counter-attacks had cost them about 650,000 men, including the cream of the officers and NCOs. Among the most terrible battles in history, the Somme had destroyed the best elements of both the British and German armies.

24 April: Not directly part of the war but arising from it was the brief but violent 'Easter Rising' of Irish nationalists in Dublin; it was suppressed by the British Army after some heavy fighting.

The Eastern Front
March: Attempting to divert German resources from the Western Front, the Russians launched an attack on 18 March in the Lake Naroch–Vilna area, but it foundered amid the mud of the spring thaw; it cost about 100,000 Russian casualties and about one-fifth that number of Germans.

4 June: With Italy under pressure from Austria, a second Russian advance was made by General Alexei Brusilov of the South-Western Army Group. Attacking on a front of 300 miles, the 'Brusilov Offensive' took the Austro-Germans by surprise, breaking their defences in two places and temporarily almost destroying the Austrian IV Army. Brusilov's troops were largely unsupported by the other Russian forces on the Eastern Front, allowing a German counter-attack to stop the Russian advance towards the north.

16 June–early August: The German counter-attack stabilized the line until Brusilov made a second drive from 28 July, pushing the defenders further back.

7 August–20 September: Brusilov attacked again and reached the foothills of the Carpathians, until Russian exhaustion and German reinforcements rushed from the Western Front stopped the Russian advance. The Brusilov Offensive was of major consequence, drawing in resources from the Central Powers' efforts on the Western and Isonzo Fronts, devastating the Austrian Army to such a degree that but for German reinforcements its collapse might have been total, and helping to cause the dismissal of the German chief-of-staff, Erich von Falkenhayn; but despite its being Russia's most successful operation of the war, the million casualties sustained contributed to the unrest which was to result in the Revolution in the following year.

27 August: Emboldened by the success of Brusilov, Roumania finally entered the war on the Allied side after much negotiation; the Austrian territory of Transylvania was invaded immediately.

August–November: Demoted to army commander, Falkenhayn stopped the Roumanian advance with the German Ninth Army, while the Bulgarian Danube Army (with German support and under the command of the German General Mackensen) attacked the Roumanians from the south.

December: The Roumanian commander Averescu, assailed by both enemy armies (which ultimately linked) and without the Russian support he required, was defeated at the River Arges (1–4 December), Bucharest was captured (6 December) and the Roumanian forces retired into Russia, with most of the country (including its oil fields and important agricultural areas) remaining in the hands of the Central Powers. Despite the Russian successes of the Brusilov Offensive, the year ended with the Central Powers in a not disadvantageous position on the Eastern Front.

The Isonzo Front

March: Italian–Austrian combat continued to lack a decisive outcome, the Italian offensive in the fifth battle of the Isonzo (11–29 March) having no more success than its predecessors.

May–June: An Austrian surprise attack from 15 May in the Trentino area broke the Italian defences, but a counter-attack and the withdrawal of Austrian units to the threatened Eastern Front recovered some of the lost territory, though Italian losses were almost twice those of the Austrians.

August: Taking advantage of the Austrian concentration for the Trentino offensive, the Italians attacked again in the sixth battle of the Isonzo (6–17 August), but it had little more effect than the previous offensives.

September–December: Renewed Italian assaults in the seventh (14–26 September), eighth (10–12 October) and ninth (1–14 November) battles of the Isonzo achieved little except to deplete the Austrian defensive capability, so that the situation at the end of the year was little changed from that at the beginning.

The Salonika Front

1915 ended with the Allies holding a bridgehead around Salonika, the Allied forces in the area being principally French and British since the withdrawal of the Serbian Army in 1915 and the crushing of Montenegro which was forced to surrender on 25 January 1916. After re-equipping, the Serbian Army rejoined the Allied forces in July and the Allies planned to break out of their positions around Salonika, but the Bulgarian-German forces, previously satisfied with a containing operation, took the offensive in August.

July–December: Independent from the main operations, an Italian force had been opposing an Austrian contingent in Albania; in November the Italians finally drove the Austrians north, enabling them to join the main Allied forces under the nominal command of the French general Maurice Sarrail (the British contingent was under its own command).

August: The Bulgarian-German offensive drove back the Allies in the Battle of Florina (17–27 August).

September–December: Sarrail's counter-attack pushed back the Central Powers, Monastir falling on 19 November, but no further progress was made, the Allies having sustained about 50,000 casualties and the Bulgarian-German forces considerably more.

The Caucasus

January–April: A Russian advance which began from Kars in early January made considerable progress, defeating the Turkish opponents at Köprukoy (18 January) and capturing Erzerum (13–16 February); a secondary movement along the Black Sea coast, supported by the Russian Navy, captured Trebizond (18 April).

May–December: A two-pronged Turkish counter-offensive was defeated, principally at Erzinjan (25 July); by the end of August fighting slackened for the winter.

The Mesopotamian Front

The advance of the British General Charles Townshend in late 1915 had ended with his withdrawal before overwhelming Turkish strength, and from 7 December his main body (less the cavalry which escaped) was besieged in Kut-al-Amara.

January–April: As Townshend's supplies ran low, continued attempts by the British and Indian armies to break through the Turkish siege-lines were unsuccessful; faced with starvation, Townshend surrendered his garrison of more than 8,000 men on 29 April.

August: A new British commander was appointed, Sir Frederick Maude; the British continued to hold their defensive positions until an overall strategy for the area had been devised.

December: It was finally decided that Maude should resume the offensive, and from mid-December he began to advance up both banks of the Tigris with more than 160,000 men, one-third British and the remainder from the Indian Army.

The Middle Eastern Front

January–August: British efforts were directed towards extending the defences of the Suez Canal into the Sinai desert, where sporadic fighting occurred when the Turks attempted to resist. Not all British resources could be devoted to this task due to a tribal insurrection by the Senussi in western Egypt, which was suppressed by March.

June: The Arab Revolt. With British and French encouragement, the Arab chieftains of the Hejaz proclaimed their independence from Turkey and a widespread guerrilla war broke out. From mid-June all Turkish lines of communication north, as far as Syria, were threatened by the fierce and mobile Arab irregulars, who received limited Allied support.

August: A Turkish attempt to attack the British in the Sinai (with German assistance and under a German commander, General von Kressenstein) was repelled at the battle of Rumani (3 August).

August–December: The British continued to advance their Sinai lines to prepare for an advance into Palestine in the following year.

The Persian Front

To relieve pressure upon the British in Mesopotamia, the limited Russian forces in Persia advanced towards Baghdad; but upon the fall of Kut-al-Amara the Turks switched many of their resources to shield the city, and after the Russian advance was beaten back at Khanikin (1 June) they retired again in the face of a Turkish counter-offensive.

On the Western Front at least, 1916 had been the most terrible year of the war to date, the combatants suffering losses which in previous ages would have been thought insupportable: it is doubtful if either the British, French or German armies ever fully recovered from the carnage of Verdun and the Somme and the loss of so many experienced personnel. Russian gains on the Eastern Front were at a price almost unbearable, the consequences of which were to become evident in the following year;

and although the Austrians were able to keep the Isonzo Front in a state of virtual stalemate, their losses in the east destroyed much of the Empire's military resource. In the war against the Turks, despite the evacuation of the Dardanelles and the disaster of Kut, the British situation was improving so that a major offensive could be contemplated in 1917.

GERMAN ARMY: ORGANIZATION

The basic German Army organization at the outbreak of war is summarized in the previous *Fotofax* title, *1914*, but as in most armies amendments were introduced as a result of the experience of combat. Infantry regimental organization was changed to maintain firepower while reducing the number of men by the increase of 'support' weapons, principally machine-guns but including grenade-projectors and mortars *(Minen-werfer)*; the crews of such 'trench artillery' were originally distributed as platoons but in September 1918 were amalgamated into a single company. The original regimental organization of three battalions of four rifle companies each, plus a 13th, machine-gun company, was amended in 1916 when the 15-gun M/G company was replaced by three 6-gun companies, so that each battalion henceforth comprised four rifle and one M/G company. From 1917 an increasing number of light machine-guns were added to each company, and in addition to the regimental M/G companies there also existed independent machine-gun *Abteilungen*, deployed virtually as artillery.

Jäger battalions originally comprised one M/G, one cyclist and four rifle companies; the bicycle companies were eventually withdrawn and a second M/G company and a *Minenwerfer* company added in August 1916.

A wartime development was the formation of *Sturmabteilungen* or 'storm-troops', specially trained assault units. Some of these were maintained regimentally but from late 1915 there existed independent *Sturmbataillone* of two or three infantry companies, a machine-gun and a mortar company, and a flamethrower detachment crewed by pioneers.

The majority of the cavalry units were dismounted during the war to form *Kavallerieschützen* units for use as infantry, each cavalry regiment forming one battalion of a new three-battalion unit, each battalion of four 'squadrons' (rifle companies) plus a machine-gun 'squadron'.

Field artillery originally consisted of regiments of two *Abteilungen* (battalions) each, each of three 6-gun batteries. During the war regiments were re-organized into three *Abteilungen* of three 4-gun batteries each, maintaining the 36 guns per regiment, with one *Abteilung* often equipped with light field howitzers, thus mixing the type of ordnance within the regiment.

GERMAN ARMY: PERSONAL WEAPONS*

After the Franco-Prussian War had proved the superiority of the French military rifle, the Germans determined to improve their standard weapon. The Small Arms Commission and the Mauser Arms Factory initially produced the Model 1871 rifle, an improvement on the French Chassepot, itself improved in 1884 (producing the Model 1871/84), and replaced it in 1888 with a smaller-bore bolt-action rifle in imitation of the French Lebel, the *Gewehr 1888*, abbreviated to 'Gew.88'. It was 7.91mm calibre and existed as a rifle with 30-inch barrel and a carbine

*Excluding machine-guns.

('Kar.88') with 18-inch barrel, the latter not equipped to take a bayonet; it incorporated the five-round Mannlicher magazine. During the First World War the Gew.88 remained in use, especially with reserve and *Landwehr* formations, never fully disappeared from service, and many were converted to accommodate the Mauser ammunition-clip.

At the outbreak of war the regulation weapon was the *Gewehr 1898* (Gew.98), designed by the Mauser factory in 1893, the principal improvements being a flush magazine (i.e., one not projecting beneath the stock), an improved clip for charger-loading and a one-piece bolt. It weighed 9lb (9lb 14oz with bayonet), retained the 7.91mm calibre and was 49.4 inches long overall (without bayonet), with a barrel-length of 29.05in. The maximum range on the adjustable backsight was 2,000 metres, and the practicable rate of fire by a trained man was between 10 and 15 rounds per minute. A significant variety was the *Karabine 1898* (Kar.98), basically the same weapon with a 24-inch barrel; it was intended for artillery and supporting services but the shorter barrel (without materially affecting performance) made it popular with infantry for trench warfare and especially with the later 'storm troops'. Another variety, confusingly styled the *1898 Karabine* (98 Kar.) was intended as a cavalry weapon, with 18in barrel; this was deemed too short and from 1909 the cavalry began to be re-equipped with the Kar.98. The Gew.98 could be fitted with telescope sights as a sniper's rifle (by 1917 three were issued to each company), with an optional down-turning bolt-handle which required a hollowing-out of the stock on the right side above the trigger to accommodate the ball-end of the bolt (as existed on the Kar.98). This *Scharfschütze* (sniper rifle) usually fired 'K' bullets *(Keru Geschlossis)* which were armour-piercing. The Gew.98 was also modified to produce the so-called *Mehrlader (Repetier-gewehr)* (repeating-rifle) which had an extra-large magazine *(Anstechmagazin)* accommodating twenty rounds in addition to the five carried in the magazine housed in the stock; but the projecting magazine made the weapon unwieldy and it was never widely used.

Automatic rifles were used in smaller numbers. The Mondragon Automatic Rifle of 7mm calibre with 10-shot magazine projecting below the stock was used principally as an aircraft weapon before the development of machine-guns adapted for aerial use. The army's main automatic weapon was the 1915 *Muskete*, as illustrated in the previous *Fotofax* title *1915*, basically a derivative of the Danish Madsen, equipped with a bipod mount and 25-round magazine; it was restricted to the *Musketen* battalions which were intended to remain behind the front line to utilize their firepower and mobility to plug any gaps in the line through which the enemy had broken. The 1915 Bergmann Automatic Rifle was used only rarely from 1916, its firepower being diluted by its tendency to overheat and jam. Even rarer was the Bergmann MP-18, a short-barrelled sub-machine-gun (the first adopted for active service), which though a successful design was introduced so late in the war that it never attained much significance.

The bayonet was used on virtually all personal firearms (even the Mondragon Automatic Rifle), the initial Gew.98 bayonet being a narrow-bladed, quill-backed weapon swelling slightly towards the point, with a 20½-inch blade, a ribbed wooden grip and a single quillon. It was modified a number of times, most notably in 1905 as the Model 1898/05, which had a much wider 14½-inch blade, again increasing in width towards the tip; the shape was such that it gave rise to the name 'butcher-knife bayonet'. Pioneer units had a version with serrated back for use as a saw, an addition seized upon by Allied propaganda which claimed it as further proof of 'Hun frightfulness'. In addition to these patterns, 'dress' bayonets existed of the same basic style but with the metal parts plated and with no provision for attachment to the rifle; they were simply ornaments for 'walking-out dress' and not even for ceremonial parades when bayonets might have to be fixed. Later in the war there existed a range of hastily produced *Ersatz* bayonets. Scabbards were normally of blackened steel, though leather was also used, as for the original 1898 pattern.

Officers and senior NCOs were armed with swords and pistols, and machine-gun crews who might find rifles an encumbrance also carried pistols, mostly of 9mm calibre, though the Walther was 6.35mm and the Mauser 7.63mm. Initially the German Army used the six-shot Model 1883 revolver of .471 calibre (and the Saxon Cavalry pattern of .433 calibre), but from 1908 the army adopted an automatic pistol as its regulation sidearm, the 9mm Parabellum, better-known by the name of a designer, Georg Luger, who developed it from the 1893 Borchardt automatic pistol, an American invention which continued to be carried by German officers even though not the official weapon. The Parabellum initially appeared in 7.65mm calibre, but from the Model 1902 was chambered for a 9mm cartridge. It contained an 8-round magazine in the grip, with a supplementary 32-round magazine which could be attached to the base of the grip; available with short and long barrels, a shoulder-stock was available to turn it into a short carbine. Though never adopted officially, an automatic which saw widespread use was the 1898 Mauser pistol of 7.63mm calibre (or re-chambered for the standard 9mm cartridge); its magazine extended below the chamber, forward of the trigger-guard, and thus its grip was narrower than that of the Parabellum, hence the nickname 'broomhandle'. The 9mm Bayard, 9mm Browning (with long and short barrels) and the 6.35mm Walther were used only in limited numbers.

Swords soon disappeared from the combat zones as their lack of use was demonstrated; cavalry swords in general were withdrawn in 1915. Artillery and train services carried a slightly curved sabre, heavy cavalry a straight-bladed *Pallasch* with triple-bar guard, and lighter regiments a slightly shorter weapon with quarter-basket hilt; infantry and other dismounted officers used the longer 1889 sword. All had metal scabbards. Lances were carried originally only by *Uhlans*, but as in many armies the weapon was extended to all regiments in 1889, the Model 1890 lance having a length (inclusive of cruciform tip) of 10 feet 6 inches, with a tubular steel shaft. It saw little combat service after the initial brief period of fluid manoeuvre early in the war.

Of all nations, Germany was the most advanced in the production of hand-grenades, so that vast stocks of hand- and rifle-grenades were available at the outbreak of war, as a result of a commission established to investigate the lessons of the Russo-Japanese War. Almost all German grenades were ignited by a time fuze, though a few percussion varieties existed, most notably the 1914-pattern Rifle Grenade, the 'disc' pattern (resembling a convex discus) and some examples of the 'stick grenade'. Though more rifle-grenades were available initially than hand-grenades, their lack of accuracy led to their decline until the manufacture of new types from 1917, discharged from a cup affixed to the rifle-muzzle with an ordinary cartridge for propellant, instead of the rod-fittings of the earlier patterns. The best-known hand-grenade was the 'stick grenade' (*Stielhand-granate*) or 'potato-masher', a metal cylinder of explosive with a hollow wooden handle protruding from the base, through which the fuze ran, ignition being caused by pulling the cord which protruded from the bottom of the handle. Another version had a solid handle and a fuze which protruded alongside the handle from the base of the cylindrical head. Other types included the spherical pattern (*Kugelhandgranate*) which was a cast-iron, 3-inch diameter segmented ball with a friction-tube inserted in the top, ignition occurring when the wire loop at the top was withdrawn; a leather wrist-loop was often attached for this purpose. The 'egg-grenade' (*Eierhandgranate*) was of similar type, but with the cast-iron body ovoid in shape; and the 'parachute grenade' had a fabric 'parachute' stabilizer attached to the bottom of the cylinder which resembled the shape of a rifle-grenade. A number of varieties of spherical gas-grenades were produced, with thin steel exteriors and containing about ⅔-pint of liquid released by the bursting-charge, but these were never very widely used. The grenade-discharger which fired a finned projectile much farther than it was possible to throw a hand-grenade was not a 'personal' weapon but, like the trench mortar, was a piece of trench artrillery.

Three basic varieties of flamethrower were used by the German Army, but one (the *Grossflammenwerfer*) was static and had to be erected in a trench, and the *Kleinflammenwerfer*, though portable, was still cumbersome: it could be carried on the back of one member of the crew and its hose and nozzle directed by another. Only the much lighter *Wex* was truly a portable 'personal weapon', with the advantage of automatic ignition, whereas the others had to be ignited by a taper or match applied to the jet of flammable liquid issuing from the nozzle.

REGIMENTS OF THE GERMAN ARMY

The various regiments of the German Army were numbered consecutively irrespective of their state of origin and the fact that some states retained a degree of independence in their organization and uniform. The following list shows the 'state' composition of the army but does not attempt to give full titles: it was usual for regimental appellations to give the name of the dignitary from whom the unit took its title (if any), then the 'state' number (e.g., 1st Brandenburg) and finally their number in the line, thus: *Grenadier-Regiment König Friedrich I (4. Ostpreussisches) Nr. 5*. The units which comprised the German Army were as follows:

Prussian Guard
1st–5th Foot Guards; 1st–5th Guard Grenadiers; Fusiliers; *Jägers; Schützen* (Sharpshooters).

Infantry: Grenadiers
Line regiments numbered: 1 (1st E. Prussian), 2 (1st Pomeranian), 3–5 (2nd–4th E. Prussian), 6–7 (1st–2nd W. Prussian), 8 (1st Brandenburg Leib-Grenadiers), 9 (2nd Pomeranian: Colberg Grenadiers), 10–11 (1st–2nd Silesian), 12 (2nd Brandenburg), 89 (Mecklenburg), 100 (1st Saxon Leib-Grenadiers), 101 (2nd Saxon), 109 (1st Baden Leib-Grenadiers), 110 (2nd Baden), 119 (1st Württemberg).

Infantry: Fusiliers
Line regiments numbered: 33 (E. Prussian), 34 (Pomeranian), 35 (Brandenburg), 36 (Magdeburg), 37 (Westphalian), 38

(Silesian), 39 (Lower Rhenish), 40 (Hohenzollern), 73 (Hanoverian), 80 (Hessian), 86 (Schleswig-Holstein), 90 (Mecklenburg), 108 (Saxon), 122 (4th Württemberg).

Infantry: line regiments

Regiments numbered: 13, 15–17, 53, 55–57 (1st–8th Westphalian); 14, 21, 42, 49, 54, 61 (1st–8th Pomeranian); 18–19, 58–59 (1st–4th Posen); 20, 24, 48, 52, 60, 64 (3rd–8th Brandenburg); 22–23, 62–63 (1st–4th Upper Silesian); 25, 28–30, 65, 68–70, 160–61 (1st–10th Rhenish); 26–27, 66–67 (1st–4th Magdeburg); 31–32, 71–72, 94–96, 153 (1st–8th Thuringian); 41, 43–45 (5th–8th E. Prussian); 46–47, 50–51, 154 (1st–5th Lower Silesian); 74, 77–78, 164–65 (1st–5th Hanoverian); 75–76 (1st–2nd Hanseatic); 78 (E. Frisian); 81–83 (1st–3rd Hessian); 84 (Schleswig); 85 (Holstein); 87–88 (1st–2nd Nassau); 91 (Oldenburg); 92 (Brunswick); 93 (Anhalt); 97, 99 (1st–2nd Oberheim), 98 (Metz); 102–07, 133–34, 139, 177–79, 181 (3rd–15th Saxon); 111–14, 142, 169–70 (3rd–9th Baden); 115 (1st Hessian Grand-Ducal *Leibgarde*); 116–18, 168 (2nd–5th Hessian Grand-Ducal); 120, 123–27, 180 (2nd, 5th–8th Württemberg); 121 (Old Württemberg); 128 (Danzig); 129, 140, 148–49, 155, 175–76 (3rd–9th W. Prussian); 130–131, 135–36, 144–45, 156–57, 173–74 (1st–10th Lorraine); 132, 137–38, 143 (1st–4th Lower Alsace); 141 (Kulmer); 146–47 (1st–2nd Masuria); 150–51 (1st–2nd Ermland); 152 (Deutsch–Ordens); 156–57 (3rd–4th Silesian); 162 (Lübeck, 3rd Hanseatic); 163 (Schleswig-Holstein); 166 (Hesse-Homburg); 167, 171–72 (1st–3rd Upper Alsace).

Jägers

Battalions numbered: 1 (E. Prussian), 2 (Pomeranian), 3 (Brandenburg), 4 (Magdeburg), 5–6 (1st–2nd Silesian), 7 (Westphalian), 8 (Rhenish), 9 (Laurenberg), 10 (Hanoverian), 11 (Hessian), 12–13 (1st–2nd Saxon), 14 (Mecklenburg).

Cavalry: Prussian Guard

Garde du Corps, Guard Cuirassiers, 1st–2nd Dragoons, Guard Hussars, 1st–3rd *Uhlans*.

Cavalry: Saxon heavy regiments

Saxon Guard Regiment, Saxon Carabiniers.

Cavalry: Cuirassiers

Regiments numbered: 1 (Silesian), 2 (Pomeranian), 3 (E. Prussian), 4 (Westphalian), 5 (W. Prussian), 6 (Brandenburg), 7 (Magdeburg), 8 (Rhenish).

Cavalry: Dragoons

Regiments numbered: 1 (Lithuanian), 2, 12 (1st–2nd Brandenburg), 3 (Neumark), 4, 8, 15 (1st–3rd Silesian), 5 (Rhenish), 6 (Magdeburg), 7 (Westphalian), 9, 16 (1st–2nd Hanoverian), 10 (E. Prussian), 11 (Pomeranian), 13 (Schleswig-Holstein), 14 (Kurmark), 17, 18 (1st–2nd Mecklenburg), 19 (Oldenburg), 20–22 (1st–3rd Baden), 23 (Hessian Guard), 24 (2nd Hessian), 25–26 (1st–2nd Württemberg).

Cavalry: Hussars

Regiments numbered: 1–2 (1st–2nd Leib-Hussars), 3 (Brandenburg), 4, 6 (1st–2nd Silesian), 5 (Pomeranian), 7, 9 (1st–2nd Rhenish), 8, 11 (1st–2nd Westphalian), 10 (Magdeburg), 12 (Thuringian), 13–14 (1st–2nd Hessian), 15 (Hanoverian), 16 (Schleswig-Holstein), 17 (Brunswick), 18–19 (1st–2nd Saxon).

Cavalry: Uhlans

Regiments numbered: 1 (W. Prussian), 2 (Silesian), 3, 11 (1st–2nd Brandenburg), 4, 9 (1st–2nd Pomeranian), 5 (Westphalian), 6 (Thuringian), 7 (Rhenish), 8 (E. Prussian), 10 (Posen), 12 (Lithuanian), 13–14 (1st–2nd Hanoverian), 15 (Schleswig-Holstein), 16 (Altmark), 17, 18, 21 (1st–3rd Saxon), 19–20 (1st–2nd Württemberg).

Field Artillery

1st–4th (Prussian) Guard; regiments numbered: 1 (Prince August of Prussia's); 2, 17 (1st–2nd Pomeranian); 3, 18 (1st–2nd Brandenburg); 4 (Magdeburg); 5, 41 (1st–2nd Lower Silesian); 6, 42 (1st–2nd Silesian); 7, 22 (1st–2nd Westphalian); 8, 23 (1st–2nd Rhenish); 9 (Schleswig); 10, 26 (1st–2nd Hanoverian); 11, 25, 47, 61 (Hessian); 12, 28, 32, 48, 64, 68, 77, 78 (1st–8th Saxon); 13, 29, 49, 65 (1st–4th Württemberg); 14, 30, 50, 76 (1st–5th Baden); 15, 51 (1st–2nd Upper Alsace); 16, 52 (1st–2nd E. Prussian); 19, 55 (1st–2nd Thuringian); 20, 56 (1st–2nd Posen); 21, 57 (1st–2nd Upper Silesian); 24 (Holstein); 27, 63 (1st–2nd Nassau); 31, 67 1st–2nd (Lower Alsace); 33, 34, 69, 70 (1st–4th Lorraine); 35, 36 (1st–2nd W. Prussian); 37 (Lithuanian); 38 (Upper Pomeranian); 39 (Kurmark); 40 (Altmark); 43 (Cleves); 44 (Treves); 45 (Laurenburg); 46 (Lower Saxon); 53 (Lower Pomeranian); 54 (Neumark); 58 (Minden); 59 (Berg); 60 (Mecklenburg); 62 (Ostfries); 71 (Komthur); 72 (Hochmeister); 73 (Masuria); 74 (Torgau); 75 (Mansfeld).

Foot Artillery

Guard Regiment; line regiments 1, 2, 4, 6 with 'personal' titles; 3 (Brandenburg), 5 (Lower Silesian), 7 (Westphalian), 8 (Rhenish), 9 (Schleswig-Holstein), 10 (Lower Saxony), 11, 15 (1st–2nd W. Prussian), 12 (Saxon), 13 (Hohenzollern), 14 (Baden).

Pioneers

Guard Battalion; line battalions numbered: 1 (E. Prussian), 2 (Pomeranian), 3 (Brandenburg), 4 (Magdeburg), 5 (Lower Silesian), 6 (Silesian), 7 (Westphalian), 8 (Rhenish), 9 (Schleswig-Holstein), 10 (Hanoverian), 11 (Hessian), 12, 22 (1st–2nd Saxon), 13 (Württemberg), 14 (Baden), 15, 19 1st–2nd Alsace), 16, 20 (1st–2nd Lorraine), 17, 23 (1st–2nd W. Prussian), 18 (Samland), 21 (Nassau).

Train

Guard Battalion, and 19 line battalions bearing the same state designations as Pioneer battalions with the same number, except: 18 (Hessian Grand-Ducal); 19 (2nd Saxon).

Bavarian Army (remained independent of the numbering of the remainder of the German Army)
Infantry: Leib-Regiment; 1st–23rd Infantry; 1st–2nd *Jägers*.
Cavalry: 1st–2nd Heavy Cavalry; 1st–2nd *Uhlans*; 1st–7th *Chevaulegers*.
Artillery: 1st–12th Field Regiments, 1st–2nd Foot Regiments.
Supports: 1st–3rd Pioneer Battalions, 1st–3rd Train Battalions.

SOURCES AND BIBLIOGRAPHY

Although this lists works applicable to the war as a whole, as noted in the earlier titles *1914* and *1915*, emphasis is given to the actions of 1916 and to the German Army which figures in the data section.

Barker, A. J. *The Neglected War: Mesopotamia 1914–18.* London, 1967

Chappell, M. *British Battle Insignia 1914–18.* London, 1986
— *The British Soldier in the 20th Century.* Hatherleigh (series) from 1987

Farrar-Hockley, A. H. *The Somme.* London, 1964

Fosten, D. S. V., and Marrion, R. J. *The German Army 1914–18.* London, 1978

Hicks, J. E. *French Military Weapons.* New Milford, Connecticut, 1964
— *German Weapons, Uniforms, Insignia 1841–1918.* La Canada, California, 1958

Horne, A. *The Price of Glory: Verdun 1916.* London, 1962

Laffin, J. *Western Front 1916–17: the Price of Honour.* Sydney, 1987

Middlebrook, M. *The First Day on the Somme.* London, 1971

Mollo, A. *Army Uniforms of World War I.* Poole, 1977 (the most outstanding modern work on the subject)

Nash, D. B. *German Infantry 1914–18.* London, 1977
— *Imperial German Army Handbook 1914–18.* London, 1980

Nash, D. B. (ed.) *German Army Handbook 1918.* London, 1977

Nicolle, D. *Lawrence and the Arab Revolt.* London, 1989

Rankin, R. H. *Helmets and Headdress of the Imperial German Army 1870–1918.* New Milford, Connecticut, 1965

Walter, A. (ed.) *Guns of the First World War.* London, 1988 (a reprint of the *Text Book of Small Arms*, 1909)

Wilson, H. W. (ed.) *The Great War.* London, 1916 (contemporary periodical containing much significant photography and artwork)

An important article especially relevant to the modification of uniforms on campaign, concerning the Lancashire Fusiliers on the Somme, by M. Chappell, appeared in the periodical *Military Illustrated*, No. 1, London, 1986.

46. ANZACs on the march on the Western Front. Although motor transport was used increasingly during the war, horse-drawn vehicles and light carts pulled manually remained in use. The troops illustrated are unmistakably New Zealanders, their slouch hats being pinched up into the four-cornered crown like the hats worn by Boy Scouts and by the US Army.

46 ▼

▲47

▲48 ▼49

47. Though British Empire forces were equipped in British style, a number of distinctive patterns existed. This is an excellent depiction of the Australian tunic, made in drab or khaki serge, flannel or cord, which after exposure to the elements often faded to its natural blue-grey shade. The equipment is like that of the British 1908 pattern, but may include leather cartridge-pouches; the slouch hat, jealously guarded throughout the war, was the most characteristic item of Australian uniform. This 'Digger's' two attractive companions are South African recruiters, photographed on an Australian visit to Durban en route to the war. Their pseudo-military uniform was calculated to attract volunteers to the enlistment-booths!

48. Perhaps the most bizarre item of equipment devised during the period was the Canadian 'tump-line' device, a webbing strap which took some of the weight off the soldier's back by supporting it on his head, a method of weight-distribution used in the wilds of north-west Canada. It was designed by Captain Archibald who had won the high jump at the London Olympics, but not surprisingly it had only a very limited use!

49. A Belgian makes a sandwich in the entrance to his dug-out in the Belgian sector of the Western Front, from Ypres to the sea. The 1915-pattern Belgian uniform was produced in khaki because Britain could supply the cloth, but was basically in French style and included the Adrian helmet, painted khaki, with an embossed lion-mask badge on the front. This man has a fabric cover over his helmet and a double-breasted greatcoat; khaki trousers were worn with matching puttees or leather ankle-gaiters. The equipment hanging by the door of the dug-out is the 1915 pattern in brown leather; British-style webbing was manufactured later. Note the trench construction,

combining ancient-style gabions and chicken-wire.

50. A Belgian trench-mortar gunner wearing the 1915-pattern khaki tunic, trousers and puttees, with ankle-boots and khaki-painted Adrian helmet. For the artillery the collar-patch was royal blue with scarlet piping, and scarlet-piped shoulder-straps. Similarly, other branches had distinctive colours: infantry scarlet patch and royal blue piping; light infantry green patch and yellow piping; engineers black patch and scarlet piping, etc. The weapon is the French '58 cal' No. 2 mortar with finned bomb; range was varied by elevation or depression of the barrel on the slide illustrated.

51. Although some Indian Army units remained on the Western Front throughout the war, much of the army's effort was concentrated in Mesopotamia and, in the case of the Gurkhas, in the Dardanelles. This depicts the pipers of an unidentified Gurkha battalion entertaining French civilians; both pipers and spectators wear knitted woollen caps in place of their

50 ▲

more characteristic slouch hats. These indomitable Nepalese soldiers were thoroughly feared by all enemies who experienced their kukri-swinging charge and war-cry 'Ayo Gurkhali!'

51 ▼

52. *Generalfeldmarschall* Paul
Ludwig von Beneckendorf und
von Hindenburg (1874–1934)
and his chief-of-staff Erich von
Ludendorff (1865–1937) had
commanded on the Eastern
Front with considerable success
until appointed to overall
command on the Western Front
after the admissal of von
Falkenheyn in August 1916.
General officers' uniform
included a gold-embroidered
fringed loop decoration on a red
collar-patch, but in typical style
Hindenburg apparently wears
the regimental uniform of the
3rd Foot Guards, with *Garde-
Litzen* on the collar-patch. His
grey greatcoat had scarlet lapels
and piping on the upper edge of
the cuff, and gold and silver
braid shoulder-straps on red
backing, bearing the silver
crossed batons of field marshal's
rank; the cap had scarlet band
and piping. Hindenburg served
as president of the republic
from 1925 to 1934, latterly
(reluctantly) accepting Hitler as
chancellor; Ludendorff, a far
less noble character, adopted
extreme nationalism and
marched with Hitler in the
abortive Munich *putsch*.

53. The French *Soixante-quinze*
(75mm) fieldpiece was probably
the most famous ordnance of
the war, but earlier models
remained in use. This gun-
position in the Argonne has a
Modèle 1877 '*Système de Bange*'
of which the 80mm and 90mm
calibre were normally employed
in the field, but this is a larger
120L variety originally intended
for siege and garrison use. Note
the plates attached to the
wheels (*ceintures de roues*) and
ramps positioned behind the
wheels to absorb the recoil of
firing and prevent the gun from
having to be re-positioned
totally after each shot.

54. The Allied armies on the
Western Front maintained
considerable mounted forces in
the hope that they might be
able to exploit the breakthrough
that never came. Among the
most anachronistic were the
French Spahis, the near-
legendary north African cavalry
who retained their singular

53▲   54▼

equipment even when serving in
Europe: this rear view
illustrates the high-backed
saddle (not dissimilar to the
European 'great saddle' of the

17th century) and the flowing
cloak, the oriental appearance
somewhat marred by the steel
helmet (which for African
colonial troops bore a frontal

badge of 'RF' within a crescent).
The carbine slung on the back is
the 8mm Model 1890.

▲55   ▲56

55. Among the best units of the French Army were the Algerian and Tunisian *Tirailleurs*. Their designations could be confusing: they were often referred to by initials, R.M.T. (*Régiment de Marche de Tirailleurs*), R.T.A. (*Régiment des Tirailleurs Algériens*), or R.M.Z.T. (*Régiment mixte de Zouaves et de Tirailleurs*).

Uniform included the 'native' *chéchia* cap and khaki clothing, though other colours were pressed into service, such as 'horizon blue' greatcoats and even uniforms of the khaki shade styled *tenue réséda* originally intended for the Greek army. The *chéchias* here bear star-and-crescent insignia, but on campaign were usually

concealed by a horizon blue cover, until the issue of the Adrian helmet, originally blue but repainted khaki as soon as possible.

56. Among the most unusual uniforms seen in Europe was that of the French Annamite infantry, part of the garrison of Cochin-China sent to the main

theatre of war. Their uniform was khaki like that of other colonial corps, but included the unique straw or bamboo-fibre hat covered with grey cloth; for active service in Europe these were replaced by berets of the style worn by the *Chasseurs Alpins*. They served both in France and at Salonika.

▼57

57. A French listening-post on the Aisne. The sentry is using a trench periscope; note the klaxon to warn of gas attack, and the sheaf of rockets to signal for support. This demonstrates a notable difference between the systems of naming trenches and posts: whereas the British used homely names often taken from the home areas of the troops involved ('Pendle Hill Street', 'Sauchiehall Street', etc), this French post is named after a fallen hero, Jean Bosche of the 2nd *Chasseurs*, with the immortal phrase on the name-board, '*Mort au Champ d'Honneur*', 4 August 1915.

58. The Irish 'Easter Rising' of 1916 was not properly part of the war, but took advantage of British preoccupation; heavy fighting occurred in Dublin before the rising was crushed. This remarkable British armoured vehicle was made in the yard of the Guinness brewery from a number of railway-engine smoke-boxes mounted on a flat lorry, with an engine-cab at the rear to protect the driver. It was loopholed to enable the crew inside to return fire with little danger of being hit in return.

59. Easily transportable light machine-guns were adopted by most armies by the middle of the war; weapons like the French Chauchat and the Madsen derivative with which the German *Muskete* battalions were armed allowed infantry to possess their own fire-support without having to rely on the heavier machine-guns. The American-designed .303 calibre Lewis gun was adopted by the British Army from 1915; weighing 26lb, it was air-cooled with an aluminium barrel-casing and a drum magazine on top, capable of 550 rounds per minute, and was operated by one man. It is shown here on an anti-aircraft mounting on a car; normally it had a small bipod mount. A spare magazine is held by the man in the background.

60. Mechanized transport was first used to a considerable extent during the war; the first military transports were requisitioned civilian vehicles, but by 1916 specially designed transport was universal. This example crewed by members of the Royal Flying Corps is a Leyland 3-ton S-type lorry with the later pattern steel disc wheels instead of the original

▼62

cast-iron spoked variety. In this photograph the canvas tilt over the cab has been folded back. Note the use of the webbing waist-belt with the RFC khaki 'maternity jacket' (extreme right).

61. Although the British Royal Flying Corps had a prescribed uniform, officers serving on attachment usually retained their regimental uniform. In this photograph of probably Britain's most famous 'ace', Lieutenant (Temporary Captain) Albert Ball wears the uniform of his 7th (Robin Hood) Battalion, Sherwood Foresters (Nottinghamshire and Derbyshire Regiment) with the bronzed regimental collar-badges, with only the goggles suggesting his attachment to the RFC. The first man to win the Distinguished Service Order three times, Ball was a shy Nottingham youth who became one of the most intrepid fighter-pilots of the war; after his death in action at the age of 20 on 7 May 1917 he was awarded a Victoria Cross.

62. The regulation uniform of the Royal Flying Corps was the khaki 'maternity jacket', cavalry-style side-cap, trousers and puttees. This group of

senior NCOs includes a number of 'active service' variations, including the use of long woollen stockings in place of puttees (central figure). Flight-Sergeant W. H. Duckworth (seated left) purchased his own uniform which was tailored privately, here without shoulder-titles and including cavalry riding-breeches and leather 'Stohwasser' cavalry leggings.

63. The Tsar (left) and General Alexeevich Brusilov (1853–1926), architect of the 'Brusilov offensive', who made his name in the 1877–8 Russo-Turkish War and in 1916 proved himself the most capable Russian general of the war; in 1917 he joined the Soviets but was not actively employed again. Both wear the officers' version of the khaki greatcoat with rigid shoulder-boards and scarlet collar-patch, khaki breeches with scarlet stripes, and khaki cap; both carry the 1909-pattern sword (uniquely the Russians carried them with the hilt towards the rear) on a brown leather belt.

64. Although the United States did not enter the war until 1917, many individuals served in the armies of other states. Russia's long history of the employment of foreign officers is demonstrated by this photograph of Dr P. Newton, who took to Russia a Field Ambulance corps paid for by American sympathisers. He wears the officers' uniform of the Russian army: khaki peaked cap with domed oval cockade with 'sunburst' edging, and a khaki tunic with standing collar and pointed breast- and side-pockets. The conspicuous rigid shoulder-boards covered with metallic lace and bearing rank-stars were often replaced on campaign by soft shoulder-straps with khaki rank-lace, or plain shoulder-straps with the insignia drawn or stencilled on.

63 ▲　　64 ▼

65. A Russian gun-team on the Eastern Front, including a youthful cadet. The grey-brown double-breasted greatcoat had a falling collar bearing a patch in the service colour (black with red piping for artillery), and the usual double-sided shoulder-straps: one side in the facing-colour (artillery red) and the other in the garment-colour with (for rank-and-file) crossed cannon-barrels and the brigade number stencilled in red. The NCO in the centre, wearing the Cross of St. George, appears to have the wide gold stripe across the top of the shoulder-strap indicative of sergeant's rank. The cadet is armed with cossack-style artillery *Shashqa*, the guard-less sabre shorter than the cavalry pattern.

66. Russian troops queue for a hair-cut by electric clippers powered by hand-cranked generator. They wear the grey-brown greatcoat with collar-patch in the service colour: black piped red for artillery and engineers, green piped red for rifle corps, and red, blue, white or green respectively for the 1st-4th regiments in each infantry division. Shoulder-straps were red for Guards, artillery, engineers and the 1st and 2nd regiments in each line division, blue for the 3rd and 4th, crimson for rifle corps and yellow for grenadier divisions; on service they were usually reversed to show khaki with badge or regimental number usually in red for artillery, yellow for infantry and brown for engineer services. The third man in the queue appears to have a coloured strap bearing the single metallic lace stripe of sergeants' rank.

67. Some images from the war are uncannily like those of a previous age: this photograph might appear to depict a scene from Napoleon's retreat from Moscow, but in fact shows a Cossack patrol in the Caucasus. Although the Steppe Cossacks (the larger group) wore a version of the standard army uniform, the Caucasian Cossacks (Kuban and Terek) retained a 'native' costume of grey or black astrakhan cap,

▲65 ▼66

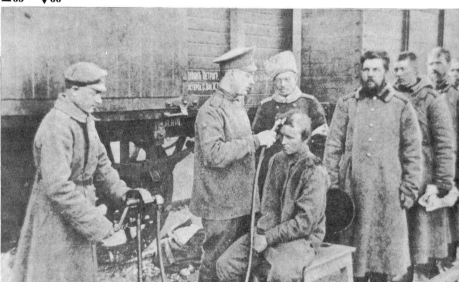

▼67

black or dark-grey kaftan (*Cherkeska*) with cartridge-tubes at each side of the breast, red shoulder-straps and collar-patch for Kuban and blue for Terek units.

68. Like the aviation services of most nations, that of the Russian forces was part of the army, trained and equipped by France. These officers affixing a bomb wear the distinctive uniform of the service, a black side-cap with red piping and silver-laced crown, dark blue shirt and red-piped black breeches, though the usual flying-dress included a leather helmet and black leather jacket. The shoulder-boards here show clearly the rank-marking of company officers: metallic lace straps with a central stripe of arm-of-service colour, with up to three stars.

69. Despite the Russians' pressing need for troops and *matériel*, they demonstrated solidarity with their allies by sending contingents to fight on the Western Front and to Salonika. They retained their national uniform, but those serving alongside the French adopted the ubiquitous *casque Adrian*. The Russian rifle was the 1891-pattern Mosin-Nagant (also known as the '3-line' or sometimes 1900-pattern even through basically identical with the 1891), a charger-loading 7.62mm calibre weapon, but to facilitate ammunition supply the Russians in France carried the French Lebel rifle.

70. An Italian infantry unit on the march, headed by the machine-gun section carrying the guns, barrels and mountings separately, on the backs of the crew. The 1909 grey-green uniform had padded rolls on the shoulders (to prevent the equipment slipping), matching trousers and puttees, and collar-patches coloured according to the branch: crimson for infantry; for machine-gunners they were pointed-ended with white stripes, blue, green and red respectively for the teams of St-Etienne, Maxim and Fiat guns. The wide black chevrons above the cuffs are the rank-insignia of senior privates (equating with lance-corporals in the British Army, for example). A black machine-gun badge was worn on the left sleeve.

68 ▲   69 ▼

70 ▼

71. An Italian light fieldpiece firing from a turf embrasure on the Italian Front. The crew wear the 1909 grey-green uniform, which for artillery had a black 'flame'-pointed collar-patch piped yellow; the field-cap bore an embroidered yellow grenade over crossed cannon-barrels, later produced in less visible black embroidery. The officers (as in right foreground, wearing leather gaiters instead of the grey-green puttees of the other ranks) had rank-insignia of one to three stars (for company officers) on the shoulder-straps, and a similar number of metallic lace bands on the cap, later changed to less visible yellow or grey lace. Note the ramps positioned behind the gun-wheels to prevent excessive recoil

72. Italian sentries manning a trench on the Italian Front in about August 1916. By now the Italian Army had adopted the French Adrian helmet, but of superior construction and without the embossed metal badge on the front as used by most nations which adopted the pattern; instead, Italian regimental insignia was often stencilled on in black paint, for infantry (for example) a crowned regimental number, backed by crossed rifles for NCOs and above. Personal equipment was produced in grey-green leather, matching the uniform-colour, with four ammunition-pouches for dismounted personnel. The rifle was the 1891-pattern 6.5mm Mannlicher-Carcano, taking a 6-round clip, though large quantities of earlier 6.5mm Vetterli rifles remained in use.

73. Italy's 6-inch 'position' guns fulfilled a similar role to the famous French '75', because despite firing a heavy shell with long range they were comparatively light and easy to transport. The gun here, en route to the Italian Front, has 'caterpillars' attached to the wheels to facilitate movement over rough or soft ground. Italian mounted troops like this artillery driver wore a tunic like that of the infantry but with shoulder-straps instead of 'rolls' at the point of the shoulder, grey-green riding-breeches, black leather gaiters and spurred ankle-boots instead of puttees.

74. A rapid mode of constructing trenches in mountainous terrain, as in the Alps: wire-netting baskets filled with sandbags. These Austrian machine-gunners apparently wear the 1909 pike-grey (*Hechtgrau*) field uniform with soft cap, though from 1915 a new uniform began to come into use, similar to the previous pattern but in field-grey, with a steel helmet initially of German pattern but later with a flatter lower edge, often styled a 'Berndorfer' helmet after its designer. Until 1917 regimental identity was indicated by the colour of collar-patch and buttons; the man at the right appears to have the two stars on the collar indicative of corporals' rank.

75. A number of armies had ski-borne infantry, the French *Chasseurs Alpins* being perhaps the most famous. This Austrian unit in the Alps appears to wear the pike-grey infantry uniform, most with the trousers with integral gaiters instead of the breeches and long stockings of the *Landesschützen* mountain troops, but the pile of equipment at the right appears to consist of rucksacks as carried by the latter, instead of the ordinary infantry pack. The piled rifles are apparently the 1895 8mm Mannlicher, a clip-loading weapon 50 inches long, rather than the 1895 short carbine of the *Landesschützen*.

73 ▲   74 ▼

75 ▼

▲76 ▼77

▼78

76. Although some units had been trained in mountain warfare earlier, the first German ski-corps were formed in 1915, the 1st–4th Bavarian Ski Battalions (*Schneeschuh-Bataillon*). The Württemberg *Gebirgs- und Schneeschuh Bataillon* was formed in October 1915 and served in the Vosges, in Roumania and on the Italian Front, being expanded to regimental strength in 1918. Their grey uniform had a black collar-patch bearing a green letter 'S' (*Schützen*: rifles) and small green shoulder-rolls; the peaked field-cap was similar to Austrian style. Equipment and arms were of infantry pattern, with rucksack instead of pack, and white and camouflaged hooded snow-suits were also used.

79 ▲

80▲ 81▼

Note the rear skirts of the 1910 tunic of the central figure, showing the false pockets each with three buttons and coloured piping. A slower but more reliable method of transport is visible at the right: ox-carts were used by all combatants in the region, and oxen were even used for hauling artillery.

78. The uniform of the Roumanian Army is illustrated in this portrait of General I. Culcer, commanding their First Army. From 1912 a grey-green field uniform was introduced, with a field-cap bearing the red, yellow and blue national cockade and piping in the arm-of-service colour for officers; a fly-fronted tunic with breast- and side-pockets in grey-green with standing colour bearing the collar-patch (red for generals, as here, and infantry); grey-green breeches (black for artillery and cavalry); and black riding-boots or brown ankle-boots and gaiters. Rank was indicated by the shoulder-strap device, here gold lace straps piped red, with three silver stars. From May 1916 a uniform of French manufacture in 'horizon blue' was authorized, but except for a number of officers it was not widely used.

79. After evacuation from its homeland, the Serbian Army was re-equipped in 1916 by the Allied nations, partly in British khaki and partly in French 'horizon blue', including the Adrian steel helmet. This depicts a cavalry unit equipped and serving as infantry at Salonika, with French-style uniform and equipment. The Adrian helmet bore an embossed metal badge on the front of the Serbian arms, a double eagle with a shield bearing a cross upon its breast, as on the standard carried here.

80. Casualty evacuation in the Salonika area utilizing a 'mule cacolet', a harness with a seat on each side to enable less severely wounded men to ride over rough country. Two Highlanders form the mule's burden; the 2nd Battalion, Camerons and 1st Battalion, Argyll and Sutherland were both with the 27th Division at Salonika from December 1915. The white labels attached to their breast-pockets would give details of injury and treatment given at the advanced dressing-station.

81. This sergeant with the rather severe haircut is using a trench periscope at Salonika, the upper part camouflaged with fabric. His unit is identified by the brass shoulder-title 'Y & L': 1st Battalion, York and Lancaster Regiment, which arrived in Salonika in early December 1915 as part of 83 Brigade, 28th Division, in which theatre it served for the remainder of the war.

▲82   ▼83

▲84

82. Prior to formation of the British Army's Corps of Signals in 1920, communications were the responsibiity of the Royal Engineers' 'signal service'. This officer operating a field-telephone at Salonika wears the white over blue 'armlet' or brassard on both upper sleeves which identified signals personnel. Rank-insignia is carried on the shoulder-strap, much less visible than on the cuff; the Sam Browne belt is worn with double shoulder-braces. The pistol by the officer's right hand is a Mauser automatic, perhaps captured from the Germans, though such weapons were also available in Britain for private purchase before the war. The man behind the officer has the ordinary brass 'RE' shoulder-titles, without the additional 'Signal Service' title underneath.

83. Although 19th-century mortars had been pressed into service by the French at the beginning of the war, 'trench artillery' was soon designed to enable infantry to have close-range artillery support, trench mortars lobbing bombs over a limited range. The German

▼85

Minenwerfer was probably the most effective, the bombs dropping with a whine (hence the British nickname 'moaning minnie'; 'minnie' = *Minenwerfer*), but all operated on a similar principle, having a flat base-plate to absorb recoil. This British officer at Salonika is somewhat gingerly about to fire a British 'Tock Emma' (T/M: trench mortar).

84. Among the most unusual items of uniform in the European theatres of war were sun-hats, both of the Australian-style 'slouch' pattern and others of more bizarre shape. This group of engineers (including some French personnel) shows British Royal Engineers in a variety of sun-hats; the location is unknown but may be Macedonia, where such head-dress was quite common with the British forces.

85. The uniform of the British forces in Mesopotamia (alias 'Mespot'!) was like that worn in India, khaki drill with topees. The heat led to the addition of other sunshades, such as the huge quilted neck-shade fastened around the topee in this photograph. The soldier illustrated has improvised a feeding-bottle for milk with which to feed this tiny gazelle, a wonderfully humanitarian scene from a bitter war.

86. Medical inspection of an Indian Mountain Battery at Salonika. The uniforms are like those worn in India despite being in a European theatre: British officers continued to wear tropical helmets (as indeed did some British units even in Italy) and khaki drill. The medical officer here wears rank-insignia on the shoulder-straps, a style eventually also seen on the Western Front, being less distinct to enemy snipers than the large rank-badges on the cuff; the crown on the shoulder-strap identifies his rank as that of major, the metal title 'IMS' indicating 'Indian Medical Service'.

87. Roll-call of an Indian infantry company in Mesopotamia. The Mesopotamian campaign was administered largely by the Indian Army, which provided the majority of the troops involved. Note here the 1903 leather bandolier equipment; unlike most of the Empire or Dominion troops, the Indian Army did not receive the 1908 web equipment until 1921. Calling the roll is an Indian commissioned officer, wearing an empty sword-frog on the

waist-belt. The British officer wears a typical uniform, including shorts, the use of which eventually spread to the

Western Front in hot weather. The cigar in an elegant holder is a non-regulation item of equipment!

86▲

87▼

88. Turkish prisoners with Indian guards in Mesopotamia. The Turks in 'Mespot' wore the same uniform as those in the Dardanelles and Palestine campaigns: greenish-khaki tunic and trousers, puttees, and the greyish-khaki cloth helmet styled an *enverieh* or 'Enver Pasha helmet', named from its designer, Enver Pasha himself, who it was said made a personal fortune out of its patent!

89. The Arab Revolt contributed considerably to Turkish discomfiture in the Middle East, and though many of the Arab troops eventually wore items of British uniform, civilian 'native' dress was most common, sometimes with a mixture of European-style garments (as at the right). The Sheikh of Mohommerah and his retainers illustrated wear the *kafiyah* head-dress, the long *dishdash* shirt and sometimes the long *abah* coat over the top, with an abundance of cartridge-belts and daggers. Firearms included British Lee-Enfields, captured Turkish Mausers and even Japanese Ariakas (supplied by Britain early in the Arab Revolt), but those illustrated carry the old British single-shot Martini-Henry.

90. The campaigns against the Germans in East Africa were conducted largely by British Empire forces. Illustrated here are two members of the 4th (Uganda) Battalion of the King's African Rifles, a splendid force formed in 1902 by the amalgamation of the Central Africa, Uganda and East Africa Rifles; 22 battalions served in the war. They wear the service uniform of light khaki jumper and shorts, khaki pillbox cap and brown leather equipment; many preferred bare feet for active service. The diminutive figure in the centre is a rifleman of the 2nd Jammu and Kashmir Infantry, one of the 'Imperial Service' units supplied by the loyal Indian states. Kashmir provided three infantry regiments, the 1st Infantry and 3rd Rifles serving in Palestine, and the 2nd and 3rd in East Africa.

▲88 ▼89

91. German signwriters at work, presumably a short distance from the front line. Trench nameboards and grave-markers gave such personnel a surfeit of work; the man on the right is finishing the decoration of a memorial cross to private Willy Pippig, apparently a member of the Hanoverian *Jäger-Battalion Nr. 10*

(Hannoversches), killed in October 1915.

92. A burial on the field of battle. Wherever possible the civilities were observed including burial in marked graves (albeit temporary ones: most were disinterred and laid to rest in proper cemeteries in due course), but all too often

proper burial was impossible, hence the huge numbers of men posted as 'missing, believed killed' who to this day have no known grave. The burial-party here are Australians, for once with no sign of the favourite slouch hat; steel helmets, some with fabric covers (as at the left) are carried instead.

90▲   91▲   92▼

Douglas Haig (1861-1928)

The abilities and conduct of few commanders have been the subject of such debate, even controversy, as those of Douglas Haig; and it is still difficult to reconcile the differing views.

Haig was born in Edinburgh, the son of a distiller, and joined the 7th Hussars after education at Clifton, Brasenose College, Oxford, and Sandhurst. Promoted to captain in 1891, he passed through the Staff College and served with the Egyptian Army in the campaign of 1898. He gained more staff experience during the Boer War, for which he received a brevet-colonelcy, C.B. and the appointment of ADC to the king. After commanding the 17th Lancers, Haig went to India as Inspector-General of Cavalry, and was promoted to major-general in 1905. At the War Office from 1906, he acted as Haldane's military advisor during the Liberal reforms of 1906–8, and was greatly concerned with the reorganisation of the army and general staff. To these political contacts he added entry to court, partly by his marriage in 1905 to Dorothy, daughter of the 3rd Lord Vivian and maid-of-honour to Queen Victoria and Queen Alexandra. After a period as chief of general staff in India, Haig took command at Aldershot; promoted to lieutenant-general in 1910, he became a KCB in 1913.

Upon the outbreak of war, Sir Douglas Haig was given command of I Corps of the British Expeditionary Force, which earned him promotion to general in November 1914. He appreciated the realities of the situation rather better than his superior, Sir John French (1852-1925), whose reactions to the events of the early stage of the war swung between unjustified optimism and depression. Haig expected a protracted war, never sharing the views of those who thought the outcome would be swift. Although prepared for the German thrust through Belgium, his handling of the retreat from Mons was not accompanied by the greatest success, but his somewhat stolid nature and imperturbability was of the greatest value in the succeeding First Battle of Ypres, when he held the line at a critical time.

Even at this period, Haig was rarely held up as an example of a great general; one contemporary view expressed admiration for his imperturbable nature, the fact that he

was not too clever, but that he was a 'safe' man who would meet reverses with the traditional 'stiff upper lip'! (See *The Great War*, ed. H.W. Wilson & J.A. Hammerton, London 1919, XIII p. 408). When the B.E.F. was divided into two armies in 1915, Haig was put in command of the First. His close contacts with the court did him no harm: he corresponded secretly with King George V in which the failings of Sir John French were not overlooked.

Consequently, when French was relieved of his command after a series of costly operations which achieved little, Haig was appointed to succeed him on 19 December 1915, and in the following year occurred the operation with which he is perhaps most often associated. The Battle of the Somme began with the bloodiest day ever suffered by a British Army (1 July 1916) and continued until November, in which Haig's tactics were perceived by some to be little more than the massacre of his army, for gains obviously not worth the losses sustained. There is some truth in this traditional view, but to picture Haig as nothing more than a cold-hearted slaughterer of his own troops is simplistic: his conduct of offensive operations lacked flair, but the constraints upon him of having to sustain strategies not of his making would have restricted even a more imaginative general; and his somewhat stern demeanour also contributed unfortunately to the image of an aloof commander. Haig was promoted to field-marshal on 1 January 1917.

The losses of the Somme were compounded in the following year, when there were again enormous casualties in the Third Battle of Ypres (better known by the name Passchendaele), arising from the need to take pressure off the French Army, which had been beset by mutiny in the wake of the failure of the 'Nivelle offensive'. Even though the terrible losses incurred produced lamentably little progress, Haig retained his supporters, notably the chief of Imperial General Staff, Sir William 'Wully' Robertson, but such confidence did not extend to the new British Prime Minister, David Lloyd George, who advocated a concentration of effort against Austria-Hungary in the east, whereas Haig was convinced that the war could only be won on the western front. Consequently, Lloyd George had

sought to establish greater control over Haig, by insisting that the 1917 offensive should be under overall French command; and at the Rapallo Conference in November 1917 he secured his plan for a Supreme War Council to conduct Allied strategy. Foch was appointed overall Allied commander on the western front. Robertson, who viewed this development with horror, was dismissed in February 1918 and replaced by the more pliant Sir Henry Wilson.

Despite Lloyd George's reservations, Haig retained his command and fortunately was able to collaborate well with Foch. The great German offensive of spring 1918 brought the Allies close to defeat, which prompted Haig to issue his memorable order of the day on 10 April 1918: 'With our backs to the wall and believing in the justice of our cause, each of us must fight to the end'. Despite heavy losses, the Allied line held, and when the German offensive was exhausted they went on to the attack, in which Haig's organizational ability and grim determination played a conspicuous part, his most successful period of command ending in the final defeat of the German Army on the western front.

Haig's military career after the war was comparatively brief; he retired as commander-in-chief of home forces in 1921, having received the earldom of Haig of Bemersyde, the Order of Merit, and a grant of £100,000. For the remainder of his life he was concerned with the welfare of ex-servicemen. His military reputation is debated still, on which perhaps the fairest view is that expressed by Winston Churchill, that although he might have been unequal to the task he had been given, there was probably no general who at the time would have been a more obvious candidate.

References

De Groot, C. *Douglas Haig 1861-1928*, London 1986.
Herwig, H.H., & Heyman, N.M. *Biographical Dictionary of World War I*, Westport, Connecticut, 1982.
Liddell Hart, Sir Basil *Reputations*, London 1928.
Marshall Cornwall, General Sir James *Haig as Military Commander*, London 1973.
Terrain, J. *Douglas Haig: the Educated Soldier*, London 1963.
Winter, D. *Haig's Command: A Reassessment*, London 1991.

WORLD WAR ONE:
1917

1. French infantry in a trench, a photograph which is interesting despite apparently having been posed for the photographer. The man at right uses a simple trench-periscope, and holds in his right hand a grenade with segmented casing (which split along the hollows to produce shrapnel) and apparently a 'striker' at one end; it is perhaps the *Grenade C. F.*, ignited by striking the projecting bar upon a solid object. The man with the periscope has two small metallic lace rank-bars on his lower sleeve, indicating a company officer (who wore one to three 35mm-long bars according to grade), rank-distinction being reduced to that size to avoid recognition by the enemy. Apparently he also wears the ordinary leather equipment, frequently another attempt to disguise rank from the enemy.

▲2

▲3

2. The French horizon-blue service uniform included a considerable number of variations: tunics appeared with both standing and turned-down collars, and the greatcoat (which could be worn as the principal garment in place of the tunic, unlike the employment of greatcoats in most other armies) was also produced in a number of styles, both double- and single-breasted, the latter originally designed for cavalry (with much longer skirts) but soon produced in infantry-length, with breast-pockets. Coloured collar-patches bearing the unit-numeral were worn on both tunic and greatcoat, generally shaped to fit the edges of the collar, but variations occurred. (The number was normally embroidered in a contrasting colour: for engineers, for example, in scarlet on black). This young French soldier, the original identified only as 'Marcel' and dated 1917, has no collar-patch but a metal numeral instead.

3. Battlefield communications had not really kept pace with the advances in weapon technology, so that some failings of the higher command resulted from an inability to alter plans quickly, according to circumstances, from the simple impossibility of contacting their troops. The field-telephone was the most advanced form of communication, though it was highly unreliable due to its land-lines which were vulnerable to enemy fire. This French telephonist sits in a folding, portable telephone-booth; the crossed-cannon badge on his companion's helmet identifies them as artillerymen. The tunic collar-patch was scarlet, with the unit-numeral at the collar-opening and two chevrons at the opposite end of the patch, these details in medium-blue for field artillery, dark-blue for horse, and green for 'foot'.

4. At the beginning of the war, machine-guns were usually of the heavy variety, fitted on a tripod or wheeled carriage and requiring a crew of at least two. A major development during the war was the emergence of the more portable light machine-gun, capable of operation by a single gunner. Unlike many Allied forces, the French used the most famous of these, the Lewis gun, only in an aviation role; for army service one of the principal weapons was the 1907 Chauchat gun, modified to produce the Modèle 1915. It used the ordinary rifle cartridge and had a characteristic, 20-round, semi-circular drum magazine positioned beneath the barrel.

▼4

INTRODUCTION

After some 28 months of carnage on a scale never previously imagined, 1917 began with neither the Allies nor the Central Powers in a position of dominance; and as before, the successes of one side during the year were largely negated by events affecting the other. The revolution in Russia not only removed that country from the Allied war effort but also overturned one of Europe's oldest monarchies; and coupled with the near-collapse of the Italian military effort, and with horrendously costly but almost resultless Allied attacks on the Western Front which included a widespread mutiny among the French armies (which, providentially for the Allies, the Germans failed to exploit), this could have been decisive for the Central Powers. Their gains in 1917, however, were offset by the increasing exhaustion of their forces, major reverses inflicted upon Turkey in Palestine and Mesopotamia, and, most decisively, by the entry of the United States of America into the war on the side of the Allies. Despite President Woodrow Wilson's attempts to keep the USA uncommitted, unrestricted German submarine warfare and a report of prospective German–Mexican collaboration to attack the USA caused the immense economic resources of the United States to be committed against the Central Powers; although it would be many months before the American military would be deployed in substantial numbers, the boost to the prospects of the Allies was immense.

The year 1917 also saw the spread of the war to other nations. Portuguese troops were committed to the Western Front (with limited effect), the internal turmoil in Greece was resolved finally by the triumph of the Venezelist faction which brought that country into the Allied camp, and many other states followed the lead of the USA. Cuba declared war on Germany on the day after the USA had declared war, and was followed by Panama, Guatemala, Nicaragua, China (22 July), Siam (4 August) and Brazil (26 October, after the German sinking of a Brazilian vessel); Costa Rica, Haiti and Honduras followed in the next year, but none of these contributed substantially to the Allied war effort save in the denying of their ports to German vessels.

Tactically, 1917 witnessed a number of developments, including the use of heavy bombers for attacking civilian or industrial targets, the advent of massed attacks by armoured vehicles, and the so-called 'Huterian' tactic of rapid advances by-passing enemy strongpoints which were neutralized at a later stage. In the field of uniform and equipment, shortages of *matériel* still resulted in wide ranges of non-official items of dress, and there was an increasing use of formation- and unit-signs, factors which make even studio portrait photographs of great interest, as can be seen from some of those illustrated here.

▲5 ▼6

▲7

BOYAU DE TOUL

5. Among the more conventional 'trench artillery' were a number of French patterns which used the somewhat unlikely propellant of compressed air. The leading French designer, Edgar Brandt, in addition to producing the 'Type 90' trench-mortar, designed the 1916-pattern Brandt air-operated projector of 75mm calibre, with a characteristically shaped barrel which narrowed towards the muzzle. The Brandt was not the only compressed-air mortar employed by the French: others included the Boileau-Debladis *Obusier Pneumatique* ('pneumatic howitzer'). Range was determined both by the pressure of the compressed air and the angle at which the barrel was positioned; a maximum practicable range was about 300 yards.

6. Grenade-projectors were used by most of the main combatant nations, ranging from simple cup-dischargers attached to the muzzle of a rifle, to mortar-like weapons such as the German *Granatenwerfer*, which fired a grenade fitted with stabilizer-fins like a mortar-bomb or 'aerial torpedo'. Far less sophisticated is this French contraption for projecting rifle-grenades, which resembles a rifle on an elevating-frame, on a principal used for artillery during the sixteenth century. The cup-shaped discharger (or *tromblon*) on the end resembles that for projecting the 'Grenade VB' or 'Viven-Bessiere'. Note the grenade-shaped cloth badge on the upper sleeve of the attendant; such badges (usually in the 'arm-of-service' colour) were worn as 'trade' badges in the French army: this indicates a grenadier, whereas trench-mortar crews wore a badge in the shape of a mortar-bomb.

7. Shortages of equipment were endemic in all armies, resulting from the expansion of forces at a rate which outstripped *matériel*. The consequences were most marked in British service in the early part of the war, but shortages were felt throughout, affecting even that most prized symbol of regimental identity, the cap-badge: to conserve nickel, all-brass badges were produced from 1916, but some recruits could not even acquire these. This member of the King's Regiment (Liverpool) wears the leather 1914-pattern 'emergency'- issue belt instead of the authorized webbing pattern, and has an ordinary tunic-button in place of a cap-badge.

8. Some recruits of remarkably unmilitary appearance were swept into all armies, such as this studious-looking member of the Durham Light Infantry. This provides an excellent illustration of the 'soft cap', introduced from 1917 to replace the earlier, stiff service cap. The 'soft cap' had a stitched peak and band, clearly shown here, and could be folded up if necessary or even worn beneath the steel helmet. The shoulder-strap bears not only the metal unit-title but also the bugle-horn badge worn by light infantry regiments; fusilier regiments wore a grenade-badge in the same place.

9. As the war progressed, a greater proportion of young soldiers were conscripted into most armies. This portrait of a youthful member of Alexandra, Princess of Wales's Own Yorkshire Regiment (Green Howards) exhibits some interesting features of uniform, including the shapeless appearance of the 1917 'soft cap with no stiffening wires to the crown and stitched peak and band; and note the use of collar badges, not usually worn upon service dress, in this case the cipher and coronet of Queen Alexandra after whom the regiment was named. The regimental cap-badge at this period was nicknamed (from its shape) 'the Eiffel Tower', the name no doubt resulting from service in France.

8▲   9▼

10. Attacks of poison gas could have an equally terrible effect upon animals as upon humans, so 'nosebag'-style respirators were designed to protect army horses. These British cavalrymen wear the later pattern of respirator, the so-called 'box' type, suspended around the neck in a rectangular bag made of webbing material, with a hose leading from the mouthpiece to the chemical canister in the bag. Although the British infantry generally wore the 1908-pattern web equipment except when it was in short supply, the cavalry retained the 1903-pattern leather ammunition-bandolier, with extra rounds carried in bandoliers around the horses' necks.

11. It was usual for gas-alarms to be positioned in every front-line trench. These varied from bells appropriated from civilian sources, hand-cranked sirens, shell-cases suspended on rope or wire to be struck like a gong when gas was detected, to simple wooden rattles. This French position is equipped with a klaxon-style alarm of a

12▲

13▲ 14▼

type carried by motor vehicles; the man demonstrating its use wears the ordinary French tunic, an Adrian-pattern helmet bearing the star-within-crescent of North African troops, and carries the gas mask in a metal canister worn on a strap around the neck, here with the top of the canister open.

12. The German army's gas mask was issued in 1915, and was carried in a metal can slung around the neck; it was considerably more efficient than the early patterns used by the Allied nations. This German wears the ordinary cartridge-containers on the waist-belt (all leather equipment was ordered to be blackened from September 1915, though this only confirmed a practice already in vogue), and carries an old-pattern bayonet, the narrow-bladed 1898 pattern which was still used despite the issue of the wider, short-bladed 1902 and 1905 modifications.

13. In most armies, among the most-respected and often bravest participants were the military nurses who served near the front line; their role was even more remarkable given the traditional place in society which women had occupied before the war. These French nurses, apparently leaving the entrance to a dugout, are equipped with gas masks and Adrian helmets, most unusual additions to their traditional costume; at the right is Mademoiselle Leladier, whose bravery was rewarded by the bestowal of the *Croix de Guerre*.

14. Many strange items of equipment were devised during the war, including this harness supporting a rope-handled cylinder to carry soup or stew from the mobile field-kitchens to the front-line trenches, in the hope that the contents would remain hot until they reached the line. The leather coat with fleece lining worn by this ration-carrier on the Western Front in the early weeks of 1917 would serve a dual role as insulation against the cold and against the heat of the soup-cylinder. Around the neck is worn the 'box' respirator, and the equipment demonstrates the continuing use even at this date of the 1914-pattern emergency leather issue.

▲15 ▼16

15. The Vickers gun remained the British Army's principal machine-gun from shortly after the commencement of the First World War until well after 1945; justly famous for its reliability, it used a standard 0.303in. cartridge, could achieve a maximum range of 4,500 yards and a rate of fire up to 500 rounds per minute. This photograph shows a gun on its usual tripod mounting, with a crew whose shoulder-titles 'MMG' identify them as members of the Motor Machine Gun service. The Machine Gun Corps was formed in October 1915 and its Heavy Branch, formed in November 1916, became the Tank Corps in July 1917.

16. George H. Leishman of the Motor Machine Gun service; the Machine Gun Corps was formed when the requirement of machine-guns and crews outstripped those which could be accommodated by individual battalions, and henceforth were used in a role not unlike that of support artillery. Private Leishman wears the heavy greatcoat sometimes styled a 'British warm', leather gaiters (commonly used instead of puttees by motorized units) and a cap bearing the brass, crowned, crossed Vickers guns of the MGC with white-metal letters 'MMG' below, plus motoring goggles. A caption on the original records that Leishman was invalided from East Africa with fever in 1917.

17. Motor-cycle combinations armed with machine-guns would have been a most valuable reconnaissance or support force had the campaigning on the Western Front not settled by the end of 1914 into a static battle of opposing trench-lines. This section of the British Motor Machine Gun service was photographed in July 1917, and includes an interesting variety of equipment: most of the men wear short overcoats and 1908-pattern web equipment, and while most have the ordinary service cap, a few have removed the wire stiffening to produce the 'Gorblimey' style favoured by experienced campaigners.

18. A Belgian machine-gun section equipped with light cars with pneumatic tyres for the transport of the guns, drawn by dogs; the tradition of canine teams persisted in the Belgian Army. The crews wear the khaki Belgian service uniform, the greatcoats with a double row of five bronzed buttons and shoulder-straps with arm-of-service piping. Brown leather equipment including multiple cartridge-pouches on the waist-belt began to be introduced from 1915, and later British-manufactured web equipment, but these men retain the original Belgian black leather equipment with large cartridge-boxes and rectangular brass belt-plates. Their French Adrian helmets probably have the Belgian lion-mask on the front.

17▲

18▲ 19▼

19. The staff uniform of the German Army is splendidly illustrated in this photograph of General Wilhelm Groener, who headed the munitions, supply and personnel branch of the War Ministry. The most distinctive feature is the staff collar-patch of gold embroidery upon scarlet backing, intended to resemble a loop of lace with tassel end, as worn in the eighteenth century. The field-grey cap had coloured band and piping and bore the universal national red/white/black cockade, plus that of the wearer's own State. The greatcoat has facing-coloured lapels (scarlet) and plaited gold and silver straps, which for general officers bore up to four silver stars (none for *Generalmajor* or major-general, one star for *Generalleutnant* or lieutenant-general, etc.) and crossed silver batons for *Generalfeldmarschall* (field marshal). The decoration at the neck is the *Pour le Mérite*.

20. Although the *Maschinengewehr 08* (machine-gun Model 1908) was a good weapon, its considerable weight and 'sledge' mounting made it less than ideal for trench warfare. The solution was the Model 08/15, introduced from 1915, basically the 1908 pattern with a shoulder-stock added, and a bipod mount instead of the 'sledge', producing a very much more mobile weapon. Its ammunition could be fed in by means of the usual belt, but to increase manoeuvrability further a 125-round drum magazine was devised. A lighter, air-cooled version was produced in 1918 (Model 08/18), but the cooling system was not very efficient and the weapon was prone to jamming. These two machine-gunners wear the tunics common in the German Army at this period of the war: the 1915 modification of the 1910 *Waffenrock* (left), and the 1915 *Bluse* with fly-front (right).

21. There was little opportunity for the employment of cavalry on the Western Front during the later stages of the war, though armies retained a mounted capability in reserve to exploit the breakthrough which was always desired but rarely achieved. These French troopers wear the mounted troops' version of the horizon-blue service uniform, like that of the infantry but with leather gaiters instead of puttees and a longer, single-breasted greatcoat with dark-blue collar-patches with numeral and two lines of braid in white, crimson, green and sky-blue respectively for dragoons, cuirassiers, *chasseurs à cheval* and hussars. Personal equipment was styled like that of the infantry; weapons included the 8mm carbine and the lance, usually of 1913 pattern.

22. The huge cavalry force with which Germany began the war could not be employed in the trench-war which succeeded the 'war of manoeuvre', so much of the cavalry was dismounted as the war progressed. Many units originally attached to infantry formations were retained in a mounted role for escort duty, but by the end of the war the remainder (about 80 per cent of the total) were grouped into dismounted units styled *Kavallerie-Schützen*, each of three battalions, each battalion

▲20　▼21

based upon a mounted regiment and comprising four dismounted (infantry) squadrons (companies) and a machine-gun squadron; each squadron included a *Minenwerfer* unit. These cavalrymen are among those who remained mounted, with the 1916-pattern steel helmet replacing their original head-dress.

23. A British artillery battery 'dug-in'. The 18pdr field-gun might be described as the workhorse of the Royal Artillery, of 3.3in calibre with a range of 7,000 yards. It was capable of an effective rate of fire of eight rounds per minute, which explains the need for huge reserves of ammunition for a concentrated bombardment. The shells here are stacked in rows, laid alternatively nose-cap to base. Presuming that the pile of shells in the foreground includes one row shielded from the camera, this huge pile of ammunition represents less than ten minutes' fire for one gun at the optimum rate, which demonstrates the enormity of the quantity of munitions required.

24. The 'weight' of artillery increased as the war progressed, with guns of immense size being used to bombard enemy positions. The British 12in siege-howitzer, for example, needed a steel box filled with 20 *tons* of ballast to hold it in position after recoil. Only the static nature of trench warfare permitted such leviathans to be used: in more mobile warfare they would have been unable to keep up with the fighting, despite the enormous range of which some were capable (giants like the German 'Paris gun', for example, could throw a shell almost 75 miles). Naval artillery had been used increasingly on land over the previous century (most notably, perhaps, with the British naval brigades in the Boer War) and were again employed: this massive British naval gun on the Western Front is stabilized by a trail of enormous weight and by huge steel wheels.

22▲

23▲   24▼

▲25

▲26 ▼27

25. A major development of the war was the mechanization of army transport, which prior to 1914 had depended almost entirely upon horse-drawn vehicles. France pioneered the mechanization of artillery transport: the first four-wheel drive artillery tractor was constructed in 1910–11 by the automobile company Panhard & Levassor, and bore the title of 'Chatillon-Panhard', the former name from the Chatillon ordnance company for which the designer of the vehicle worked, Lieutenant-Colonel Deport. Although the French Army had experimented with lorry-drawn artillery from 1907, the Chatillon-Panhard was the first satisfactory off-road vehicle and at the outbreak of war the 50 such tractors in artillery service represented almost a quarter of the total mechanized transport of the French Army.

26. The German Army introduced a new range of ordnance in late 1916, from 7.7cm to 15cm calibre, initially styled the 'KiH' (*Kanone in Haubitzlafette*: 'gun on howitzer carriage'), and a modified design known as 'FK 16' (*Feld-Kanone* – field-gun – Model 1916). The gun illustrated (complete with limber which accommodated 24 rounds) was one of twelve overrun and captured at Feuchy, near Arras, on 9 April 1917 by an attack mounted by the 7/8th (Service) Battalion, King's Own Scottish Borderers, at a cost of 5 officers and 100 other ranks. This battalion was formed on 28 May 1916 by the amalgamation of the previous 7th and 8th Battalions, both raised in Berwick-upon-Tweed in September 1914, resulting in the somewhat unusual numbering '7/8th' of the combined battalion.

27. The personalization of artillery pieces with homely names was as old as the science of gunnery, and even led to such names becoming alternative generic terms, such as the 'Long Toms' of the Boer War. *Dicke Berta* (lit. thick or large Bertha), known alliteratively as 'Big Bertha' to the British, was an immense variety of German siege-gun, the 42mm *Mörser*, designed originally to throw shells of sufficient force to penetrate the most modern of fortifications. The gigantic size of shell is illustrated here: note the crane needed to lift it into the breech of the gun.

28. Classed as auxiliary trench artillery was the *Albrecht Mörser* (mortar), a curiously constructed German weapon produced in three calibres, 25, 35, and 45cm. The barrel of this device was made of wood (the staves, as in a cask, ran the length of the barrel and are clearly visible here), bound with wire and reinforced by metal hoops. Manufacture was unsophisticated, even crude, and by the last year of the war the weapon was generally regarded as obsolescent. The elevating-mechanism is shown clearly: to absorb the shock of recoil it was equipped with a heavy base-plate like that of a more conventional trench-mortar.

29. The Hindenburg or Siegfried Line was one of the most heavily fortified systems of the period, with many defended positions of great strength, which caused the Allied attackers to suffer very heavy casualties. This is a typical 'pill-box' (named from its shape), basically a machine-gun position made of concrete around a framework of steel grids which stiffened the concrete to a most formidable degree, impervious to all but a direct hit by artillery or an audacious and hazardous infantry assault.

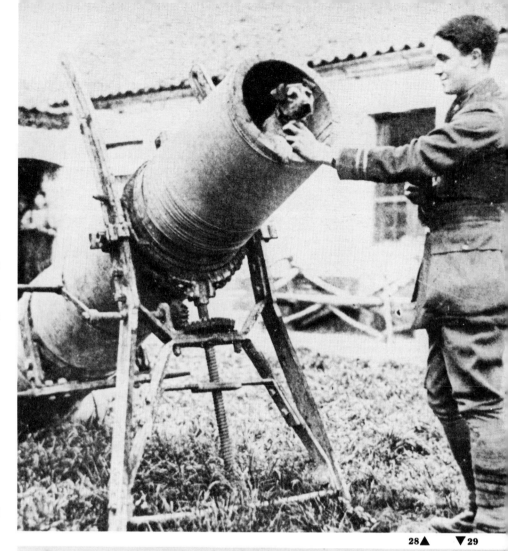

28▲   ▼29

30. A German 'assault detachment'. Groups of hand-picked men were formed for trench-assaults in 1916, when companies of *Sturmtruppen* ('stormtroops') were deployed at regimental level, each comprising an officer and three platoons of 40 men. By 1918 most formations on the Western Front had *Sturmbataillone*, each consisting of four *Sturmkompanie* plus a light trench-mortar platoon, flamethrower section, machine-gun company, headquarters and an artillery detachment with a 3.7cm gun. This unit is grouped around their 1908 machine-guns on the ordinary carriage, plus (left foreground) a 1908/15 gun with bipod mount. Most wear the fly-fronted 1915 *Bluse*, though at least one retains the 1910 *Waffenrock*; many have bags around the neck, fashioned from sandbags, to carry the hand-grenades which were one of the principal weapons of the stormtroops. Shorter carbines were popular, being less unwieldy than the long rifle for use in the confines of the trenches.

31. A trench gas-alarm made from a bell. The sentry, wearing his equipment over the greatcoat and with a fabric cover over the steel helmet, is a South African. The chalked inscription on the bell ('Duck Ye Nut') is a typically British piece of graffiti, exhibiting the humour which led to sign-boards such as 'Trench Mansions' being erected outside the filthiest and most decrepit of dugouts.

32. British troops receiving hot food from a camp-kettle or 'dixie', an oval iron pot in which stew, tea, soup and porridge could be boiled (but not necessarily simultaneously!); the flat lid could be used to fry corned beef or bacon, or make a variety of 'puddings', often the rock-hard army biscuit pounded into crumbs, bound with fat and mixed with dried fruit or jam to produce makeshift 'duff'. Stew was usually produced from 'bully beef' (corned beef) and tins of 'Maconochie' (vegetable stew in thin gravy), which with tinned jam (colloquially styled 'Tickler's' from the name of a manufacturer) and the hard biscuit formed the staple diet. Like so much of the British Army's argot, the term 'dixie' came from India: from *degshai*, a cooking-pot.

33. British staff and infantry officers. This picture is most interesting because of the display of unit-insignia on the helmet of the officer at centre, an example of battalion- and formation-signs which proliferated in the later stages of the war; the position at the rear of the helmet, like similar badges on the back, below the collar, was to aid recognition by troops following. The Maltese Cross insignia is often associated with the Wiltshire Regiment (worn by the 1/4th Battalion in dark green, or red on the helmet), but was also used by the 1/7th Sherwood Foresters (dark green), 1/Rifle Brigade (yellow), 1/12th London (Rangers) (a slightly different shape, in black), and 70 Field Ambulance (orange-yellow), among others.

34. 'Tommies' entering the wrecked town of Péronne in March 1917. They wear the typical winter campaign uniform of the British Army: khaki greatcoats worn over the tunic (or a sleeveless leather jerkin instead of the greatcoat, as worn by the lance-corporal at right), with 'box'-type respirator in light khaki webbing bag slung around the neck and carried on the breast. The man second right carries the platoon's Lewis gun wrapped in canvas or sacking; the man in the background carries (doubtless with great care) the unmistakeable rum-jar.

32▲

33▲   34▼

35. Unlike the remainder of the French Army, the 'African' units of the colonial forces eventually were prescribed a mustard-khaki uniform of a shade not dissimilar from British khaki; this involved not only the indigenous troops but also the Foreign Legion, which was regarded as a 'colonial' corps. The complete issue of khaki was delayed so that it was probably not universal until the end of 1916, until when horizon-blue and khaki were worn together; the first Adrian helmets were issued in horizon-blue and re-painted later. This Moroccan *tirailleur* wears an unusual amount of camouflage and carries the original Lebel bayonet with hooked quillon, which was removed to produce the 1916 Lebel modification.

36. Although armoured warfare was not new in 1917 – British tanks had been deployed in the previous year – the action at Cambrai can probably be regarded as the first massed use of the arm. Developments in armoured warfare occurred rapidly: in addition to successive 'marks' of the original design, both France and Germany manufactured tanks, and a new variety of 'light tank' appeared, such as the British 'Whippet'. This vehicle, viewed from the rear and somewhat the worse for wear, retains the initial basic design but exhibits one of the first modifications, in the removal of the large steering-wheels from the tail.

37. German infantry stalking a British tank on the Western Front. The Germans are identified easily by the shape of their steel helmets; the man second from left is the operator of a 'Wex' *Flammenwerfer*, the most portable of the German flamethrowers, introduced in 1917 and easily distinguishable by its circular configuration with a gas-canister in the centre. Note also the 'unditching beam' fastened to the rear of the tank, intended to facilitate manoeuvring the vehicle clear if it became bogged-down.

38. Mud assumed a great importance in 1917, especially in the British offensive from Ypres, so that for the British 'Passchendaele' became synonymous with seas of shifting, glutinous mud. A typical problem is illustrated here on the Aisne front, with a French two-wheeled wagon bogged to its axle. The men endeavouring to free it carry carbines shorter than the Lebel rifle (as found especially handy for trench-service); note the cartridge-pouch carried at the rear of the waist-belt, and the fabric-covered, 1877-pattern canteen with its characteristic double spout, shown clearly on the central figure. All wear a

▲ 35

▲ 36   ▼ 37

rolled blanket, bandolier-
fashion.

39. The popular concept of
'trenches' is very different from
what actually existed in many
cases: after bombardment and
bad weather, trench-lines might
resemble nothing more than
scrapes in the earth or shell-
holes sometimes connected by
shallow gullies. This French
position is not unusual. The
poilu in the foreground wears a
helmet with a dent which
presumably demonstrates its
efficacy as shrapnel-protection.

40. German officer prisoners of war with British escorts (left). The central figure, wearing his gas mask-canister slung over the shoulder, appears to wear the 1915 *Bluse* with the unplaited shoulder-cords of silver lace bearing the single star of *Oberleutnant*'s rank; *Leutnants* had no stars, *Hauptmann* (captain: *Rittmeister* in the cavalry) two. Field officers had plaited cords with none, one and two stars for *Major*, *Oberstleutnant* and *Oberst* respectively. Note the cuff-title 'Gibraltar', a battle-honour worn by units descended from the Hanoverian regiments which helped defend that place in the great siege of 1779–83, most ironically when serving under British command.

41. The effect of bombardment and soft terrain is shown by this photograph of a captured German position with a French

▲40

▲41 ▼42

soldier attempting to dig out of the mud a piece of German 'trench artillery' which has apparently been half-buried by collapsing earth. The weapon is a *Minenwerfer*, of 24.5 or 17cm calibre, both of which saw extensive use as close-support howitzers, achieving a maximum range of more than 1,500 yards. The name *Minenwerfer* (lit. 'bomb-thrower') led to the common British nickname 'Minnie' for such weapons.

42. The Polish army was formed in France from June 1917, its personnel transferring from French or Russian service, recruited from German or Austrian ex-prisoners of war, or from Polish volunteers from the USA. Being organized by the French, their uniform was of French style, plus the traditional Polish *czapka* cap (peaked for officers, cavalry and artillery) in the same horizon-blue as the remainder of the uniform, piped in the colour of the numeral and piping on the collar-patch: infantry (*chasseurs à pied*) green (plus a horn), artillery light-blue, engineers scarlet and the remainder white; the collar-patches were horizon-blue for infantry, scarlet for artillery, light-crimson for cavalry and black for engineers. These *chasseur* buglers wear the green horn-badge at the point of the collar-patch and apparently have the same insignia on the *czapka*.

43. Aviation services suffered terrible losses in action and from accident. The French hero Georges Guynemer was lost in 1917, being credited with 54 victories. Attending the commemorative parade at the field from which he made his last flight are two more highly decorated 'aces': Capitaine Heurtaux, supported on sticks, and René Fonck, probably the greatest of all fighter pilots, with 75 acknowledged victories (though his own estimate exceeded that number by more than 50). Heurtaux wears the original dark-blue uniform (often, as in British service, combined with items of uniform

from the individual's original regiment), while Fonck has the 1915 horizon-blue uniform: the aiguillette on his left shoulder is the *fouragère* (lanyard) of the *Croix de Guerre*.

44. A French decoration-parade at Noyon, about 70 miles northeast of Paris (overrun in the German offensive of 1918). The central figure, next to the French general in horizon-blue, is H. R. H. Prince Arthur of Connaught, who served as Extra ADC to the C-in-C, British Expeditionary Force (1914–17) and as a staff officer (GSO 2) 1917–18. Prince Arthur's appointment is indicated by his scarlet gorget-patches on the lapels (hence the nickname 'red-tabs' accorded to all staff officers), but otherwise wears the uniform of the regiment in which he was a major, the Royal Scots Greys, whose badge is shown clearly on his cap.

CHRONOLOGY: 1917

The strategy of the Allies for 1917 was decided towards the close of the previous year, at a conference at Chantilly convened by the French Marshal Joseph Joffre before his retirement on 31 December 1916. It was agreed that the main thrust for 1917 would be an Anglo-French push on the Western Front, concerted with Russian and Italian offensives. A secondary (though major) offensive was planned by Britain against the Turks in Palestine. Allied planning was complicated greatly by Joffre's retirement and the appointment in his stead of General Robert Nivelle, whose grandiose schemes clashed with those of the British commander, Douglas Haig. David Lloyd George, the recently appointed British Prime Minister, mistrusted Haig and thus settled the affair by placing the British forces under French command, which appalled Haig and the British Army. In contrast, and because Nivelle's pronouncements had revealed the planning of an offensive in the west, the Central Powers decided to adopt a defensive posture in both east and west, with their offensive manoeuvres limited to what they hoped would be a decisive drive against Italy.

Before serious operations commenced in 1917, a diplomatic development of crucial importance occurred: the entry of the USA into the war on the Allied side. Despite the efforts of President Woodrow Wilson to keep the USA neutral, the German proclamation of unrestricted U-boat warfare and the resulting destruction of US vessels, and the discovery of a plan for German support of a Mexican invasion of south-western United States in the event of US–German hostility, tipped the scales and led to a declaration of war by the USA upon Germany (6 April; war was not declared upon Austria until 7 December). The unpreparedness of the US military establishment, however, meant that although an American Expeditionary Force was planned for service on the Western Front, it was some considerable time before the vast resources of the United States could have a marked effect upon the war.

The Western Front

February–April: In accordance with their decision to defend on the Western Front, the Germans withdrew some twenty miles to a new, heavily fortified defensive position, the Hindenburg or Siegfried Line, which being shorter than the previous 'front' was easier to defend. The withdrawal was completed by 5 April.

9–15 April: As a preliminary to the Anglo-French 'Nivelle offensive', the British made progress in the Battle of Arras, including the capture of Vimy Ridge, but no breakthrough was achieved.

16–20 April: The 'Nivelle offensive' by more than a million French troops was a total failure, costing immense casualties and gaining hardly anything, proving that Nivelle's over-confident predictions were false.

April–May: After the carnage of the Nivelle offensive, wide-spread mutiny swept through the French armies; Nivelle was replaced by Henri Pétain, but for two weeks almost the whole of the French front was in a state of anarchy. Fortunately for the Allies, the unrest was quelled by Pétain before Ludendorff, the German commander on the Western Front, was able to exploit the situation.

7 June: After an intense bombardment, a British attack stormed Messines Ridge as a preliminary for Haig's major offensive on the Ypres salient, partly intended to break through the German lines towards the North Sea coast, and partly to divert German attention from the French, who were still disorganized following the mutinies.

31 July–November: The Battle of Passchendaele (3rd Ypres). An immense British offensive gained about five miles of territory in three months' intense fighting, latterly in an utter quagmire resulting from prolonged heavy rain, wich caused the offensive to founder in a sea of mud. After suffering some 300,000 casualties, the British called off the offensive after the capture of Passchendaele village on 6 November.

20 November–3 December: Haig continued to pressure the German defences, still attempting to deflect German attention from the disorganized French, by an offensive which led to the first widespread deployment of tanks, at Cambrai. Great advances were made at the start of the attack, a genuine 'surprise' due to the lack of preliminary bombardment; but the Germans marshalled their reserves, counter-attacked, and with many of the tanks breaking down or being neutralized by artillery fire, the British made a partial withdrawal from their initial gains. Both sides had lost something under 50,000 casualties, but new tactics had been established: an offensive without a massive bombardment, and the use of armour as the primary striking-force.

The Eastern Front

March–May: The most climactic events of 1917 resulted in the collapse of one of the 'Great Powers' in the Russian Revolution. Triggered in part by the immense losses of the 'Brusilov offensive' of 1916, and based upon long-standing unrest, turbulence in Russia led to the abdication of the Tsar and the estblishment of a Provisional Government (12 March). This determined to continue the war against the Central Powers, but the influence of Bolshevik agitation (sponsored by Germany to destabilize the new government) undermined the authority of the military command, leading to the widespread murder of officers.

July: Despite the chaotic state of the Russian forces, the newly appointed war minister, Alexander Kerensky (head of the Provisional Government from 20 July), mounted an offensive in Galicia, commanded by Brusilov. The 'Kerensky offensive' initially made progress, but a German counter-attack from 19 July not only threw back the Russians but totally routed their now-demoralized forces.

September–October: A German offensive on the northern sector towards Riga had the same effect as that in Galicia: the Russian forces collapsed almost totally as their personnel deserted and fled. A new tactic named after the German General von Hutier was used in this operation, a rapid advance which by-passed strongpoints and left them to be neutralized by the German reserves, allowing for more rapid offensives. Faced with the complete disintegration of the army, the Kerensky administration fled from Petrograd to Moscow, and the Bolsheviks began to assume power.

7 November: The Bolsheviks, under Lenin and Trotsky, seized power and began to negotiate peace with Germany. (According to the Russian calendar, this occurred on 25 October 1917.)

15 December: an armistice was agreed at Brest Litovsk, ending hostilities on the Eastern Front. The total removal of Russia from the war allowed the Central Powers to concentrate henceforth on the Western Front.

The Balkan Front

January–11 June: Operations by the Anglo-French and Serbian

forces were inconclusive, co-operation between the Allied contingents was poor, and Greece was split with internal dissent between the factions wishing to support the Allies and those of King Constantine's party which favoured the Central Powers. Allied attacks at Monastir and Djoran (March) and in the Battle of the Vardar (5–19 May) made little progress.

12 June: Allied pressure finally caused the abdication of Constantine; his successor, King Alexander, re-appointed as Prime Minister the Allied sympathizer Eleutherios Venizelos.

27 June: Greece finally declared war on the Central Powers, thanks to the pro-Allied Venizelist faction. Although the Greek Army joined the Allied forces, no major progress was made before the end of the year, though in December the somewhat ineffective French commander-in-chief, Sarrail, was replaced by the more proficient Guillaumat, who began to institute a reorganization of the Allied forces.

The Italian Front

May–June: Despite fearing a major Austrian offensive with German assistance, after plans were made for French and British reinforcements if this should eventuate, the Italian commander Cadorna again launched an attack against the Austrian positions in the tenth Battle of the Isonzo. It had no more success than the previous nine.

August–September: Finally, the Italians broke through in the eleventh Battle of the Isonzo, making significant territorial gains and bringing the Austrian forces to the brink of collapse; Austria requested German assistance.

24 October–12 November: The arrival of considerable German forces enabled an Austro–German counter-attack in the Battle of Caporetto (twelfth Isonzo); using 'Huterian tactics' of by-passing strongpoints, the German spearhead smashed through the Italian lines, causing the total disintegration of many of the Italian formations. After a precipitate flight by much of the Italian Army, thanks to British and French support by mid-November Cadorna managed to construct a defence-line; but Caporetto was a colossal defeat, costing Italy more than 300,000 men (against 20,000 Austro-German casualties), and had the forces of the Central Powers been able to push on without outmarching their supports, the Italian defeat could have been total despite the sterling efforts of the Anglo-French reinforcement. It also cost Cadorna his command.

The Mesopotamian Front

22–23 February: Maude's Anglo-Indian advance continued its march to Baghdad, driving back the Turks at the Second Battle of Kut.

11 March: Baghdad fell to Maude's army.

27–28 September: As Turkish reinforcements were diverted to Palestine, Maude advanced up the Euphrates, threatening the Mosul oil-fields, and winning the Battle of Ramadi. In the midst of his triumph, Maude died of cholera (18 November). Contrasting with the reverses of the previous year, thanks to Maude's skill British progress in Mesopotamia in 1917 had been extremely successful.

The Palestine Front

January: With Lloyd George's encouragement, the British prepared to launch a major offensive in Palestine. At the Battle of Magruntein (8–9 January) the Turks were finally ejected from the Sinai.

March–April: Advancing on the Turkish positions between Beersheba and Gaza, the British were twice repelled at Gaza (First Battle, 26 March, Second, 17–19 April). The British commander, Sir Archibald Murray, was replaced by Sir Edmund Allenby, a general of very great ability in both tactics and leadership.

October: Having reorganized his forces, including a strong cavalry force, the Desert Mounted Corps, Allenby left a contingent to watch Gaza and attacked the Turks at Beersheba (31 October). Breaking through, he compelled them to retire from Gaza as well as from Beersheba.

November–December: Despite the arrival of the German General von Falkenhayn to revitalize the Turkish command, Allenby drove the Turks back upon Jerusalem, winning a significant victory at Junction Station (13–14 November). He attacked Jerusalem on 8 December; the Turks withdrew on the following day, and after a Turkish counter-attack was beaten off on 26 December, British possession of the city was assured. Allenby's brilliance had laid the foundation for total victory in the succeeding year.

The Turkish Fronts

In addition to Palestine and Mesopotamia, the Allies were in conflict with the Turks in the Caucasus and in Persia, but the turmoil of the Russian Revolution ended the former campaign totally, and planned Anglo-Russian co-operation in Persia was abandoned; both released Turkish resources for the more important Fronts.

As in previous years, 1917 ended with neither side in a position of dominance, though the gradual exhaustion of the main combatant nations was having an effect. For the Allies, the great successes in Palestine and Mesopotamia could not compensate disappointments on the Western Front, with only limited British gains at appalling cost, nor for the critical situation in Italy. Despite the Central Powers' major success in 1917, the elimination of Russia from the war, the entry of the United States offset the advantage gained, although it would be some considerable time before US resources could make much difference to the overall progress of the war. Both sides gathered themselves for a final effort in 1918.

FRENCH ARMY WEAPONS

The principal rifle of the French army was the Lebel pattern, which originated in 1886, designed under the aegis of the 'Commission for Repeating Weapons' established in 1883 to provide the French army with a new rifle. The work of a number of military weapons-specialists, its title 'Lebel' is somewhat curious, as the colonel whose name it bore (commandant of the Weapons School at Châlons-sur-Marne), though a member of the Commission, was less concerned with the design than were other members. The first small-bore military rifle to be adopted by any nation (8mm calibre), with a charge of smokeless powder, it was superbly produced and engineered so that its parts were interchangeable, facilitating mass-production. It was, however, probably too good, and retained far too long, being introduced into service at the very time when the superior Lee magazine was coming to prominence in other armies. The Lebel was an eight-shot repeater (a ninth could be loaded by actually placing it in the breech), but unlike the superior clip-loading weapons, the Lebel's cartridges (carried under the barrel) had to be loaded individually; thus in the time taken to discharge eight shots, it was only a limited improvement over a single-shot rifle and was thus virtually obsolete before it even came into universal use with the French forces, and remained inferior in rate-of-fire if not accuracy when compared with the weapons of the other major European powers. Minor adjustments to the original model were introduced in 1893, resulting in the official designation '1886 M.93'. It had an overall length (without bayonet) of 51.1 inches and a weight of 9lb 3½oz.

The Lebel was not the only rifle to be used by the French forces. Three patterns of shorter carbine existed, all of the Modèle 1890 specification and of similar design, with slightly differing weights: a Cavalry pattern, a Cuirassier pattern and a Gendarmerie pattern, with no bayonet save for the Gendarmerie; all used the Mannlicher-type three-round clip. Two patterns of Musketoon (Modèle 1892, for Artillery and Gendarmerie) were very similar, modified in 1916 to produce a new Artillery Musketoon with an enlarged clip for five rounds (Modèle 1916). Colonial troops (Indo-China units) were issued with the Modèle 1902 rifle, known as the 'Mannlicher-Berthier' system; these were the basis for successors to the Lebel which were used during the war, the Modèle 1907/15, with a clip of three rounds, and the Modèle 1916 with a five-round clip; though these did not supplant the Lebel throughout the army. In order to accommodate the clip, the magazine on the later models was sited beneath the breech, necessitating an increase in the depth of stock. The shorter carbines and musketoons were not restricted to those arms of service for which they had been designed: their reduced length was found to be especially useful in close-quarter trench-fighting.

The bayonet for the Lebel had a long, needle-like blade of cruciform section (sometimes styled an 'épée bayonet'), constructed for the thrust and thus having no cutting-edge; blade-length varied slightly (some broken bayonets were re-tipped and re-issued), but in general the blades were about 20½ inches. The hilt and locking-mechanism varied slightly according to the model of rifle to which it was issued, but usually had a grip of white-metal alloy (sometimes termed 'German silver'), though steel and brass grips were also produced; with a hooked quillon, which was removed to produce the 1916-pattern bayonet. The scabbard was steel, circular in cross-section, and with a steel button at the chape. This was not the only pattern to be used: musketoons and others were equipped with a more conventional 'knife' bayonet, with blade-length either 10 or 16 inches, with wooden or 'composition' grips (the latter a plastic-like material) and steel quillons.

Pistols were carried not only by officers but by other troops such as artillery and gendarmerie. The standard weapon was the Modèle 1892 revolver, of 8mm calibre, though the earlier patterns were also carried: the Modèle 1886 (similar to the 1892, also 8mm calibre), and even the Modèle 1874, of 11mm calibre. Automatic pistols were also used, such as the 7.65mm calibre Ruby, a nine-shot weapon very similar in appearance to the Browning.

Swords had little employment in the war, and were soon discarded; some, like those of the light cavalry, were still based on the 1822-pattern with brass hilt and triple-bar guard, while the 1880 modification of the Modèle 1854 cavalry sabre was common. Officers of all services officially carried swords, but these were rarely used on campaign, and almost never after 1914. Although the cavalry's firearm was by far the most effective of their weapons, three patterns of lance were in service: that of 1823 (with triangular blade and ash shaft), that of 1890 (quadrangular blade, bamboo shaft, largely restricted to a training role) and the most prolific, the 1913 pattern (triangular blade and shaft of browned steel).

As in most armies, the French used a wide variety of hand-grenades, varying from home-made 'jam-tin bombs' to 'racket' grenades (a charge tied or wired to a wooden paddle shaped like a butter-pat or table-tennis bat), spherical grenades ignited by a friction fuze activated when the grenade was thrown, the fuze attached to a leather loop around the thrower's wrist, to more sophisticated patterns of the egg-shaped variety, with either smooth or segmented casing. The Grenade 'CF' Modèle 1916, shaped like a segmented egg-grenade with a lower projection, was ignited by striking the base upon a hard object, which depressed an internal plunger to ignite the fuze; the Modèle 1916 incendiary grenade, shaped like a tin can with a tube projecting from the base, was activated in the same manner. Others had the more usual ignition of a spring-loaded plunger held in position by a lever secured by a pin, such as the Modèle 1915 egg-grenade or the Modèle 1916 'Automatic' incendiary and smoke-grenade. Rifle-grenades were also used: the 'VB' (Viven-Bessière) existed in the usual explosive version, and also a non-explosive variety for transmitting messages, contained within a jar-shaped head. These were fired from a cup (*tromblon*) attached to the muzzle of the rifle, propelled by a cartridge fired from the rifle, the fuze of the grenade being ignited by the bullet passing through the body of the grenade.

A number of patterns of machine-gun were used by the French forces. The Modèle 1900 Hotchkiss gun used a rigid brass ammunition-clip holding 24 or 30 8mm cartridges; the Modèle 1905 (Puteaux) and Modèle 1907 (St-Etienne), named from the arms factories which had designed them, used metal bands holding 25 cartridges. The St-Etienne, being air-cooled, was found to be especially useful in hot climates; and the Hotchkiss was modified to produce the Modèle 1914.

In addition to these conventional machine-guns, all of which used a variety of (generally tripod) mounts, the French used several light machine-guns or automatic rifles, though unlike many Allied forces only used the 1915 Lewis gun in an aviation role. The first of these was the 1907 Chauchat, named after its designer, which was modified to produce the Modèle 1915 CSRG. This weapon, using the standard 8mm rifle cartridge, had a simple mechanism and a 20-round semi-circular drum magazine positioned on the underside of the barrel; it was air-cooled with an aluminium radiator over the barrel, and had a flash-suppressor on the muzzle. Rate-of-fire was 240 rounds per minute. The next pattern was the Modèle 1908 or Berthier-Pacha, which had a magazine holding 20 to 30 rounds, placed under the stock; in some cases its shoulder-stock was replaced by a metal tube with a butt-plate. Rate of fire was about 450 rounds per minute; and like the Chauchat, it had a bipod mounting.

A lighter Hotchkiss machine-gun was developed in 1909, using a rigid band for 24 or 30 cartridges; its rate of fire was 650 rounds per minute, but its use was restricted to fortifications, tanks and aircraft. An automatic rifle of considerably limited use was the Modèle 1910 A-6 gun, utilizing a 7mm cartridge, but though designed in 1910 was not actually issued until late 1917, and manufacture soon ceased. A further automatic rifle was the Modèle 1917 or RSC gun, using the ordinary 8mm cartridge, actually adopted in 1916 but not produced in sufficient quantities for distribution until March

1917. It resembled an ordinary rifle (even to the provision of the Lebel bayonet) but had a magazine holding a clip of five rounds, accommodated in a projection beneath the barrel. An improved (shorter and lighter) version was styled the Modèle 1918.

FRENCH ARMY RANK MARKINGS

Although several variations of rank marking existed (for example, the amount of lace carried on the kepi of officers), the basic system of insignia was as follows:

Private 1st class (equating with lance-corporal): one rank-bar on cuff (for cavalry, one chevron).

Corporal (*caporal*, or *brigadier* in cavalry): two bars/chevrons on cuff.

Sergeant: one or two bars/chevrons of metallic lace on cuff.

Warrant officer: *adjutant*, metallic lace ring with red central stripe above cuff, the lace in the 'opposite' colour to the buttons (i.e., silver lace for units with yellow buttons and vice versa); *adjutant-chef*, as adjutant but lace of the button-colour.

2nd lieutenant: one metallic lace ring around top of cuff.

1st lieutenant: two rings.

Captain: three rings.

Field officer: four or five rings.

General of brigade: two silver stars above cuff.

General of division: three stars (cavalry generals also wore the stars on the helmet).

Marshal: seven silver stars above cuff.

From the adoption of the 'horizon-blue' uniform, rank-badges were reduced in size and the infantry-pattern bar was adopted by all; for officers, rank-bars could be worn on the front of the kepi and even on the steel helmet:

Private 1st class: one red rank-bar on the cuff.

Corporal: two red bars on cuff.

Sergeant: one or two metallic lace bars on cuff.

Warrant officer: one metallic lace bar with interwoven scarlet rectangles on cuff and kepi.

2nd lieutenant: one metallic lace bar on cuff and kepi.

1st lieutenant: two bars.

Captain: three bars.

Field officer: four or five bars.

General (more distinctions with increase in number of grades): two to six gilt metal stars above cuff.

Marshal: seven gilt stars above cuff.

In both systems of rank marking, warrant and commissioned officers wore lace rank-chevrons on their side-cap, the number of chevrons equating with the number of rings or later bars worn upon the sleeve.

FRENCH ARMY BADGES AND INSIGNIA

Badges affixed to the front of the *casque Adrian*: impressed in relief, often on an oval or circular disc, and often somewhat indistinct or crudely finished.

Top row, left to right:

1. France: infantry and cavalry; for gendarmerie, the grenade was often painted white.
2. France: artillery.
3. France: *Chasseurs à pied.*
4. France: North African troops.

Middle row, left to right:

5. France: colonial troops.
6. France: engineers.
7. France: unofficial style of rank-designation: two bars indicate lieutenant's rank.
8. Belgium.

Bottom row, left to right:

9. Russia.
10. Serbia.
11. Polish troops in France.
12. Roumania (cipher of Ferdinand I).

Other varieties included French medical services (rod of Aesculapius within a wreath of laurel (left) and oak (right)); Czechoslovak troops in France

(letters 'SC' from April 1918, replaced by arms of Bohemia, Slovakia, Moravia and Silesia from July 1918); Greece (crowned shield bearing cross); and the US troops equipped with the Adrian helmet used the French infantry badge, but an unofficial

US badge consisted of the national 'stars-and-stripes' shield within a laurel-wreath. French generals wore a number of stars on the front of the helmet to indicate their rank, often with the infantry grenade.

FRENCH ARMY FACING-COLOURS

With the adoption of the 'horizon-blue' uniform, arm-of-service distinguishing-colours were generally restricted to the collar-patch, which had piping and regimental numeral in a contrasting colour:

Cavalry: dark-blue patch, with piping and numeral crimson (cuirassiers), white (dragoons), green (*chasseurs à cheval*) or sky-blue (hussars).

Infantry: yellow patch with dark-blue piping and numeral; changed almost immediately to horizon-blue with dark-blue piping and number.

Chasseurs à pied: iron-grey patch with yellow piping and number.

Artillery: scarlet patch with bright-blue piping and numeral (field), dark-blue (horse), green (foot) or white (alpine).

Engineers: black patch with scarlet piping and numeral.

Train: green patch with scarlet piping, crimson numeral.

Medical service, administration, labour corps: crimson patch, grey-blue numeral.

Gendarmerie: black patch bearing white grenade.

French collar patches. *Top left:* the shape of the patch worn in 1914, colouring varying with arm-of-service. For infantry, for example, blue numerals on red; the 45th Regiment in 1914 served in the 8th Brigade, 4th Infantry Division, in II Corps of Lanrezac's Fifth Army. *Top right:* greatcoat and tunic collar-patch of the 'horizon-blue' uniform; for infantry, ultimately dark-blue numeral and braid on horizon-blue. *Bottom:* more usual shape of greatcoat collar-patch, coloured as before.

French officers' rank-marking is shown by this photograph of Ernest-Jacques Barbot (killed 10 May 1915) as colonel of the 159th Line Regiment (headquarters Briançon), which in 1914 formed part of the 88th Brigade of the 44th Infantry Divison. He wears the officers'-pattern black tunic with regimental numeral on the collar. Rank-distinction was carried on the kepi, which had a lace knot on the crown continuing as vertical lines of lace at the top of the sides of the cap: for subalterns these lines and knot were of a single strip of lace, for captains two and field officers three. One or two horizontal rings of lace encircled the sides of the cap for subalterns, three for captains, four for majors and (as here) five for colonels; lieutenant-colonels had five rings of which the innermost and outer rings were in the regimental lace-colour and the alternate rings in the contrasting 'metal', i.e., for a unit with gold lace (yellow buttons) the inner and outer rings were gold and the alternate ones silver.

FRENCH ARMY ORGANIZATION

Infantry Division

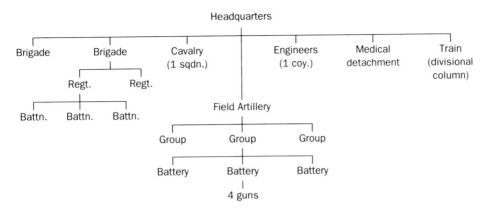

Headquarters

- Brigade
- Brigade
  - Regt.
    - Battn.
    - Battn.
    - Battn.
  - Regt.
- Cavalry (1 sqdn.)
- Field Artillery
  - Group
  - Group
    - Battery
    - Battery
      - 4 guns
    - Battery
- Engineers (1 coy.)
- Medical detachment
- Train (divisional column)

Cavalry Division

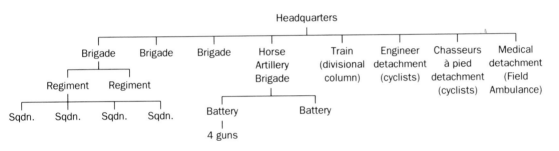

Headquarters

- Brigade
  - Regiment
    - Sqdn.
    - Sqdn.
  - Regiment
    - Sqdn.
    - Sqdn.
- Brigade
- Brigade
- Horse Artillery Brigade
  - Battery
    - 4 guns
  - Battery
- Train (divisional column)
- Engineer detachment (cyclists)
- Chasseurs à pied detachment (cyclists)
- Medical detachment (Field Ambulance)

Corps Organization

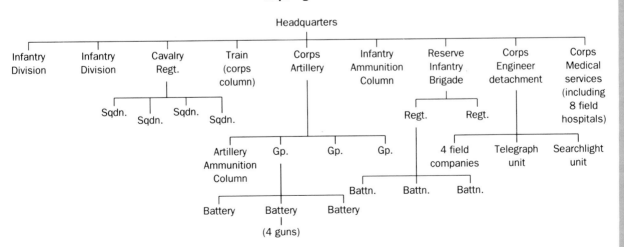

Headquarters

- Infantry Division
- Infantry Division
- Cavalry Regt.
  - Sqdn.
  - Sqdn.
  - Sqdn.
  - Sqdn.
- Train (corps column)
- Corps Artillery
  - Artillery Ammunition Column
  - Gp.
    - Battery
    - Battery
      - (4 guns)
    - Battery
  - Gp.
  - Gp.
- Infantry Ammunition Column
- Reserve Infantry Brigade
  - Regt.
  - Regt.
    - Battn.
    - Battn.
    - Battn.
- Corps Engineer detachment
  - 4 field companies
  - Telegraph unit
  - Searchlight unit
- Corps Medical services (including 8 field hospitals)

Note: the artillery and services (engineers, medical corps, etc.) noted above are those attached at Corps level: those attached at Divisional level were separate.

SOURCES AND BIBLIOGRAPHY

As noted in the previous titles of this series, much interesting material can be found in the illustrated periodicals of the time, for example the *Illustrated War News*, *War Illustrated* and *The Great War* among those published in Britain; but a comparison with earlier issues reveals a change in the selection of illustrations: those published in Allied countries now rarely depict 'enemy' subjects as they had earlier in the war, even though suitable illustrations were available, presumably, from neutral sources. Increasing censorship is evident in the later issues, with units frequently not identified and including what appears to be the occasional deliberate obliteration of cap-badges on pictures released for publication. As in previous titles, certain of the many 'campaign' histories applicable to the year in question are included below:

Barker, A. J. *The Neglected War: Mesopotamia 1914–18*, London 1967.

Bullock, D. L. *Allenby's War*, London 1988 (Palestine campaign).

Chappell, M. *British Battle Insignia 1914–18*, London 1986.

— *The Battle Soldier in the 20th Century*, Hatherleigh, series from 1987.

Fosten, D. S. V., and Marrion, R. J. *The British Army 1914–18*, London 1978.

— *The German Army 1914–18*, London 1978.

Gladden, N. *Ypres 1917*, London 1967 (personal account).

Hicks, J. E. *French Military Weapons*, New Milford, Connecticut, 1964.

Jones, I. *The Australian Light Horse*, Sydney 1987 (Palestine campaign).

Laffin, J. *Western Front 1916–17: the Price of Honour*, Sydney 1987.

Lawrence, T. E. *The Seven Pillars of Wisdom*, London 1935 (orig. 1926) (the Arab revolt).

Macdonald, L. *They Called It Passchendaele*, London 1978 (among the best studies of the period).

Macksey, K. *The Shadow of Vimy Ridge*, London 1965.

Mollo, A. *Army Uniforms of World War I*, Poole 1977 (the most outstanding work on the subject).

Nash, D. B. *German Infantry 1914–18*, Edgeware 1971.

— *Imperial German Army Handbook 1914–18*, London 1980.

Walter, A. (ed.). *Guns of the First World War*, London 1988 (reprint of the *Text Book of Small Arms*, 1909).

Williams, J. *Mutiny 1917*, London 1962 (the French Army mutinies of 1917).

Wilson, H. W. (ed.) *The Great War*, London 1917 (contemporary periodical, containing much significant photography and artwork).

Most useful for the campaigns of the whole war are the atlases:

Banks, A. *A Military Atlas of the First World War*, London 1975.

Gilbert, M. *First World War Atlas*, London 1970.

▼45

▼46

45. Even 'ordinary' photographs such as this group of three British soldiers can provide interesting information regarding the uniforms of the period. This group reputedly dates from 1917 (certainly no earlier than the previous year, as the sergeant-major (left) wears the ribbon of the Military Medal, instituted in March 1916 as a decoration for 'other ranks' one grade less than the Distinguished Conduct Medal); yet the seated man wears the shoulder-title of the Army Service Corps in woven cloth instead of the usual brass, the cloth title generally ceasing to be worn in 1907. The bar on the lower sleeve of the sergeant (right) indicates that he had been wounded.

46. Portugal remained committed to the Allied war effort even after the *coup d'état* of 9–12 December 1917 (the new president, Sidonio Paes, was assassinated on 15 December 1918). Here the Portuguese war minister, General Norton de Mattos (centre) is seen in London; much was made of Portugal's participation in the war and of their being Britain's traditional oldest ally, a connection reinforced by the close co-operation between British and Portuguese armies in the Peninsular War a century before: even the general's name reveals a British ancestor. His uniform is the national grey-blue similar to the French horizon-blue; officers could also wear a tunic with British style lapels, grey shirt and black tie, and another version had large side-pockets as worn by the officer at right. Generals' rank-badges were stars above the cuff; lower ranks had lace bars as at right.

47. Portuguese infantry in France in June 1917. The Portuguese service uniform comprised a single-breasted tunic with fly-front, trousers and puttees in light-grey-blue; a peaked cap of similar material was the usual wear, replaced here by the unique, fluted steel helmet of the Portuguese Army.

The two men at the end of the front rank are NCOs, identified by their blue shoulder-strap slides with silver lace bars (one to four according to rank). The light khaki web equipment is the Portuguese 1911 style, based on the British 1908 pattern, plus British respirators. The regulation arm was the 1904-pattern Mauser-Virguiero of .256in calibre (a carbine was also produced), but these men appear to carry British Lee-Enfields, adopted to facilitate ammunition-supply.

48. General Tamagnini, commander of the Portuguese Expeditionary Force. Officers wore a light-grey-blue tunic similar to that of the other ranks (here with four pockets: other ranks had only breast-pockets), with the usual light-grey-blue peaked cap, brown riding boots or (as here) ankle-boots and gaiters, and 'Sam Browne' belt. The rank-insignia of general was a silver star on the cap and three stars above the cuff. The somewhat unmilitary appearance of General Tamagnini and his ilk perhaps explains the somewhat derisory British nickname for the Portuguese troops, 'the Pork-and-Beans'!

49. The Canadian forces sent to Europe were not based initially upon existing units but comprised 'CEF' (Canadian Expeditionary Force) battalions, to which volunteers from civilian life and from the existing units were allocated; later whole battalions were organized by the pre-war regiments. Many of these CEF battalions were Scottish in composition and uniform, as shown in this photograph of Private Norman Rand of the 43rd Battalion, CEF (Cameron Highlanders), raised in Winnipeg. He wears the 'general service' brass maple leaf badge on the collar, but regimental insignia is carried on the sporran and on the blue glengarry: a rampant lion within a crowned strap bearing the battalion name and number, backed by a saltire and wreath of thistles and maple.

47▲

48▼

49▼

▲50

▲51

50. The insignia of the Canadian Expeditionary Force is illustrated in this photograph of William Irving of the 37th Battalion CEF (Toronto). The cap- and collar-badges are the Canadian 'general service' pattern (a brass maple leaf bearing a crown over a scroll inscribed 'Canada'), with brass battalion-insignia on the shoulder-straps, '37' over 'INF' (infantry). Note the Canadian-issue buttons (bearing a maple leaf within a crowned Garter, with 'Canada' above), and the standing collar rather than the more usual fold-down style.

51. Although it was more usual for New Zealand troops to wear the khaki slouch-hat with the crown punched up into a point (as ordered after Gallipoli), it could also be worn (as here) Australian-style, with the brim not folded up. Private Harry

Crozier wears the ordinary service uniform with the brass crowned fern-leaf badge enclosing the letters 'NZ', which served as the official insignia of the New Zealand Expeditionary Force, though his hat appears to bear a regimental badge. The waist-belt is from the 1908 web equipment.

52. Private William B. Perrin of the New Zealand Machine-Gun Corps, wearing the slouch hat in its familiar 'lemon-squeezer' style with crown punched up, and the unit badge: crowned, crossed Vickers guns with 'NZ' below, worn on the hat and collar; the brass shoulder-titles are 'NZMGC'. In British style the unit's companies wore identification-patches below the rear of the collar, of a star on a black square, the stars yellow, pink, green and red for 1st-4th companies respectively, a blue

star for headquarters, and a black star on red for the 5th company. The original of this photograph describes the subject as 'A Rum 'Un', a term which might be applied to other members of the splendid ANZAC forces!

53. Although Canada provided more Scottish units than any other nation save Scotland, overseas Scottish corps were not restricted to Canada. This picture shows Private James Edge of the South African Scottish (4th South African Infantry), raised in 1915 as the Scottish battalion of the South African Infantry Brigade for service on the Western Front. Shown here is the khaki kilt-apron (the button fastening its frontal pocket is visible), concealing the Murray of Athol tartan kilt (the 'government' or Black Watch set with a red

overstripe); the bonnet does not bear the regimental badge (a rampant lion upon a shield backed by a saltire and thistles with 'Mors Lucrum Mihi' on a scroll below) but the South African 'general service' badge, a springbok head within a wreath inscribed with the bilingual motto 'Union is Strength' and 'Eendracht Maakt Macht'.

54. The military medical services were supplemented by volunteer organizations, which in British and Empire service were usually referred to by the initials 'VAD' irrespective of their official appellation ('Voluntary Aid Detachment'). This Canadian ambulance-driver wears the cap-badge of the Canadian Red Cross Society, and has the insignia of a winged wheel with the initials 'VAD' on her lower sleeve.

54 ▼   52 ▲   55 ▼   53 ▲

55. Perhaps the most far-reaching result of the war was the collapse of imperial power in Russia, and the subsequent establishment of a Communist state; the Tsar abdicated and a Provisional Government was created in March 1917. Illustrated here is Grand Duke Michael, to whom the Tsar initially relinquished the throne; he wears the ordinary khaki tunic and breeches (cavalry officers were officially directed to wear green breeches, but in effect the khaki was almost universal), with the soft cloth shoulder-straps which replaced the more conspicuous, metallic-laced, rigid shoulder-boards during the war. Clearly shown here is the officers' version of the cap-cockade, domed and with a vandycked edge, in white, black and orange.

▲ 56   ▼ 57

56. Russian forces served on other fronts than the east: units were sent to Salonika and to the Western Front, and naval personnel had even supported the Dardanelles landing (the cruiser *Askold*, immortalized from its five funnels by its British nickname 'the packet of Woodbines'!) The abdication of the Tsar and the formation of the first democratic government marked the beginning of the end of Russian participation in the war: here, a priest administers the oath of allegiance to the new government to General Lokhvitsky and his staff of the Russian forces in France.

57. Alexander Kerensky (1881-1970) was originally war minister, and later head of the Provisional Government after the abdication of the Tsar. He attempted to maintain Russia's committment to the Allies, but the 'Kerensky Offensive' was not a success and his administration was overthrown by the Bolsheviks. In this photograph he wears a style of officers' tunic patterned on British lines, which came into use during the war, with pleated breast-pockets, large side-pockets and six metal or leather-covered buttons on the breast, something after the fashion of an English 'Norfolk jacket'.

58. Although internal unrest manifested itself in several of the combatant nations, it was nowhere so severe as in Russia, where fighting occurred between the rival factions. This is a scene in Petrograd: a street-barricade is fortified by artillery and over the wall of packing-cases there flies a red flag. Such scenes were only a precursor of years of civil war which followed the seizure of power by the Bolsheviks.

59. The war had an immense effect upon the role of women in European society, as the occupations normally filled by men passed to women when the men were called to the Colours; but although several armies included units of female personnel, they were employed mostly in medical or administrative duties. Not so in Russia, where a 'Battalion of Death' of ostensible combatants was formed. This illustrates the battalion commandant, Madame Botchkareva (seated, second from right) with her staff; the uniform is like that of the ordinary Russian troops, presenting an exceptionally unfeminine appearance.

▲60 ▼61

60. In many instances, units of the Russian Army disintegrated totally in mid-1917, dissolving into fugitive mobs. Some remained loyal and attempted to cover the retreat of the fugitives, in which they were aided by the armoured cars of the British Royal Naval Air Service, led by Commander Oliver Locker Lampson. In this illustration members of the RNAS, recognizable by their khaki British uniform, aid loyal Russian troops attempting to stop the surge of deserters, one of whom (second right) is being threatened by the rifle of an RNAS officer (centre). The large barrel protruding over the loyal Russian's shoulder belongs to a Lewis gun carried by another RNAS man.

61. Italian infantry of the 'Lombardia' Brigade with their Colours; this brigade comprised the 73rd and 74th Infantry Regiments, with the distinctive white collar-patch with central light-blue stripe and white-metal five-pointed star at the front. These men wear the grey-green service uniform, including a wide variety of overcoats and Adrian-style helmet. New rank-badges were introduced from 1916, officers' insignia in the form of small, metal, five-pointed stars on the cuff, one, two or three for sub-lieutenants, lieutenants and captains respectively; and one to three stars on a patch bordered with metallic lace for majors, lieutenant-colonels and colonels. The colour-bearer has the single star of a sub-lieutenant; on his left is a lieutenant (two stars) and on his right a colonel (three stars within a lace border).

62. The Italian *Alpini* (mountain troops) were regarded as an élite formation and distinguished by grey-green felt Tyrolean-style hats bearing on the front an embroidered grey badge of an eagle atop a hunting-horn backed by crossed rifles, with a metal regimental numeral in the 'curl' of the horn. At the left side of the hat was a pompom coloured red, white, green, blue or yellow for the 1st-5th battalions of a regiment respectively, with a black crow-feather (eagle-feather for officers). Their green collar-patches or *'mostrines'* were flame-shaped and bore a white-metal star. This illustrates Italian NCO rank-insignia: a large (16mm wide) black chevron above the cuff with two 5mm chevrons above, indicating *caporale maggiore* (senior corporal); privates 1st class had just the large chevron, corporals one large and one narrow, and sergeants and *sergente maggiore* the same as corporals but in metallic lace.

63. An Italian sentry amid the Alpine snows. The Adrian steel helmet was first worn by the Italian Army in October 1915, imported from France, bearing French insignia and painted horizon-blue. From early 1916 they were supplied without badges and uncoloured, the Italians painting them grey-green. Later in the same year an Italian-manufactured helmet was produced, superior to the French original in having the skull and peaks made from a single piece of steel, with the comb soldered on instead of riveted, producing a much more robust item. Regimental insignia was sometimes painted on the front, and rank-markings on the left side, in black. This sentry, complete with leather and fur coat as a shield against the Alpine climate, wears his helmet back-to-front!

64. King Ludwig III of Bavaria meeting Austrian officers. From 1915 the Austrian Army began to replace its pike-grey uniform with one of field-grey, basically the same in cut but for a turn-down collar; German-style steel helmets (slightly modified in their Austrian manufacture) came into use at the same time, though were initially the preserve of storm-troops, the soft kepi remaining the standard head-dress. King Ludwig wears the *Pickelhaube* with a field-grey service cover; although it was withdrawn from the army's service uniform upon the issue of the steel helmet, it remained the semi-ceremonial head-dress and was still worn by staff officers.

62 ▲　　　　　　63 ▲　　64 ▼

▲ **65**

65. A British dispatch-rider or 'Don R' in Italy. Despite Italy's being a European theatre of operations, the uniform of the British forces could take on a definite 'colonial' style: felt slouch hats and even topees were worn, with shorts, as here. The abbreviation 'Don R' was one of many resulting from the phonetic alphabet designed to improve the transmission of messages over telephone-lines: hence 'Ack Emma' (a.m.), 'Pip Emma' (p.m.), 'Ack-Ack' (anti-aircraft), 'O Pip' (observation post), etc.

66. Probably the most unusual member of the Serbian army was Flora Sandes, a middle-aged English gentlewoman who went to Serbia as a volunteer nurse but who progressed to a combat capacity, rising to the rank of sergeant-major, being wounded and receiving the Star of Karageorge (worn here on its red ribbon). In this photograph she wears Serbian uniform with the three four-pointed yellow metal stars of sergeant's rank on the shoulder-strap. Flora was promoted to lieutenant in 1918 and continued to live in Serbia after marrying a Russian officer, only returning to Britain after the Second World War.

67. The re-formed Serbian Army in Salonika was re-equipped by the Allies, their uniforms a mixture of British khaki and French horizon-blue. Like so many other nations, they adopted the *casque Adrian* like that worn by the French Army, but with the Serbian coat of arms (a crowned double-eagle with a shield bearing a cross upon its breast) applied in stamped metal on the front. This man at Salonika is equipped with the sky-rockets used for signalling.

68. A British trench-mortar on the Salonika front. The 'Tock Emma' (T/M) was a major development of the war, the best-known configuration being probably the Stokes pattern.

▼ **66**

▼ **67**

Although some types (such as the German *Minenwerfer*) had firing-mechanisms at the base of the tube, a common variety was 'drop-fired', i.e., the projectile was dropped down the tube and launched by a propellant charge ignited by a percussion cap in the base. The most familiar mortar-projectile was the 'bomb' resembling a finned shell (the fins to stabilize flight) but this variety, considerably prone to 'dudding' or failing to explode, was for obvious reasons known as a 'football' or 'toffee-apple' (from the rod which fitted down the barrel). The heavy base-plate absorbed the recoil. Note the variety of 'trench cap' worn by these men, with ear-flaps fastened over the top.

69. The Allied landings at Salonika had been frustrated by the unexpected declaration of Greek neutrality, and some internal conflict occurred between the Greek factions. On 12 June 1917 King Constantine was forced to abdicate and the appointment by his successor Alexander of the pro-Allied premier Eleutherios Venizelos resulted in Greece joining the Allies on 27 June. Before this, however, 'Venizelist' forces had been supporting the Allies. The Greek Army wore a khaki-green tunic, trousers and puttees (or gaiters) and brown leather equipment, and either a khaki peaked cap (replacing a kepi) or a khaki or light-blue side-cap. The standard arm was the 1903-pattern Mannlicher-Schoenauer rifle of 6.5mm calibre, and a similar carbine, modified slightly in 1914 to produce the Model 1903/14. The Venizelist forces (as here) were equipped largely by France and thus wore French-style accoutrements including the Adrian helmet with Greek arms on the front. The man at left foreground appears to carry anti-gas goggles around his left upper arm.

70. The Central Powers in the Balkans: from left to right, Bulgarian, Austrian and German, at the station of Uskub, Macedonia. The Bulgarian wears a uniform of Russian influence; although a greyish-green service uniform had begun to be issued in 1908, earlier, brown uniforms and supplies provided by Germany were also utilized. The Austrian wears the national pike-grey uniform and kepi with the standard infantry waist-belt with two brown leather cartridge-pouches at each side of the buckle. The German wears the 1915 alteration of the 1910 *Waffenrock*, still with buttons visible on the breast but with turned-up cuffs, and with the tropical hat more usually associated with German

units in the African colonies. Khaki drill uniforms were also used by the Germans in Macedonia, Palestine and Bulgaria, not dissimilar from the ordinary uniform except for patch breast- and side-pockets, with either khaki caps with brown peaks, or brown cloth-covered topees.

71. Armoured cars might have exerted a greater influence than they did had not much of the campaigning degenerated into static trench-warfare. The value of such vehicles was proven in more mobile roles, in the Middle East and with the Russians. While the British Rolls-Royce cars were probably the best-known, many other varieties existed, notably (in British service) Lanchesters. This unit was photographed in North Africa, in operations against the Senussi rebels, who waged a sporadic war against the Allies over a considerable area around their Cyrenaica stronghold. With Turkish encouragement, the Senussi effort occupied the attention of perhaps in excess of 100,000 Allied troops (Italians, British and French in order of numbers) until at least mid-1917. Armoured cars performed most successful mobile operations against this enemy.

72. An anti-aircraft position in the Sinai. Although the slouch hat was not restricted to the Australian and New Zealand forces but was worn also by some British units, the tunics with pouch-pockets and waist-belts are typically Australian, the first pattern of drab serge, flannel or cord fading from its light khaki-drab dye to its original blue-grey colour. Legwear includes leather gaiters (left), puttees and shorts, the latter sometimes made by simply hacking off the lower leg of the trousers. The gun mounted on a post is the ubiquitous Lewis: the spotter (left) carries binoculars and the man wearing the service cap (with ear-flaps or neck-shade tied up over the top) carries a flare-pistol.

▲70

▲71 ▼72

73. Despite the increase of mechanization of army transport, horse-drawn vehicles remained vital assets, and in some theatres of war were more reliable than motor vehicles. This field ambulance, drawn up for inspection, formed part of the Allied forces in Palestine; the men wear slouch hats made famous by the ANZACs, but they were also worn by British units. Note the large red-cross flag affixed to the ambulance; and although the drivers do not appear to wear them, white brassards bearing a red cross are clearly visible on the left upper arms of the personnel drawn up on foot.

74. The 'Desert Mounted Corps' became famous for its actions in Palestine, but did not normally resort to mounts of this nature. This Worcestershire Yeoman, photographed probably in early 1917, poses for a typical 'tourist' image with pyramid and sphinx in the background. Note the lack of rank-badges on the sleeves: unlike the uniforms worn on the Western Front, officers' insignia on tropical dress was almost invariably carried on the shoulder-straps. The 1/1st Worcestershire Yeomanry landed in Egypt in April 1915, served at Suvla, and then with the 5th Mounted Brigade in the Imperial (later Australian) Mounted Division in Palestine until May 1918, when they became Corps cavalry of XX Corps.

▲75

75. A column of Turkish troops on the march, headed by a band of very mixed appearance. Although the Turkish forces wore a mixture of head-dress, including the Arab *burnous*, the fez or fur tarboosh (*kalpac*) was usually replaced on active service by the so-called 'Enver Pasha helmet' or *kabalak*, initially a loose turban but later stitched into shape to produce a cloth sun-helmet, further amended by arranging the folded cloth around a light, plaited straw framework, to produce a light but very effective sun-helmet.

76. A Turkish machine-gun company near Beersheba. Although the Turkish Army was armed and equipped in a predominantly German fashion, the cloth sun-helmet shown here was uniquely Turkish, owing little to European styles (though Enver Pasha, whose name it bore, reputedly based the idea upon the Italian topee); its great similarity to

the turban is shown clearly here. Note the boxes of ammunition (in belts) at the right of the central gun-team; the central man in the right-hand group is the observer, sighting and ranging upon the enemy.

77. Captain Oskar Teichman, the highly decorated medical officer of the Worcestershire Yeomanry (DSO, MC, *Croix de Guerre, Croce di Guerra*). This shows the typical service uniform worn in Palestine and Mesopotamia: resembling the ordinary uniform but in lighter-weight material and with rank-badges mounted on the shoulder-straps. The sun-helmet in this case has a quilted surface. Medical officers, though attached to regiments on an almost permanent basis, remained members of the Royal Army Medical Corps and wore the appropriate insignia, visible here as lapel-badges (a crowned

wreath with the rod of Aesculapius in the centre, bronzed for service uniform).

78. Many members of the Allied forces in Palestine found it a most moving experience to be campaigning in the Holy Land, around the places about which they had learned from infancy. This view of the Australian Light Horse on the road from Bethlehem to Jerusalem, but for the uniforms of the slouch-hatted ANZACs, might almost have occurred at any time over the previous two thousand years.

76 ▲   77 ▲   78 ▼

▲79

79. A Mesopotamian scene: Turkish prisoners of war are bound and blindfolded before being escorted to the compounds established behind every front-line for the temporary accommodation of prisoners. Blindfolding was not generally used in the war, except in the cases of envoys who crossed to enemy lines under flags-of-truce, and who

▼80

would return to their own lines after their negotiations had been completed.

80. The uniform worn by the British forces in the Middle East (Palestine and Mesopotamia) was very similar to that used in India. This group wear a typical hot-weather campaign dress: shorts, puttees, shirt-sleeves instead of

the tunic, and topee, here with various additions in the form of additional sun-protection for the neck. Note the NCO chevrons worn on the shirts: rank badges were often attached very loosely to tropical uniforms to permit easy removal for the frequent washing of these garments.

81. Camel-transport had long been used by the British Army

in the Middle East and India. This scene from 'Mespot' (Mesopotamia) shows an Indian Army camel and 'driver' (the original photograph is annotated 'dispatch rider'!), with a British soldier in typical 'Mespot' tropical uniform: shirt-sleeves, shorts, puttees and topee, the latter with a quilted sun-shade added. This uniform was also worn in Palestine, frequently with the ordinary tunic instead of 'shirt-sleeve order'.

82. Methods of aircraft-detection were not sophisticated: whereas visual observers were sometimes provided with reclining chairs, this Indian soldier in Mesopotamia has no such luxuries, having what appears to be an extremely uncomfortable resting-place from which to use the large telescope which comprises his only equipment.

83. One of the most outstanding commanders of the war was Paul Emil von Lettow-Vorbeck (1870–1964), a veteran of the Boxer Rebellion and campaigns against the Hottentots. In 1914 he commanded in German East

Africa (Tanganyika) and though immensely outnumbered waged an aggressive guerrilla campaign with the greatest skill. In 1917 he was driven into Portuguese East Africa, but refused to submit and continued to fight (having marched into Northern Rhodesia) until after the armistice, only halting operations when the British convinced him that the war had ended. Here he wears the uniform of the German troops in the African colonies, field-grey (originally 'sand-grey' or khaki-yellow) with a grey felt hat, trimmed with the colony's facing-colour (cornflower-blue, poppy-red and white respectively for South-West Africa, Cameroons/Togoland and East Africa).

81▲   82▼   83▼

▲84

84. The campaigning in East Africa produced images which might have originated in the Boer War or on the North-West Frontier of India. This section of British infantry defending a blockhouse wear Indian-style uniform of light khaki tunic and shorts, puttees and topee, with 1908-pattern web equipment and, at least in the case of the man in the foreground, the 1907-pattern bayonet with hooked quillon which was generally removed in 1913. The bugler at the rear is an interesting relic of the old practice of conveying orders by bugle-call.

85. Operations in East Africa occupied large numbers of Allied forces and in many ways resembled an old-style 'colonial' campaign. Mechanization was introduced even here, however, for example this traction-engine hauling the British gun-boat *Mimi* across a bridge constructed for the purpose. Although the two British boats thus transported were established on Lake Tanganyika at the turn of 1915/16, hostilities continued until after the Armistice in Europe.

86. Although it took some considerable time for the physical presence of the United States' entry into the war to take effect, from the outset the boost to Allied morale was enormous. The first US troops arrived in France in late July 1917; by May 1918 there were more than half a million in France, and by late July more than double that number. This sentry wears the national field uniform of khaki tunic and breeches, puttees or leather or canvas leggings, and khaki felt hat with a cord around the crown in the arm-of-service colour (infantry light blue, cavalry yellow, artillery scarlet, etc.). The 1910-pattern web equipment was also khaki; the standard rifle was the Pattern 1903 Springfield of .30in calibre, but shortages of weapons led to the issue of adapted British P.14 rifles, styled by the Americans as the Model 1917 Enfield, also of .30in calibre.

87. Among the first drafts of United States troops to arrive in Europe was this engineer unit, seen here in London where they were received with rapture, a civic welcome and a parade past Buckingham Palace. They wear the US khaki service uniform, the Colour-bearers with leather gaiters and the others with canvas gaiters. The New Zealand-style felt campaign hat was not especially popular, and was replaced by the 'overseas cap', a peak-less side-cap; officers wore khaki peaked caps with light khaki band and brown peak and chinstrap, with bronze eagle badge. Steel helmets were not originally part of their equipment; these were issued in Europe, either the British pattern or the French Adrian helmet. Hat-cords for engineers (as here) were mixed scarlet and white, but officers of all branches wore cords of gold or gold and black.

85▲   86▲ 87▼

▲ 88

▲ 89 ▼ 90

respectively, and a silver eagle for colonel; 2nd lieutenants had no badges. The insignia was also worn on the 'overseas cap', and greatcoats bore black Austrian knots on the cuffs (brown for 2nd lieutenants), increasing in number with rank.

89. The year 1917 saw another terrible development to warfare: aircraft-bombardment of civilian and industrial targets, a far more significant innovation than the earlier Zeppelin raids. German 'Gotha' heavy bombers raided Britain and caused much consternation, presaging the events of 1939–45. This piece of burned-out fuselage belonged to a machine which fell in an attack on London on 6 December 1917; the man observing it wears the side-cap, 'maternity jacket' and greatcoat of the Royal Flying Corps (note the black shoulder-title bearing the unit-designation in white embroidery), while the sentry wears the brass royal coat of arms cap-badge authorized for local volunteer corps in 1916 but often ignored in favour of the retention of those units' badges. He carries the P.14 rifle, as issued to many such second-line formations, and wears the 1914 leather equipment.

90. This remarkable Heath Robinson-style device is a sound-detector, operating like a giant ear-trumpet to assist the detection of enemy aircraft. The German with his ear to the 'trumpet' demonstrates a late use of what appears to be the 1871-pattern bayonet with S-shaped quillon, which existed in two lengths plus a pioneer weapon with serrated back (*Pionierfaschinenmesser*). Note the woollen sword-knot (*Troddel*), the colour-combinations of which identified the owner's company.

91. Home-defence forces were formed by most nations. In Britain, these were generally styled 'Volunteer Training Corps' but initially were not part of HM Forces, officers were not commissioned and bore singular titles such as 'Platoon

88. A field-kitchen of some sophistication: an 'automobile cooker' of the US Army in France. In hot weather US troops could wear a khaki shirt instead of the tunic (with a light khaki tie for officers), and officers could also use a khaki-drill version of the ordinary tunic, of the same cut but with pointed cuffs. The men illustrated appear to have light khaki canvas gaiters instead of leather gaiters or puttees. Officers' rank-insignia was worn on the tunic shoulder-strap and shirt-collar, one or two silver bars for 1st lieutenant and captain, a gilt or silver leaf for major and lieutenant-colonel

91

Commander', and the force wore a grey-green uniform with unique rank-insignia and badges. From April 1916 their utility was recognized and they became part of the army under the title 'Volunteer Force', officers received ordinary ranks in September, but not until December 1916 were khaki uniforms introduced, and even then the older clothing and insignia remained in use for some considerable time. Here,

Commandant W. Bradley (seated, second right) and his officers of the Blackpool battalion are shown in the grey-green uniform, except Adjutant Shankland who wears the glengarry of the Argyll & Sutherland Highlanders, a tunic cut to resemble a Scottish doublet but with 'English' regular army rank-badges and (apparently) the cap-badge of the Blackpool battalion worn on the lapels, which with the khaki

kilt-apron produces an unusual uniform.

92. Prisoners of war on both sides retained their ordinary uniform, in this case with identifying numerals on large panels stitched to the tunic. This group of French, Russian and British prisoners was photographed by a German commercial photographer, Strauss of Cassel, at the Langensalza camp in June 1917.

Included are a corporal of the Hampshire Regiment (seated, second left) and a sergeant of the East Lancashire Regiment (seated right); the men wearing kepis are French and the remainder Russian, including one in Cossack dress (standing right) and an officer (seated, second right) with two-tone 'co-respondent' shoes!

92

John Joseph Pershing (1860-1948)

The most significant event of 1917 was probably the entry into the war of the United States of America. Although American military preparedness was insufficient to permit any immediate substantial deployment, the morale implication was immense, as the American commitment promised irresistible force in both men and industrial might. The most prominent representative of that force was John Joseph Pershing, who was appointed commander of the American Expeditionary Force on 26 May 1917.

Pershing was born near Laclede, Missouri, the son of a merchant, and graduated from West Point in about the middle of his class in 1886. Posted as a 2nd lieutenant to the 6th Cavalry, he served in New Mexico against the Apaches and against the Sioux in the Dakotas, and in 1891 was appointed professor of military science at the University of Nebraska, where he remained for four years, during which time he also took a law degree. He returned to the U.S. Military Academy at West Point in 1897 as instructor in tactics, but requested active duty upon the outbreak of the Spanish-American War. He served in Cuba with the 10th Cavalry (a Negro unit, from which he gained his nickname 'Black Jack'), and in the Philippines, where he gained valuable experience in a number of organisational posts.

In 1903 Pershing returned to the United States as a member of the general staff, attended the War College in 1904-5, went to Japan in the latter year as attaché to the U.S. embassy, and acted as a military observer with the Japanese army in Manchuria during the Russo-Japanese War. In 1906, as reward for his achievements in the Philippines, President Theodore Roosevelt advanced him in rank from captain to brigadier-general over the heads of some 862 more senior officers. Pershing was sent back to the Philippines as commander of the Department of Mindanao and governor of Moro Province, where he campaigned successfully against the Moro tribesmen. Appointed to command the 8th Infantry Brigade at San Francisco, while serving temporarily on the Mexican border, Pershing lost his wife and three daughters in a terrible fire (only his son being rescued); his subsequent taciturn demeanour reflected the name 'Black Jack'.

Pershing's previous career and experience led in March 1916 to his appointment to command the punitive expedition to Mexico, in pursuit of the bandit Francisco (Pancho) Villa, after the latter's raid upon Columbus, New Mexico. Pershing was promoted to major-general, and later assumed command of the entire military force on the Mexican border, which with the mobilisation of the National Guard involved a total of about 150,000 men.

Upon the entry of the U.S.A. into the World War, Pershing was the obvious candidate for the role of commander of the American Expeditionary Force, and he went to France in June 1917 to prepare for the arrival of U.S. troops. From the beginning, President Woodrow Wilson gave Pershing the authority to organise his forces as he chose, to cooperate with the Allied military system but not to integrate the A.E.F. into it, maintaining the American position that they were an associated, rather than a fully Allied, power. This insistence upon American integrity of command was maintained against urging from the Allies to commit American forces piecemeal, as they arrived in Europe; instead, Pershing resisted all appeals and instituted a programme of intensive training to enable the A.E.F. to take the field as an independent army. (As an exception to this general rule, some units did serve with other armies, two divisions with the French IV and VI Corps, and one regiment in Italy.) Pershing's reorganisation of regimental and divisional structure, conforming more to European practice, was a considerable improvement, which economised on field and staff officers, and he had a refreshing attitude towards subordinates, ruthlessly removing inept or mediocre commanders, to the great benefit of the army.

The plight of the Allies during Ludendorff's 'Michael' offensive in spring 1918 prompted Pershing to relax the insistence upon independence and to offer troops as a support to the French. Otherwise, he retained his position so strongly that, despite the American baptism of fire in late May and early June 1918, not until mid-September 1918 did a major, wholly American operation occur, in the capture of the St. Mihiel salient. Pershing requested that the Americans be allowed to conduct this action as

much for reasons of national pride and the consequent boost to morale as for combat experience; and as overwhelming American forces were deployed against Germans who were already withdrawing, the task was not difficult. More serious was the next major offensive made by the A.E.F., in the Meuse–Argonne sector, although their progress was sufficiently slow for the French premier, Georges Clemenceau, to petition (unsuccessfully) for Pershing's removal. The armistice followed some three weeks later.

Pershing's influence upon the American contribution to the western front was crucial, though he was not without his critics: his relations with the army chief of staff, General Peyton March (originally a brigadier-general of artillery in the A.E.F.) varied from uneasy to hostile, with conflict occurring over Pershing's desire for the power to promote general officers, which March believed was within his own jurisdiction. Pershing also aroused some criticism over his decision to press for Germany's unconditional surrender, without reference to higher authority. A skilled tactician with an appreciation of the importance of logistics, Pershing delayed the entry of American troops into combat by refusing to commit his forces before they were ready, but ensured by so doing that their participation would have been decisive. He retired from military life in 1924, fully deserving of the unique rank of General of the Armies bestowed upon him after the war.

References

Herwig, H.H., & Heyman, N.M. *Biographical Dictionary of World War I*, Westport, Connecticut, 1982.

Liddell Hart, Sir Basil *Reputations*, London 1928.

Pershing, General J.J. *My Experience in the World War*, London 1931.

Smythe, P. *Guerilla Warrior: the Early Life of John J. Pershing*, New York, 1973.

Vandiver, F.E. *Black Jack: The Life and Times of John J. Pershing*, College Station, Texas, 1977

WORLD WAR ONE: 1918

1. At the beginning of 1918, operations on the Western Front were still governed by the static trench-warfare which had existed for the previous three years. This rocket-post in a snow-covered British trench is attended by two 'Tommies' wearing typical uniform for the season: the ordinary service dress plus a sleeveless (and often fleece-lined) leather jerkin, worn over the tunic but underneath the equipment. Both carry the improved pattern of respirator in its 'box'-shaped khaki canvas case suspended around the neck and resting upon the upper breast, the case having an opening upper flap to facilitate instant readiness. Rockets were an important method of signalling, more reliable than telephone land-lines which were greatly vulnerable to shell-fire.

▲2

2. One of the most infamous ailments which arose from the war was 'trench foot', a result of prolonged exposure to cold and dampness which caused the flesh on the feet to become gangrenous and rot away; at its worst, amputations of toes or feet could result, or even death if the condition went untreated. Regular inspections of feet were undertaken, and as the condition was deemed preventable it was possible for men to be punished for contracting the condition, though generally such sanctions were not enacted. The officer inspecting here is a member of the British Royal Army Medical Corps: the regimental badge on the lapel of the tunic is clearly visible.

3. The use of dogs in war was a theory which enjoyed considerable currency; the Belgian Army made use of dog-drawn machine-gun carriages, but most common were the red-cross dogs trained to seek out the wounded on the battlefield. There was, however, little opportunity for them to be used. These dog-handlers in a zigzag trench wear the ordinary French uniform; note the chevrons carried on the upper left sleeve of two of the men. These were not insignia of rank: NCO rank-markings were small diagonal bars on the cuff, one or two red bars for 1st class privates and corporals respectively, one or two metallic bars for sergeants, and a metallic bar with scarlet squares for warrant officers. The blue chevrons on the left sleeve indicated length of service, one chevron for every six months.

▼3

INTRODUCTION

At the beginning of 1918 both the Allied and Central Powers were suffering severely from more than three years of unremitting, attritional warfare. The exit of Russia from the war following the 1917 revolution might have been a crucial blow against the Allies, allowing Germany to concentrate on the Western Front; but probably the most decisive factor was the entry of the United States into the war on the side of the Allies. Although some in the Allied camp might regard America's entry unduly delayed, especially in the light of the length of time which elapsed between their declaration of war and the committing of substantial numbers of troops to combat, the effect was profound.

The material resources of the United States were immense, but although there was a considerable delay before the huge numbers of American troops had any effect on the fighting, the intervening period was used for training and ensuring that when they were committed they were present in sufficient numbers for their intervention to be truly effective. Equally important was the boost to the morale of the other Allied nations, and the equivalent discouragement to the Central Powers.

Military developments continued even in the closing stages of the war. There was an increasing use of armoured fighting vehicles, with both France and Germany utilizing vehicles of their own manufacture, adumbrating the events of succeeding conflicts. The almost static trench warfare of the previous three years and more was replaced by a war of greater manoeuvre from the spring of 1918, with the beginning of the huge German offensive intended to defeat the French and British before the effect of the Americans turned the war irrevocably against the Central Powers. For the Allies, this was one of the most critical periods of the war; but they held on, the German offensive faltered, and the resulting Allied counter-attack ended the German capacity for continued resistance. The end came comparatively rapidly as the weakened Central Powers collapsed on all fronts, Germany itself being riven by internal unrest and mutiny even before the Armistice of 11 November 1918 mercifully brought an end to a war of unprecedented carnage.

Some of the images of 1918 are considerably different from those of 1914, the eagerness and militaristic fervour being replaced by resignation. Wilfred Owen's 'drawing-down of blinds' in *Anthem for Doomed Youth* is an appropriate analogy for the war, which drew down the blinds of the old order and changed completely the course of history. The greatest tragedy of a tragic war, however, is perhaps the fact that the 'Great War for Civilization' was followed less than 21 years later by the outbreak of a war equally terrible as that ended by the Armistice of November 1918.

4. Antonio at the Front: a Portuguese rocket-position on the Western Front. Portuguese troops served alongside the British in the later stages of the war, and their weaponry and personal equipment was of British design: in this case including a British Lee-Enfield rifle, light khaki web equipment modelled on the British 1908 pattern and introduced into the Portuguese Army in 1911, and apparently British steel helmets rather than the variety with fluted crown most usually associated with the Portuguese Army. The tunic, trousers and puttees were of a shade similar to the French 'horizon-blue'. Just as the French soldier was nicknamed '*poilu*' and the British 'Tommy', so the Portuguese was styled 'Antonio'; or, more scathingly by the British who had no great opinion of their military capabilities, 'the Pork and Beans'.

5. Belgian troops moving finned mortar-bombs or 'aerial torpedoes'. They wear the later khaki service uniform of the

Belgian Army, with the French-style Adrian helmet bearing the Belgian lion-mask insignia on the front. The use of light railways of various gauges (some with locomotives) was considerable, right along the Western Front, as here in the Belgian sector near the North Sea coast. This is a narrow-gauge version to facilitate the transport of ammunition to a battery. In the background is a camouflaged screen of straw or grass, of a style used at least as early as the eighteenth century and sometimes termed a 'blind', i.e., a screen to conceal from the enemy the activities progressing behind it.

6. Shortages of equipment affected most armies throughout the war. In British service, for example, insufficient sets of the regulation 1908-pattern web equipment led to the introduction of the 1914-pattern leather equipment, intended originally only for use by troops at home, but which was actually worn in all theatres of war. Occasionally even more unusual items had to be pressed into service: this Royal Fusilier wears a leather belt with a large

metal plate bearing what appears to be the insignia of the Order of the Thistle, perhaps a set of old equipment from a Scottish volunteer battalion re-issued as part of a set of 1914-pattern equipment.

7 and 8. The change of appearance of the service uniform occasioned by the war is illustrated in these photographs of two wounded officers who passed through the King's Lancashire Military Convalescent Hospital at Blackpool in 1918. Lieutenant Henry Cardwell of the Lancashire Fusiliers (originally a law lecturer at Manchester University) wears the 'regulation'-style cap; note the large size of collar-badge with 'T' (Territorial) beneath. Contrastingly, Lieutenant F. Brooks-Turner of the East Lancashire Regiment has a somewhat disreputable, unstiffened cap, as worn on active service, and an identification-sign on the shoulder. (The 7th Battalion, East Lancashires wore such a triangle in red, with yellow border.)

6▲

7▼   8▼

9. A wartime development in the British Army was the conversion of some infantry battalions to pioneers, to act in suppport of the engineer services. By 1916 each division had one pioneer battalion on its establishment, equipped with eight Lewis guns (twelve by 1918) instead of the twelve, ultimately 36, of ordinary infantry battalions. A new badge was designed for pioneers, a brass crossed rifle and pick on the collar, as illustrated most clearly in this photograph of a member of the Durham Light Infantry; note the bugle badge above the 'Durham' title on the shoulder-strap. The 11th (Service) Battalion DLI served as pioneers for the 20th Division, and the 22nd (Service, 3rd County) Battalion for the 8th Division.

10. Despite the exigencies of the war, maintenance of pre-war regimental uniform was an important part of the preservation of *esprit de corps*. This uniform is typical: Private John Gregg of the 2/7th (Fife) Battalion, Black Watch (Territorial Force) wears a service tunic with skirts cut back to resemble the Highland doublet; and though he has khaki puttees in place of the pre-war stockings, he wears the sporran, comparatively rarely seen with service dress, an item of no functional use but an example of the distinctions guarded jealously by most British regiments. The 1/7th Black Watch served in France and Flanders from May 1915, but the associated 2/7th remained at home, spending the period from March 1916 until its disbandment in April 1918 in East Anglia.

11. The recent innovation of motor transport produced some singular uniforms, as some of the existing regulation dress was not completely suitable for use in open vehicles or on motor cycles. Civilian-style garments were pressed into service; this driver of the British Army Service Corps wears an unusual 'uniform' in the form of a civilian coat, apparently of waterproof material, with a fur collar and (presumably) fur lining, fastened on the breast by metal clips.

▼10

▼11

12▲

12. Although the wearing of shorts is commonly associated with service in tropical climates, there was quite widespread use of this garment by British troops on the Western Front in hot weather. This is a typical group showing the wearing of shorts with puttees in the place of stockings: the crew of a motorized anti-aircraft battery, photographed in France. Most are identifiable by their cap-badges as members of the Royal Artillery, but the vehicle-drivers (e.g., second row from rear) are members of the Army Service Corps.

13. An unusual British formation was the 63rd (Royal Naval) Division, formed in 1914 from naval reservists, who were employed as soldiers. They were transferred from Admiralty to War Office superintendence on 29 April 1916, and received the number '63' that July. They served with distinction in the Dardanelles and from late 1915 on the Western Front.

Battalions bore the names of famous British admirals, Anson, Benbow, Collingwood, Drake, Hawke, Hood, Howe and Nelson, but apart from insignia, uniform and equipment was of army pattern. Non-naval units were included in the division

(from 1916 one army brigade, and the 14th Battalion, Worcestershire Regiment were the divisional pioneers), but the division's Machine-Gun Corps emphasized their identity by using the MGC cap-badge with the 'RND' shoulder-title below,

shown in this rare photograph which depicts this insignia in use. The RND machine-gunner is accompanied by gunner J. H. Carleton of 476 Siege Battery, Royal Garrison Artillery.

13▼

▲14

on the breast. The unit is unidentified but the costume is absolutely typical; the collar badge appears to include a wreath of fern-leaves, indicating that the men are New Zealanders. The platoon officer (second row from the front, fourth from left) wears his single rank-star (2nd lieutenant) on the shoulder-strap, less conspicuous than the alternative laced cuff. The platoon Lewis gun is posed in the foreground.

16. One of the most distinctive items of uniform was the Australasian slouch hat, worn by the New Zealand forces with the brim flat and the crown punched up into 'lemon-squeezer' shape, a style generally adopted after Gallipoli. This New Zeland sergeant was photographed in France in February 1918. The unit is unidentified, but the shape of the hat- and collar-badge probably represent either one of the 'reinforcement' units, or perhaps the badges are those of the 10th North Otago Rifles, a regiment which contributed companies to the composite

14. Major-General Sir H. S. Jeudwine (front row, centre) and his staff of the 55th (West Lancashire) Division, Auchel, April 1918. This illustrates the use of the staff brassard or 'armlet', which in this case bears the division's rose insignia as on the name-boards, foreground; it is most clearly

▼15

visible on the right arm of Lieutenant-Colonel S. H. Eden (front, second left) but is worn by almost all the officers in the group. The author of the history of the British General Headquarters (*G.H.Q.* by 'G.S.O.', London 1920) stated that no less than 62 brassard-designs were authorized,

exclusive of divisional varieties like that shown, which he referred to somewhat scathingly as being in 'crude stained-glass-window colours'!

15. An infantry platoon in Western Front battle order, wearing helmets with fabric covers and the 'box' respirator

16▲

17▲

Otago Regiment which, after service at the Dardanelles and in Egypt, served on the Western Front until the end of the war.

17. British Empire troops generally wore the service uniform of the British Army, but distinctions existed. In this photograph E. Craig (left) and W. Van der Walt (right) wear Canadian and South African uniform respectively. Craig's tunic has more breast-buttons than the usual British pattern, and his shoulder-straps bear the brass unit-title '12 INF' over 'Canada'; his spurred boots indicate the regimental transport section. Cap- and collar-badges are the ordinary brass maple-leaf insignia. Van der Walt wears the insignia of the 3rd South African Infantry and the springbok-head cap-badge. Both wear the white-metal 'Imperial Service badge' on the left breast, initially designed to indicate members of a Territorial unit which had volunteered for active service overseas, at a time when the

ordinary condition of enlistment of Territorial units was for home service only.

18. Perhaps the most famous unit of the French Army, the Foreign Legion was honoured extensively. As a result of appalling losses, the original Legion regiments were amalgamated in October 1915 into the *Régiment de Marche de la Légion Etrangère*, usually known by the initials 'RMLE'. In late 1917 the unit was awarded the red *fourragère* (lanyard) of the *Légion d'honneur* in recognition of their conduct at Verdun. This RMLE colour-party consists entirely of holders of the *Légion d'honneur*, including two of the corps' greatest heroes: Lieutenant-Colonel Paul Rollet holds the flag, and at extreme left is the most decorated NCO in the French Army, *Adjutant-chef* Mader, a German, who in April 1917 with ten companions captured a German battery. All wear the ordinary French uniform in the khaki colouring

of North African units; Rollet wears his old, lightweight North African uniform, an idiosyncracy for which he was

well known. He became the Legion's first Inspector-General in 1931 and is regarded as 'the Father of the Legion'.

18▼

▲19   ▲20   ▼21

19. To replace the immense number of casualties sustained by the later stages of the war, youths were enlisted into the combatant forces. This group of Germans, probably photographed towards the end of the war, is typical: the two seated soldiers appear little more than schoolboys. Note three styles of tunic worn concurrently: the 1910 *Waffenrock* with 1915 cuff-modification (seated left)), the 1915 *Bluse* (standing) and apparently the continuing use of the pre-war blue tunic (seated right), here with apparently field-grey trousers; re-issue of the blue was an emergency measure, worn by recruits at depots, if no field-grey were available. (Dr. John Hall)

20. Body-armour was not prolific, but some use was·made of it by the German Army. This is a typical set, of the type introduced in 1916; it could also include a reinforcing-plate attached by the ventilation-lugs on the helmet and strapped around the rear, providing a double thickness of armour for the front of the head. The great weight of such armour (35lb) was not popular, and it was used mostly by sentries on the Western Front. This illustration shows the continuing use of the 1910-pattern *Waffenrock* with three-button cuff-flap of 'Brandenburg' pattern.

21. Field Marshal Hindenburg presents awards of the Iron Cross. Hindenburg wears his regimental uniform of the 3rd Foot Guards, and the breast-star of the Iron Cross. The Grand Cross of the Iron Cross was awarded only five times, including that to Hindenburg and one to the Kaiser, the latter at the request of the General Staff; the eight-pointed silver-gilt breast-star with an Iron Cross superimposed was unique to Hindenburg and was conferred in March 1918. The Iron Cross was not an award of the German Empire but purely Prussian, re-instituted at the beginning of each war and discontinued at its end (until it was revived in 1939 when it applied to the whole of Germany). During the First World War more than 160,000 awards of the 1st Class and about five million of the 2nd Class were given. The recipients in this photograph wear the 1915 *Bluse*, the officer (extreme left) having pleated breast-pockets.

22. This German, posed in the barrel of a massive piece of ordnance, wears the *Stahlhelm* (steel helmet) introduced from 1916; note that the chinstrap was not attached near to the internal head-band, but to lugs sited low down on the 'skirts' of the helmet. The soldier seems to be wearing a tunic with shoulder-straps removed, a measure undertaken sometimes to prevent unit-identification in case of death or capture.

23. Despite the use of more sophisticated methods of communication, message-carrying by pigeon remained in use. The British Army used motorized pigeon-lofts (trucks with a wooden 'loft' constructed at the rear) to transport them near to the battlefield, but an even swifter method of transport is shown here, a pigeon-basket carried on the back of a 'Don R' (dispatch-rider).

22▲ 23▼

▲24

▲25 ▼26

24. Armoured vehicles were unique to the British Army for only a short period. France had two varieties of heavy tank, the Schneider and St-Chamond, both virtually armoured boxes mounted upon tractor units; neither was especially effective and from October 1917 French resources were concentrated on the production of the Renault light tank. Illustrated here, the St-Chamond had a 75mm gun and could carry in addition four Hotchkiss machine-guns, one on each side of the field-gun and one protruding from each side of the body. It had a maximum speed of 5mph, but its off-road performance was not impressive, the tracks not being sufficiently wide.

25. Colonel J. E. Estienne, one of the leading exponents of armoured vehicles in the French Army, conceived the idea of a 'light tank' to act in a role akin to that of cavalry skirmishers. The result was the Renault light tank, illustrated here, first used in action in May 1918. Weighing only 7 tons, it had a crew of two and was armed either with a Hotchkiss machine-gun or a 37mm gun, mounted upon a revolving turret. Despite achieving considerable popularity, they were essentially armoured machine-gun posts, with a road speed of but 6mph, and compared unfavourably with the British 'Whippet' light tank, the Medium Mark A which carried three crew, four machine-guns and had a maximum speed of 8mph.

26. The German Army adopted the concept of armoured warfare only late in the war, and the largest part of their eventual armoured capacity was in the form of captured British vehicles styled *Beute-Panzerkampfwagen* (lit. 'looted tanks'). In addition, an enormous tank was designed by the German War Department, the A7V, which first saw action on 21 March 1918. This monstrous vehicle weighed 33 tons and carried 18 crew (a huge number), and was armed with a converted Russian 57mm field-gun and six 1908-pattern machine-guns, two on each flank and two at the rear. Despite the poor performance of these lumbering vehicles, a leviathan was under construction when the war ended, the 165-ton 'K' model, armed with four 77mm guns. This captured A7V is being inspected by French troops.

27. One of the German Army's most common pieces of artillery was the *Mörser*, a 21cm calibre howitzer, used by the Foot Artillery. It had a comparatively short barrel (about 8½ feet) with a recoil system mounted above. It had a shield mounted above the recoil mechanism, but this was frequently removed (as here); its projectile was a shell weighing 184lb, with a maximum range of 10,280 yards and a rate of fire of two shots per minute. Shown to good effect here are the steel wheels, handspike at the end of the trail (for traversing) and the recoil plate affixed to the underside of the trail.

27▲

28. Among the war's many technological innovations were some which never fulfilled the role for which they were designed. One of the biggest failures was the tunnelling machine designed by the British to automate the driving of tunnels under the German lines on the Western Front; the machinery failed completely. A similar device was this French trench-excavator, consisting of a line of shovels on a belt or chain to scoop out earth automatically. The man at the left wears the French Army's horizon-blue, peakless side-cap, a popular and comfortable 'undress' head-dress.

28▼

29. British officers examining pieces of a German Gotha bomber destroyed in a raid on London on 28 January 1918. Royal Flying Corps officers frequently retained the uniform of their original regiment (unless commissioned directly into the RFC); in this case, Captain G. H. Hackwill (centre) and Lieutenant C. C. Banks (right), who were responsible for the destruction of the German machine, wear their regimental uniform of the Somerset Light Infantry and Royal Welch Fusiliers respectively, with the addition of the RFC 'wings' above the left breast-pocket; Hackwill appears to have replaced his regimental cap-badge with that of the RFC, and retains cuff-style rank-marking; Banks carries his rank-insignia on his shoulder-straps.

30. Georges Madon was France's fourth highest-scoring pilot, with 41 'kills', behind only René Fonck (75), Georges Guynemer (54) and Charles Nungesser (45); only 22 pilots of all nationalities scored more victories than Madon. In this photograph he wears the dark-blue tunic with its distinctive insignia of the French aviation corps: a winged, five-pointed star on the collar (the badge of qualified pilots) and a gold propeller on the lower right sleeve (normally, though not here, with gold wings attached to hub of the propeller blade). Similar insignia was worn by the enlisted men, in red and gold for NCOs and red and white for other ranks; those who were not qualified aviators wore a winged grenade on the collar. Note the French red/white/blue roundel on the lower surface of the wing of the aircraft in the background.

31. The war had a profound effect upon the role of women in society, both with the widespread employment of women at home, filling the occupations of men who were in the armed services, and as part of the military forces of several nations. Womens' duties in the services had hitherto been

restricted to a medical and nursing capacity, but was widened during the war to include other non-combatant duties. Many wore military-style uniform, but few had the elegance of this French *automobiliste* (driver), whose belted greatcoat appears somewhat incongruous with the fashionable high heels and beret, the latter with 'A' insignia.

32. Many women were engaged upon 'war work' (in the munitions industry, for example) but many others served voluntarily, especially in various medical duties. Many volunteer nurses served near to the theatre of combat; others, like these ambulance-women, served at home, in this case to assist casualties from the air raids which increased in the later part of the war. The costume illustrated here is very military, including even puttees.

32 ▲

33. China declared war upon Germany and Austria in August 1917, but the internal unrest in the country precluded any military action against the Central Powers. Large numbers of Chinese labourers were employed by the Allies, however: by early 1918 almost 100,000 by the British on the Western Front, about the same number by the French and 5,000 by the Americans; they served also in Mesopotamia and East Africa. This photograph depicts a Chinese labour battalion embarking for service with the Allies.

33 ▼

34. By no means all the personnel from the overseas colonies of the Allied nations were employed in a combat capacity: large numbers of 'native' labourers were enlisted for the more mundane manual tasks, especially from the British territories in the East and from French possessions in North Africa. Photographed in France was this detachment of British-Indian labourers, wearing a somewhat incongruous mixture of civilian and quasi-military clothing and equipment.

▲34 ▼35

35. Massive pieces of ordnance were used by the Germans to bombard Paris from March 1918. The immense range of such guns, up to 80 miles, was possible by the use of high-velocity projectiles fired into the upper atmosphere, where because of reduced air-resistance greater ranges could be achieved. The projectile was surprisingly small: the so-called 'Paris gun' shell was 21cm calibre, only half that of the 42cm *Mörser*. Contrary to popular belief, it was the latter that was nicknamed 'Big Bertha', not the 'Paris gun'. In this photograph of the moment of discharge, two of the German gunners cover their ears against the blast.

36. The employment of huge pieces of artillery later in the war was made possible by the almost static trench-warfare which permitted these ponderous leviathans to be moved into position. Some were mounted on railway carriages, such as this German 38cm gun. The most commonly used British railway-mounted gun was the 12in howitzer, which threw a shell of 750lb weight over eight miles; a very much more massive railway gun was the French 40cm howitzer (approximating in calibre to the British 16in gun) which projected a shell weighing almost 2,000lb to a distance of almost ten miles.

36 ▲

37. The difficulties of handling huge railway-mounted guns are illustrated by this photograph of an American gun in France: shells had to be lifted by crane, and the barrel had to be returned to the horizontal every time for loading, and elevated anew for each shot. Traversing within the framework of the carriage was limited, so that this had to be achieved by the use of railway turntables or by running the carriage along a curved spur of track. Some 144 rail-mounted guns were used by the US forces in France, the largest in calibre being 14in guns and 16in howitzers; the latter had a limited traverse but the former's breech projected so far beyond the trunnions that a 15° elevation was the maximum which could be achieved.

37 ▲   38 ▼

38. John Joseph 'Black Jack' Pershing (1860–1948) was America's leading soldier of the war; his success in the expedition to defeat the Mexican bandit Pancho Villa led to his appointment to command the US Expeditionary Force in Europe. His command was marked by an unwillingness to commit US troops until they were sufficiently numerous and well-trained to make a decisive contribution; his reward for his invaluable service was promotion to the singular rank 'General of the Armies'. Here he wears the service uniform including khaki peaked cap with khaki mohair braid, brown peak and chinstrap and bronze eagle badge; high-collared khaki tunic with patch breast- and side-pockets and five bronzed buttons on the breast; khaki breeches and leather leggings or riding boots. The original leather waist-belt was often replaced by a British Sam Browne belt. Rank insignia for general officers was borne upon the shoulder-straps, one to four silver stars.

▲39

▲40 ▼41

39. In the words of a popular song, 'the Yanks are coming'. The contribution of the United States to Allied victory should never be overlooked, even if their active military participation was delayed until large numbers of US troops were established in Europe. By mid-July 1918 more than a million US troops were in Europe, later twice that number; almost 850,000 were disembarked at Liverpool alone. This unit, marching off for active service, wears the New Zealand-style felt 'campaign hat' which was neither functional nor popular, and was often replaced by the 'overseas cap' or side-cap. For bad weather gabardine raincoats or khaki trench-coats could be worn instead of the ordinary greatcoat.

40. US troops in France, wearing their national khaki or olive-drab service uniform (which existed in both serge and lighter-weight cotton), plus the British-pattern steel helmet. Gas masks were also copied from the Allies: both British and French patterns were used. Visible here are the canvas gaiters or leggings with which the US troops were issued originally; khaki puttees were often preferred on active service. The 1910-pattern canvas web equipment included a 'long pack' which protruded so far below the waist that sitting was difficult!

41. US troops fitting gas masks. There being no steel helmet issued before leaving the USA, both British and French styles were utilized, the latter in the original horizon-blue colour and with French insignia on the front. The latter became the distinctive insignia of the US 93rd Division, a blue Adrian helmet upon a black disc; such insignia was authorized from 19 October 1918, confirming a practice already in existence unofficially: the wildcat badge of the 81st Division was worn before the formation left the USA, in July 1918. Sometimes such badges were painted on the helmet, but the general use of sleeve-

insignia was not widespread before the cessation of hostilities. French weapons were also adopted by some American units serving with the French, to facilitate ammunition-supply, for example the Lebel rifle and the Chauchat gun. The man in the left foreground wears the French-style 'overseas cap' often preferred to the brimmed hat.

42. American officers photographed in England with the survivors of the transport *Tuscania*, which had been torpedoed by a U-boat off the coast of Ireland when bringing American troops to Europe; providentially, only 166 of the 2,235 people aboard were lost. This illustrates the US officers' greatcoat, a long, khaki garment with falling collar and two rows of five horn buttons converging towards the waist, with a half-belt at the rear. Rank was indicated by black Austrian knots on the cuffs, three to five lines of braid for field ranks, one or two for company officers, increasing in number with the grade; for general officers the braid was brown mohair with the appropriate number of white-metal stars. The felt campaign hat had cords of mixed black and gold for officers.

43. One of the most famous aviation squadrons was the French *Escadrille Lafayette* formed from American volunteer pilots who entered French service prior to the involvement of the USA in the war. Illustrated here is Raoul Lufbery, an American of French origin, who was one of the squadron's 'aces' and who transferred to the US aviation service when the USA entered the war. The 'Aviation Section' was part of the US Signal Corps and wore ordinary army uniform (a distinctive collar-badge was not authorized until April 1918), plus a silver-embroidered 'wing' on the left breast, a 'Union shield' bearing 'US' in gold, with two wings for pilots and one for observers. (The former was designated as the badge of 'Military Aviator', the latter 'Junior Military Aviator'; others, representative of different grades, also existed.) Lufbery scored 17 victories but was killed in 1918 when he jumped from his blazing aeroplane rather than be burned to death during the aircraft's descent.

CHRONOLOGY: 1918

At the beginning of 1918 the military situation was critical for both Allied and Central Powers. The Allies' hopes for 1917 had been unfulfilled, for despite major successes against Turkey, little progress had been achieved on the Western Front, Russia had been removed from the war, Italy had almost suffered total defeat. Despite the great boost to Allied morale provided by the United States' entry into the war their forces were not yet present in sufficient numbers to have an effect, and they refused to be integrated into the overall Anglo-French military structure. Similarly, the Central Powers were insecure, badly affected by the Allied naval blockade, and more than ever Germany was compelled to be the dominant power, for Austria was nearing exhaustion and Turkey and Bulgaria were in scarcely better condition. Hindenburg and Ludendorff now exercised almost total control over not only Germany's military effort but also over the actions of the other partners.

The Western Front

Hindenburg and Ludendorff realized that Germany's one hope lay in a massive attack against the Anglo-French armies, to destroy them before the American presence turned the war by weight of numbers. To this end, Ludendorff planned a series of major offensives.

March–April: Ludendorff's first (Somme) offensive. On 21 March, using 'Hutier' tactics of infiltration by-passing strong-points to be neutralized at a later stage, three German armies attacked on a 60-mile front aimed at breaking through the British right flank and separating them from the French. At first the attack enjoyed spectacular success, rolling over the stretched British Fifth Army and making major territorial gains. Despite an undertaking for mutual support, the French commander Pétain made the defence of Paris his main priority and thus French assistance was not forthcoming until the appointment as Allied co-ordinator of Marshal Ferdinand Foch (26 March), from 3 April supreme comamnder of Allied forces in France (to which appointment even the Americans acceeded). The subsequent co-ordination of Allied effort was one reason for the halting of the offensive; but equally, the Germans found that a rapid advance was made difficult by the roadless sea of mud over which they had to pass (a consequence of more than three years' war), and that despite the collapse of Allied resistance in places, their supports could not keep pace to permit the drive to continue. After establishing a salient 40 miles deep, Ludendorff halted his advance on 5 April. Though it had cost the Allies immense losses (especially the British who bore the brunt of the attack), German casualties, especially among the hardened assault divisions, had been almost as severe.

April: Ludendorff's second (Lys) offensive. Beginning on 9 April, the next German drive was farther north, along the Lys sector held by the British. Again substantial gains were made; but inspired by Haig's famous 'backs to the wall' message, the British held on and despite a 10-mile German advance, a breakthrough to the Channel ports was prevented.

May–June: Ludendorff's third (Aisne) offensive. The next attack was against the French along the Aisne, on a 25-mile front, beginning on 27 May. Driving onwards to the Marne, the German attack was halted after major territorial gains, when US troops were hurried forward to support the French, scoring their first major successes at Château-Thierry and Belleau

Wood. Ludendorff halted, having established a 20-mile salient some 30 miles wide, and prepared for a further effort against the French before making his planned decisive offensive against the British in the north.

June: Ludendorff's fourth (Noyon–Montdidier) offensive. From 9 June Ludendorff attacked from the salients gained by his Somme and Aisne offensives, against the French forces between them; but by 13 June the attack had been halted by Franco-American counter-attacks.

July: Second Battle of the Marne. From 15 to 19 July Ludendorff attempted to take the Rheims area by his fifth (Marne) offensive, to the south of the salient established by the Aisne offensive, but although German forces penetrated to the Marne, Franco-American resistance stemmed the advance. It was Ludendorff's final attempt to smash the Allies, costing him half a million men; but despite all the territorial gains it had failed to breach decisively the Allied lines.

July–August: The Allied counter-attack. As soon as the German Marne offensive ran out of steam, the Franco-American forces counter-attacked and recovered the German gains along the Marne. To the north, Haig launched an Anglo-French attack from 8 August which throughout the remainder of the month drove the Germans from their newly won territory, so that by early September they were back at the Hindenburg Line, with Ludendorff and the more realistic German commanders realizing that, with the collapse of their final major effort, the war was lost.

September–October: Foch began his final advance, based on two major offensives, Anglo-French to the north and Franco-American to the south, with supplementary advances elsewhere along the front, beginning with a successful Franco-American operation at St-Mihiel, to the east of Verdun. On 26 September the main French offensive opened in the Meuse-Argonne area, and on the following day Haig's advance began, followed on 28 September by a British supplementary attack in Flanders. This concentrated pressure on more than one sector casued the final collapse of the German effort on the Western Front; successive defensive-lines were breached until the Germans were in full retreat, and as early as 6 October an armistice was requested. Ludendorff resigned on 27 October to facilitate the process.

November: Despite continuing stubborn resistance from elements of the German forces, their collapse was irrevocable. From late October mutinies and riots erupted within Gemany itself, arising partly from Communist agitation; a republic was proclaimed on 9 November, and on the following day the Kaiser fled to exile in the Netherlands. After four days of negotiation, an armistice was declared in force from 11 a.m. on 11 November; and for the first time in more than four years, the guns fell silent on the Western Front.

The Eastern Front

Although the Russian Revolution had removed that country from the war, hostilities did not end in 1917. Germany insisted that former Russian provinces along the Baltic, the Ukraine and Poland be granted autonomy, all of which were openly hostile to the Bolshevik regime. The Bolsheviks were compelled to comply under the threat of renewed hostilities, so that a final peace was signed only on 3 March; Germany continued to occupy the Ukraine and appropriate its agricultural resources. This was merely the preliminary for a prolonged and bitter civil war in Russia between the Bolsheviks and their opponents, which involved not only the internal warring factions but many foreign expeditionary forces in opposition to the Bolsheviks. These included British, French and Americans who landed in north Russia, Americans and Japanese in Siberia, together with a huge force of Austrian ex-prisoners known as the Czech Legion, and involved in addition the Finnish War of Independence (aided by German forces prior to the Armistice in Europe) and the Russo-Polish War which won independence for those states. Russia was torn apart by heavy fighting until 1920, and not until late 1922 did the last of the foreign contingents leave.

The Italian Front
June: After the near-collapse of the Italian military in 1917, the Germans withdrew their forces to the Western Front, leaving Austria to operate alone. In June 1918 they launched a double offensive on the Trentino and Piave fronts, but being unable (from the terrain) to make these mutually supportive, the division of resources allowed neither attack to be decisive. The major Austrian effort (15–22 June) made only limited progress before it was compelled to withdraw.

October: Despite the increasing demoralization of the Austrian state and the exhaustion of its forces, and despite urgings by Foch, the Italians made no counter-attack immediately after the Austrian offensive had faltered. In late October, however, spearheaded by British and French units, the Italians attacked in the Battle of Vittorio Veneto, and though they were stopped along the Piave, the British and French broke through the Austrian lines; Austrian resistance collapsed utterly.

November: With Austrian forces shattered and the morale of the state in ruins, and with Allied forces sweeping the opposition before them, an armistice was granted on 3 November, and hostilities ceased on the following day.

The Balkan Front
September: Following years of inconclusive operations, the Allies (now commanded by the capable Fench general Franchet d'Esperey) mounted a decisive offensive as the war neared its end. Most German front-line troops had been withdrawn, so that the Bulgarians were left virtually unaided; and from 15 September the Allied forces (principally Serbian, French and British) attacked in the Battle of the Vardar. By 29 September the Bulgarian Army was in complete rout, and an armistice was agreed on that day.

October–November: Despite the end of hostilities with Bulgaria, the Allied forces continued to march northwards, crossing the Danube on 11 November, and were preparing to advance further when Germany's surrender ended operations in the Balkan theatre.

The Palestine Front
January–September: After the capture of Jerusalem in December 1917, Edmund Allenby's offensive was delayed by the transfer of resources to the threatened Western Front. In this period, Turkish attention was occupied by the Arab rebellion which caused chaos, especially along the Hejaz railway, commanded and assisted by the British, notably T. E. Lawrence.

September–November: Superbly organized and commanded, Allenby's forces burst through the Turkish defensive-lines at the Battle of Megiddo (19 September), taking the Turks completely by surprise; by 21 September much of the Turkish forces had ceased to exist as cohesive units, so that the

German General Liman von Sanders (who had replaced von Falkenhayn in overall command) had only his tiny German contingent still capable of resistance. As the Turks fled, Allenby pursued with vigour, taking Damascus (1 October) and Beirut (2 October), so that on 30 October Turkey signed an armistice, ending the campaign.

The Mesopotamia Front
October: Following the Turkish defeats of 1917, operations in Mesopotamia were limited until, with Turkish surrender imminent, a British force was pushed forward to secure the Mosul oil-fields before the conclusion of an armistice. Although Mosul had not been taken when the armistice was declared, the British still marched in and occupied it.

The Caucasus Front
A British force from Mesopotamia was sent northwards from Baghdad in January, intent on preventing Turkish possession of the oil-fields of western Persia, and even crossed the Russian border to occupy Baku in early August. From February the Turks advanced into Armenia, and a German force was even landed on the Black Sea coast. The British evacuated Baku after heavy Turkish attacks (August–September), and operations ceased after the Turkish armistice on 30 October.

East Africa
The last sphere of campaigning in the World War (not including the conflict in Russia following the Revolution) was in East Africa, where the very capable German commander, Paul von Lettow-Vorbeck, had for four years been waging a guerrilla war against vastly superior Allied forces. After being driven into Portuguese East Africa in 1917 he re-equipped his tiny force with captured Portuguese supplies and marched into Northern Rhodesia, until he was informed of the armistice by the British on 14 November; he surrendered his command nine days later.

The Reckoning
The cost of the World War cannot be measured simply in terms of financial expenditure and military casualties; its consequences were incalculable, and it marked the end of the European 'old order' which had existed for centuries. Following the fall of the two oldest European empires, Austria–Hungary and Russia, the political map changed unrecognizably, and the triumph of the Bolshevik faction in Russia would exert an influence which far outstripped the boundaries of Europe. In purely military terms, the casualties cannot be estimated exactly, but even approximate figures are so enormous as to defy belief. Over 65 million men had been mobilized for the war (12 million Russians, 11 million Germans, almost nine million British, more than 8 million French, almost eight million Austro-Hungarians, more than 5½ million Italians and almost 4½ million Americans). Germany had suffered more than 1,800,000 dead, Russia 1,700,000 (plus two million civilian dead), France more than 1,350,000; Britain and her Empire, and Austria–Hungary, more than 900,000 each; Italy 460,000, Roumania 335,000 (plus 275,000 civilians), Turkey 325,000 (plus more than two million civilians), Serbia 45,000 military dead plus 80,000 from disease and 650,000 civilians. The wounded numbered almost three times the dead: almost five million Russians, four million Germans and French, almost four million Austro-Hungarians, more than two million British and almost a million Italians. Yet the ultimate tragedy of the 'war to end wars' was that less than 21 years after the armistice, another World War began.

ORDERS OF BATTLE

It is interesting to compare orders-of-battle for the later war period, which show the allocation of 'supporting services' on permanent attachment to the divisional structure, a refinement of the system which operated at the beginning of the war, and which included autonomous machine-gun and trench artillery companies instead of the previous practice of having these supports as integral parts of regimental structure. The following orders-of-battle are of the German 36th Division and the British 36th (Ulster) Division, which by strange coincidence were opposed to each other just south of St-Quentin in the start of Ludendorff's great offensive on 21 March 1918:

German 36th Division

Infantry: 71 Brigade: Regiment No. 5 (King Frederick I's Grenadiers) (3rd East Prussian); Regiment No. 128 (Danzig); Regiment No. 175 (8th West Prussian).

Artillery: Field Regiment No. 26 (2nd West Prussian); 1 Abteilung, 4th Reserve Foot Regiment; 824, 1209 and 1229 Light Ammunition Columns.

Cavalry: Hussar Regiment No. 5 (Prince Blücher's) (Pomeranian) (4 squadrons).

Engineers: Pioneer Battalion No. 17 (1st West Prussian) (3 & 5 companies); Trench-mortar Company No. 36; Searchlight Section No. 206.

Signal Service: No. 36 Telegraph Detachment; No. 62 Wireless Detachment.

Train: No. 569 Motor Transport Company.

Medical services: No. 43 Field Ambulance Company; Nos. 288 and 290 Field Hospitals; No. 36 Veterinary Hospital.

36th (Ulster) Division

Infantry: 107 Brigade: 1st Battalion, Royal Irish Rifles; 2nd Battalion, Royal Irish Rifles; 15th (Service) Battalion, Royal Irish Rifles (North Belfast); 107th Trench-mortar Battery.

108 Brigade: 12th (Service) Battalion, Royal Irish Rifles (Central Antrim); 1st Battalion, Royal Irish Fusiliers; 9th (Service) Battalion, Royal Irish Fusiliers (County Armagh: later titled 9th North Irish Horse Battalion, though had absorbed this regiment (dismounted) in September 1917); 108th Trench-mortar Battery.

109 Brigade: 1st Battalion, Royal Inniskilling Fusiliers; 2nd Battalion, Royal Inniskilling Fusiliers; 9th (Service) Battalion, Royal Inniskilling Fusiliers (County Tyrone); 109th Trench-mortar Battery.

Artillery: CLIII Brigade Royal Field Artillery ('A', 'B' & 'C' field batteries, 'D' howitzer battery); CLXXIII Brigade, Royal Field Artillery ('A', 'B' & 'C' field batteries, 'D' howitzer battery); X/36 and Y/36 Medium Trench-mortar Batteries; 36th Divisional Ammunition Column; No. 36 Battalion, Machine-Gun Corps (107th, 108th, 109th and 266th Machine-gun Companies).

Engineers: 121st, 122nd & 150th Field Companies, Royal Engineers; 16th (Service) Battalion, Royal Irish Rifles (2nd County Down) (Pioneers).

Signal service: 36th Divisional Signal Coy.

Train: 36th Divisional Train.

Medical services: 108th, 109th & 110th Field Ambulances, Royal Army Medical Corps; 48th Mobile Veterinary Section.

(Comprehensive orders-of-battle can be found in *History of the Great War: Orders of Battle* (A. F. Becke, London 1934–8), and *Histories of . . . Divisions of the German Army . . .* (Washington 1920), though in neither case are regimental and battalion titles given as fully as in the above).

ORDERS OF BATTLE: RUSSIA, AUSTRIA-HUNGARY AND USA

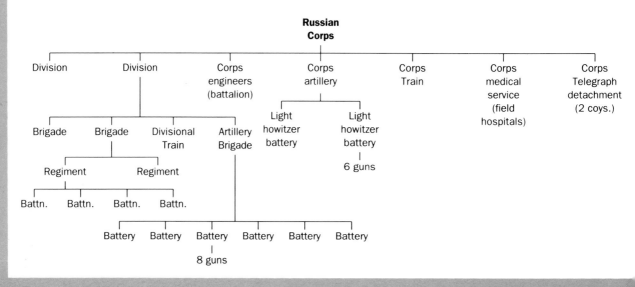

Russian
Cavalry Division

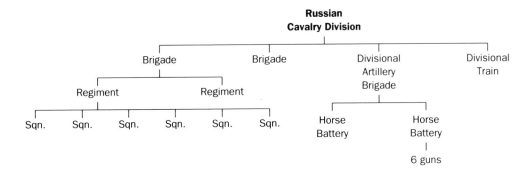

```
Russian
Cavalry Division
├── Brigade
│   ├── Regiment
│   │   ├── Sqn.
│   │   ├── Sqn.
│   │   └── Sqn.
│   └── Regiment
│       ├── Sqn.
│       ├── Sqn.
│       └── Sqn.
├── Brigade
├── Divisional Artillery Brigade
│   ├── Horse Battery
│   └── Horse Battery
│       └── 6 guns
└── Divisional Train
```

Austro-Hungarian
Cavalry Division

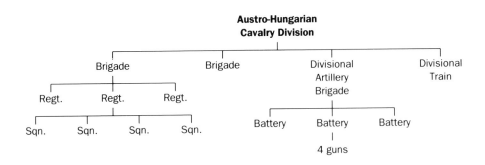

```
Austro-Hungarian
Cavalry Division
├── Brigade
│   ├── Regt.
│   │   └── Sqn.
│   ├── Regt.
│   │   └── Sqn.
│   └── Regt.
│       ├── Sqn.
│       └── Sqn.
├── Brigade
├── Divisional Artillery Brigade
│   ├── Battery
│   ├── Battery
│   │   └── 4 guns
│   └── Battery
└── Divisional Train
```

Austro-Hungarian
Corps

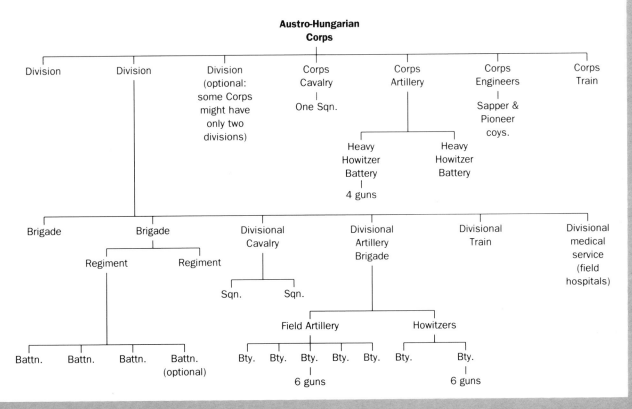

```
Austro-Hungarian
Corps
├── Division
├── Division
│   ├── Brigade
│   ├── Brigade
│   │   ├── Regiment
│   │   │   ├── Battn.
│   │   │   ├── Battn.
│   │   │   ├── Battn.
│   │   │   └── Battn. (optional)
│   │   └── Regiment
│   ├── Divisional Cavalry
│   │   ├── Sqn.
│   │   └── Sqn.
│   ├── Divisional Artillery Brigade
│   │   ├── Field Artillery
│   │   │   ├── Bty.
│   │   │   ├── Bty.
│   │   │   ├── Bty.
│   │   │   │   └── 6 guns
│   │   │   ├── Bty.
│   │   │   └── Bty.
│   │   └── Howitzers
│   │       ├── Bty.
│   │       └── Bty.
│   │           └── 6 guns
│   ├── Divisional Train
│   └── Divisional medical service (field hospitals)
├── Division (optional: some Corps might have only two divisions)
├── Corps Cavalry
│   └── One Sqn.
├── Corps Artillery
│   ├── Heavy Howitzer Battery
│   │   └── 4 guns
│   └── Heavy Howitzer Battery
├── Corps Engineers
│   └── Sapper & Pioneer coys.
└── Corps Train
```

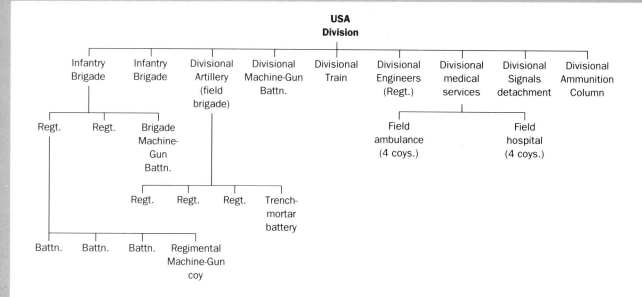

USA
Division

- Infantry Brigade
  - Regt.
    - Battn.
    - Battn.
    - Battn.
    - Regimental Machine-Gun coy
  - Regt.
- Infantry Brigade
  - Brigade Machine-Gun Battn.
- Divisional Artillery (field brigade)
  - Regt.
  - Regt.
  - Regt.
  - Trench-mortar battery
- Divisional Machine-Gun Battn.
- Divisional Train
- Divisional Engineers (Regt.)
- Divisional medical services
  - Field ambulance (4 coys.)
  - Field hospital (4 coys.)
- Divisional Signals detachment
- Divisional Ammunition Column

BRITISH FORMATION SIGNS

The later stages of the war saw the increasing use of 'formation signs' in the British and Empire, and latterly American, forces. These set the style for the worldwide use of such insignia later in the century. Such signs were originally painted on corps or divisional vehicles, and many were worn as uniform-insignia, though in some cases the two were dissimilar or existed in different colouring. It is interesting to consider the origin of some of these signs, though not all the stories regarding their design would appear to be true. Some had no especial motivation behind their design; others were originally puns, such as the letters 'ATN' worn by the 18th Division. Illustrated here are typical examples:

Top row, left to right:

1. III Corps. Triangle (representing '3') in red (left), white and black, these being the racing colours of General Sir William Pulteney.

2. VIII Corps. Green hunting-horn with red mouth, neck and strings; from the family crest of General Sir Aylmer Hunter-Weston.

3. XI Corps. White numerals on dark green; typical of the 'numeral' type of sign.

4. XIII Corps. Horseshoes red (left) and white; good-luck emblems arranged to represent the name of the commander, Lieutenant-General Sir Walter Congreve, VC ('CC' = 'Congreve's Corps'). The 13 nail-holes reprsent the number of the Corps.

2nd row, left to right:

5. XIV Corps. Dark-blue and white chequers, the code-flag for 'N', the fourteenth letter of the alphabet.

6. XVIII Corps. Black 'M' over crossed axes on white: pun on the name of the commander, Lieutenant-General Sir Ivor Maxse ('M-axes').

7. XIX Corps. White question-mark on red: pun on the name of the commander, Sir Herbert Watts (hence 'what's').

8. Guards Division. White eye on blue ground, upon red shield. Apparently no definite reason for this design, which gave rise to the Guards' nickname 'Old Eyes'. (Possible connection with the Guards' 18th-century oath, 'Damn my eyes and blue breeches'?.)

3rd row, left to right:

9. 5th Division. Yellow bar on blue ground. An order prohibiting the painting of names, etc., on transport vehicles led to this division painting a yellow bar through such marks; later adopted as the divisional sign.

10. 11th (Northern) Division. Red Egyptian hieroglyph *ankh* (the sign of life and resurrection), adopted to commemorate the division's service in Egypt.

11. 14th (Light) Division. White lines on

1.

2.

3.

4.

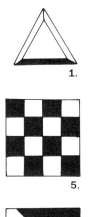
5.

6.

7.

8.

9.

10.

11.

12.

green, green being the traditional colour of light infantry; and white lines were said to represent the 14th proposition of Euclid, though this may well not be the case.

12. 16th (Irish) Division. Badge worn on uniform: green shamrock on khaki, the symbol of Ireland.

4th row, left to right:

13. 17th (Northern) Division. White rectangles on red (or vice versa): said to represent the top of the number '17', but apparently actually originated with the 17th Divisional Supply Column, composed of Australians, and is the Morse sign for 'A'.

14. 31st Division. Composed of Lancashire and Yorkshire units, hence the county symbols of red and white roses; for Lancashire units the red rose overlapped the white, and for Yorkshire vice versa.

15. 33rd Division. White domino: from the numerals '33'.

16. 36th (Ulster) Division. The red hand

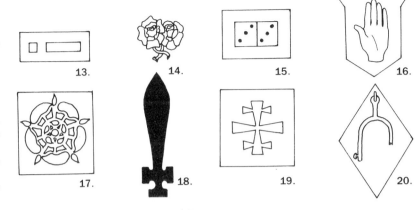

13.   14.   15.   16.

17.   18.   19.   20.

of Ulster, symbol of the province.

5th row, left to right:

17. 49th (West Riding) Division. White rose of Yorkshire.

18. 56th (London) Division. Red sword, taken from the Arms of the City of London.

19. 59th (North Midland) Division. Yellow cross of Offa, King of Mercia (reigned AD757–796), who reigned over the area from which the division was recruited.

20. 74th (Yeomanry) Division. White broken spur on black, representing the conversion of the division from cavalry to infantry.

BRITISH BATTALION INSIGNA

As noted in *1915*, British units on active service were distinguished by cloth panels or badges worn on the sleeve, rear of the tunic, or helmet. In many cases these were simply geometrical shapes, but the tradition of regimental identity was so strong that many 'battalion signs' were based upon the regimental badge, or insignia representing the unit's function. Some of these were quite crude in execution and included asymmetrical designs. Examples of this element of regimental tradition are shown here:

Top row, left to right:

1. 12th Battalion, Northumberland Fusiliers: red 'V', representing the regiment's pre-1881 number as the 5th Regiment of Foot.

2. Shamrock: red, light-blue, violet and black for the 24th–27th Battalions, Northumberland Fusiliers respectively (1st–4th Tyneside Irish): representative of the Irish identity. The amalgamated 24/27th Battalion (formed August 1917) wore a black shamrock on red disc.

3. Grenade: red, yellow, blue-grey and green for the 17th, 22nd–24th Battalions, Royal Fusiliers respectively, taken from the regimental cap-badge design.

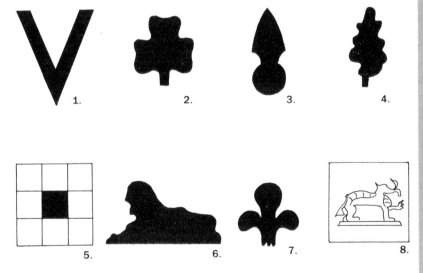

1.   2.   3.   4.

5.   6.   7.   8.

4. 2nd Battalion, Cheshire Regiment: dark-green oak-leaf, taken from the regimental cap-badge. Worn on the back; 1st Battalion wore a similar design on a white oblong on the helmet. 11th Battalion insignia was a green oak-sprig with acorn.

Second row, left to right:

5. 1/4th (Border) Battalion, King's Own Scottish Borderers: red cross with black centre upon white square, worn on the helmet; presumably imitating the diced band of Highland glengarry caps and bonnets.

6. 8th Battalion, South Lancashire Regiment: crimson sphinx, taken from the battle-honour 'Egypt' on the regimental cap-badge. (The 2nd Battalion, wore white numerals '82' on a red oval, this being the battalion's old regimental number, not used officially since 1881!)

7. 1st Battalion, Welsh Regiment: red Prince of Wales's plumes, from the regimental cap-badge.

8. 2nd Battalion, Berkshire Regiment: blue square bearing red dragon marked in black; from the regimental cap-badge.

9. 8th Battalion, King's Own Yorkshire Light Infantry: dark-green 'French' bugle, from the regimental cap-badge. The 6th Battalion wore a similar but slightly different dark-green bugle.

10. 1/7th Battalion, Manchester Regiment: dark-green fleur-de-lys, worn on helmet; from the regimental cap-badge, the 7th Battalion wearing a fleur-de-lys for a considerable period before it was adopted by the regiment's regular battalions in 1923.

11. 10th Battalion, Durham Light Infantry: red patch in the shape of the crowned-bugle cap-badge.

12. 1st Battalion, Leinster Regiment: white maple-leaf on dark-green rectangle, worn on helmet; a reference to the regiment's subsidiary title 'Royal Canadians', the old 100th Foot (later 1st Battalion, Leinsters) being raised in Canada in 1858. The 7th Battalion wore a green maple-leaf of different design.

Bottom row, left to right:

13. 1st Battalion, Monmouthshire Regiment: black dragon, from the regimental cap-badge.

14. 173rd Machine-Gun Company: black crossed machine-guns and crown on medium-green square; from the corps' cap-badge. Similar badges were used by other M/G companies, e.g., 8th (yellow on green triangle), 10th (green on khaki), 23rd (red on green, guns marked in black), 24th (red on white), 25th (red on yellow), 33rd (white on

9.   10.   11.   12.

13.   14.   15.   16.

dark green), 43rd (red on khaki), 143rd (white on blue triangle), 172nd (black on yellow), 174th (black on red). Among those using the crossed guns without the crown were the 34th (black on yellow) and 218th (black on red disc).

15. 25th Trench-Mortar Battery: dark-blue grenade on yellow square, the grenade (insignia of the Royal Artillery) representing the projectile used by the battery. Similar designs were used by other T/M batteries: 23rd (black on green arc), 24th (blue on white disc), 70th, 112th and 148th (blue on khaki) and 111th (blue on khaki oval, right sleeve).

16. 18th Ammunition Sub-Park, Army Service Corps: red shell on black triangle, representing the ammunition-supply function of the unit. Similar shell badges were worn by trench-mortar batteries, e.g., 63rd (yellow shell over blue grenade on khaki oval), 111th (blue shell, left sleeve).

Details of many similar insignia can be found in *British Battle Insignia 1914–18*, M. Chappell, London 1986; and in *Identification Pamphlet No. 2: British Miscellaneous Cloth Formation Signs and Titles*, Major J. Waring, privately published, n.d.

SOURCES AND BIBLIOGRAPHY

As noted in the previous titles of this series, much interesting material can be found in the illustrated periodicals of the time, for example the *Illustrated War News*, *War Illustrated* and *The Great War* among those published in Britain. (It is interesting to observe that the former, which had run weekly from the beginning of the war, ceased publication in mid-April 1918, the reason given being a need to conserve paper). As in previous *Fotofax* titles, there is space to list only a few works below, of which some concern the 1918 campaigns, while others are of more 'general' use:

Barker, A. J. *The Neglected War: Mesopotamia 1914–18*, London 1967.

Bullock, D. L. *Allenby's War*, London 1988 (Palestine campaign).

Chappell, M. *British Battle Insignia 1914–18*, London 1986.

— *The British Soldier in the 20th Century*, Hatherleigh, series from 1987.

Fosten, D. S. V., and Marrion, R. J. *The British Army 1914–18*, London 1978.

— *The German Army 1914–18*, London 1978.

Dunn, J. C. *The War the Infantry Knew 1914–19*, 1938 (new edn., ed. K. Simpson, London 1987) (outstanding account of the war from battalion level).

Hicks, J. E. *French Military Weapons*, New Milford, Connecticut, 1964.

Laffin, J. *Western Front 1917–18: the Cost of Victory*, Sydney 1988.

Livesey, A. *Great Battles of World War I*, London 1989 (good introduction to the major actions of the whole war).

Middlebrook, M. *The Kaiser's Battle: 21 March 1918: The First Day of the German Spring Offensive*, London 1978 (major study of Ludendorff's opening offensive).

Mollo, A. *Army Uniforms of World War I*, Poole 1977 (the most outstanding work on the subject).

Nash, D. B. *German Infantry 1914–18*, Edgeware 1971.

— *Imperial German Army Handbook 1914–18*, London 1980.

Nash, D. B. (ed.) *German Army Handbook April 1918*, London 1977.

Walter, A. (ed.). *Guns of the First World War*, London 1988 (reprint of the *Text Book of Small Arms*, 1909).

Wilson, H. W. (ed.) *The Great War*, London 1918–19 (contemporary periodical, containing much significant photography and artwork).

Most useful for the campaigns of the whole war are the atlases:

Banks, A. *A Military Atlas of the First World War*, London 1975.

Gilbert, M. *First World War Atlas*, London 1970.

44. The partnership between Paul von Hindenburg (1847–1934) and Erich von Ludendorff (1865–1937) began when the latter was sent to Hindenburg as chief of staff in late 1914; it remained of considerable significance, if not quite in the Blücher/Gneisenau mould of a century before. Here, Hindenburg (left) is pictured with Ludendorff (right) at Avesnes, the town in northern France (midway between Brussels and Rheims) which was the site of the German general headquarters. Hindenburg retains the 1910-pattern tunic with buttons visible; Ludendorff and the officer in the background wear the 1915 *Bluse* with fly-front.

44▲　45▼

45. German infantry double forward to an attack with hand-grenades. Grenades increased greatly in importance in the later stages of the war, forming a principal weapon of the German 'assault detachments' or stormtroops, who were often equipped with haversacks fabricated from sandbags in which the grenades were carried, as used by the man second from the front of this file. Equipment was often reduced to a minimum; it was common for pistols to be carried by grenadiers instead of rifles. The metal cylinders are containers for gas masks. Despite the late date of the photograph, at least two of these men wear the 1910 *Waffenrock* with its decorated rear pocket-flaps.

▲46 ▼47

46. Members of a German assault detachment with French prisoners, dated 26 June 1918. This shows the equipment of the 'stormtroops' extremely well: all wear the 1910 *Waffenrock*, two with shoulder-straps removed (probably to prevent easy identification), and some have puttees in place of the high boots. The helmets have fabric covers, and the minimum of equipment is carried, including grenade-sacks probably fabricated from sandbags. The small rectangular box carried on the front of the tunic by two of the stormtroops is a portable torch. The French prisoners wear a variety of styles, but where collar-insignia is visible it identifies them as members of the 65th Chasseurs. (Dr. John Hall)

47. Ferdinand Foch (1851–1929) was appointed commander of the Allied armies on the Western Front, and later overall. His elevation was primarily an attempt to co-ordinate Allied effort, rather than from any obvious military genius, but undoubtedly he had very considerable talents indeed. In August 1918 he was promoted to Marshal, and was accorded the rank of Field Marshal by Britain in recognition of his invaluable efforts. Here he wears the horizon-blue service uniform with a British-style Sam Browne belt, and the scarlet staff kepi with dark-blue band bearing the two rows of gold oak-leaves of a *général de division*; *générals de brigade* had one row, marshals three. The cord around the neck was for his *pince-nez* spectacles.

48. *L'entente cordiale* at its most visible: French infantry provide the covering-party for a British Vickers gun team during the German spring offensive. Intermingling of Allied troops was common at this period, whereas in the previous static trench warfare, each army had its own designated section of the line. The central figure lying behind the ditch is an officer, apparently consulting his map-case.

49. The German spring offensive which broke the Allied line heralded a period of fluid manoeuvre not seen since the establishment of the trench-systems in 1914. This canal-crossing is protected by a British 18pdr field-gun in a most exposed position. It shows how the gun was crewed; the gunner with his back to the camera is sitting upon a seat attached to the carriage. Visible at the end of the tubular trail is the handspike for traversing the gun, and the spade-shaped base-plate which would sink into soft terrain to stabilize the trail.

50. Armoured cars found useful employment only in mobile warfare, not the static conditions of the Western Front trenches; but the fluid campaigning following the German breakthrough of March 1918 allowed them to be used with more success. Here, Canadian infantry file past a somewhat unusual, semi-protected vehicle mounting two Vickers guns. The 1st Canadian Armoured Machine Gun Brigade was equipped with light trucks manufactured by the Autocar Company of Pennsylvania, with armoured cab and hinged, folding side-panels. These proved useful in the attempts to halt the German advance, but their casualties were considerable, as unlike most conventional armoured cars they had no armoured turret but were open at the top, and thus resembled a mobile machine-gun nest rather than an armoured fighting vehicle.

48▲

49▲   50▼

51. Typical of the mobile warfare which followed the great German attack is this scene of French infantry dug into small trenches, sometimes styled *trous de loup* or 'wolf-pits'. This hastily established position has been set up to sweep the road with fire from the light-machine gun at left, apparently a Modèle 1915 or Chauchat gun. An observer with binoculars is in the forward position.

▲51

52. A German machine-gun battery overlooking the coast at Zeebrugge. Several nations employed naval units in a land-based role, most notably the British Royal Naval Division. Not all such formations wore military-style uniform: these German sailors, equipped with the 1908 *Maschinengewehr*, wear naval uniform, including the 'sailor's collar', a relic of the neckerchief worn by mariners in the eighteenth century, visible on the uniform of one of the men in the trench between the two guns.

▲52　▼53

53. One of the most famous warships of the period was HMS *Vindictive*, a 2nd-class cruiser of 1897 used in the operations to wreck the German U-boat offensive by blocking their access to the North Sea at Zeebrugge and Ostend. *Vindictive* was used in the raid on Zeebrugge on St. George's Day, 1918 (23 April), and was sunk as a blockship at Ostend on 10 May. This, the most audacious amphibious operation of the war, was conducted by Roger Keyes, perhaps the most able naval commander of the period. This illustration shows *Vindictive*, shot to pieces, at Ostend; the vessel was broken up in 1920.

54. An unusual vantage-point on the Western Front: a Scottish infantry outpost. A Lewis gun is positioned in the foreground; the lance-corporal (standing by the tree) has a khaki apron over his kilt, but the lookout up the tree wears the kilt uncovered. All appear to wear the sleeveless leather jerkin, and the lookout may be carrying his equipment bandolier-style in a rolled blanket.

55. The passage of wheeled vehicles over terrain devastated by shell-fire was extremely difficult, or sometimes impossible. Illustrated here is a British artillery team struggling along by the Canal du Nord near Cambrai; a destroyed bridge is visible in the background. At the left is a British digging-party, with their officer at the right of the group; despite the heavy nature of this work, all wear helmets and carry the respirator on the breast, presumably evidence of the comparative proximity of the enemy.

54 ▲   55 ▼

56. A somewhat unmilitary-looking German soldier surrenders to British troops. The collapse of the German spring offensive and the end of trench warfare led to much more 'open' fighting, during which large numbers of Germans surrendered once their position became hopeless; between July 1918 and the end of the war about 385,000 prisoners were taken. As was not unusual in hot weather, these British troops wear shorts, in this case with knee-length woollen stockings instead of puttees; their equipment is reduced to a minimum for combat, basically the 1908-pattern cartridge-pouches and belts and the gas mask on the breast.

▲56　▼57

57. Despite the introduction of the steel helmet, the *Pickelhaube* remained in use, as worn here by Field Marshal Hindenburg at an inspection of his own 3rd Foot Guards on 18 August 1918. This ceremonial parade marked the anniversary of the battle of Gravelotte-St-Privat (1870) in which the Prussian Guard made a series of heroic attacks against the French defenders of St-Privat la Montaigne: an echo of a war in which German arms had markedly more success than being enjoyed at the time of the parade. The men in the ranks appear to wear the 1915 fly-fronted *Bluse*, but the officer on Hindenburg's right has the 1915 modification of the *Waffenrock*, with turned-back cuffs like the *Bluse* but with buttons visible on the breast. Note the white lace bars (*Litzen*), dull silver for officers, indicative of Guard status, visible on the collars and on Hindenburg's cuffs.

58. Despite the increasing use of motorized transport, horse-drawn vehicles continued to represent a major portion of the mobile capacity of most armies. This French wagon-train is parked outside the church of Lassigny, a short distance from Noyon, a town which passed into German hands in late March – early April 1918, almost at the junction of the zones of operation of the British Fifth and the French Sixth Armies. Devastating as this damage appears, it was not as severe as that in other towns which were virtually erased from the map by successive bombardments.

59. The entry into the war of a number of smaller nations resulted in large numbers of military attachés and missions visiting the Western Front, increasing the number of uniforms on view. It was reported that one Roumanian observer arrived at the Western Front wearing a plumed head-dress and a spectacular sky-blue cloak, much to the astonishment of the Royal Artillery battery detailed to look

58▲

after him! This group of Allied observers, obviously watching an aircraft, includes British, French, American (with the felt 'campaign hat'), possibly a Portuguese (with the muffler) and, in the light-coloured trench-coat, Major Prince Amoradhat of Siam.

60. Siam entered the war

against Germany on 22 July 1917. Siam's King Chulalongkorn was succeeded in 1910 by Crown Prince Somdetch Maha Vajiravudh, who took the title of King Rama IV in 1917; being Sandhurst-educated, he doubtless felt some sympathy towards Britain. A Siamese mission to the Western Front in early 1918 was led by

Major-General Phya Bijai Janriddhi (seated left, with other members of his mission), and despite the very limited size of the Siamese armed forces an expeditionary force landed at Marseilles in August 1918, comprising an ambulance unit and aviators who were trained by the French. The war ended before they saw action.

59▼　　　　　　　　　　　60▼

▲ 61

61. A wedding group featuring officers of the King's Own Scottish Borderers. Accompanying the original photograph of this happy scene is an extract from Lieutenant-Colonel W. D. Croft's *Three Years with the 9th (Scottish) Division* (London 1919) which records the heroic death in action during the German spring offensive of 'that firebrand' A. C. Campbell, an 'incomparable leader whom we could ill spare'. Captain (Temporary Major) Aubone Charles Campbell, DSO, 1st Battalion, KOSB, died on 3 April 1918 on attachment to the 11th Battalion, Royal Scots. Recording the association of this extract with the photograph reproduced here seems almost to be an intrusion into private grief; but it was shared by millions of families between 1914 and 1918.

62. An especial poignancy is attached to the fate of soldiers killed immediately before the cessation of hostilites. Lieutenant Donald Stuart McGregor of the 6th Battalion, Royal Scots (attached 29th Battalion, Machine Gun Corps) was killed at Hoogmolen on 22 October 1918, less than three weeks before the Armistice, in circumstances of great gallantry, bringing his guns into action in the face of impossible fire. He was awarded the Victoria Cross. Six days before his death he had celebrated his 23rd birthday. In this photograph he wears the uniform of the Royal Scots, the small letter 'T' beneath his collar-badge indicating a Territorial battalion.

63. Some of the most difficult terrain over which the war was waged was on the Italian Front, where units of specialist mountain troops were especially valuable. This Austrian alpine outpost shows

▼ 62

▼ 63

several items of distinctive equipment: rucksacks appear to be carried in place of the ordinary pack, an alpenstock is visible, and white camouflage coats or smocks are in evidence. As far as can be seen, the men wear the standard Austrian legwear of trousers with integral gaiters, not the breeches and long woollen stockings favoured by the *Kaiserschützen* units (the original *Landesschützen*, in 1917 granted the 'imperial' title

as a mark of distinction for their excellent service).

64. The terrain of the Italian Front made transportation of weapons and supplies difficult, but the existence of passable roads and motorized transport made feasible even the movement of such heavy ordnance as illustrated here. This Italian gun is accompanied by motor-lorries with solid wheels. The standard military lorry developed for the Italian

Army was the Fiat 18BL (and derivatives), of which hundreds were manufactured and which were also employed by the French and British forces on the Italian Front.

65. French light infantry on the Italian Front, distinguished by their dark-blue berets, originally a mark of alpine troops. At the head is a bugler carrying a small trumpet-banner on his bugle, an item normally used only on ceremonial occasions. Note the

hooked alpenstocks carried strapped to the side of the knapsack; a unit *fanion* (marker-flag) is just visible, attached to the bugler's rifle. At left is an Italian wearing the grey-green uniform with fly-fronted tunic; at right is a British soldier whose cap-badge identifies him as a member of King Edward's Horse (King's Overseas Dominions Regiment), which served with XI Corps in Italy from December 1917 to March 1918.

64▲

65▼

66. The opportunities for employing cavalry were so limited after the opening months of the war that most armies dismounted many of their horsed regiments and used them as infantry. Cavalry divisions were kept in being, however, and in some areas – for example Palestine – were of immense value. The Northamptonshire Yeomanry, shown here fording a river in Italy, served as 'divisional cavalry' (i.e., attached to infantry divisions) from early 1915; moving to Italy in November 1917, they served until the end of the year as 'corps cavalry' of XIV Corps.

67. 'Kaiser Bill' in unusual guise, wearing Austrian uniform in honour of the Emperor Karl's visit to the German headquarters at Spa in August 1918. Kaiser Wilhelm II (1859–1941) was vilified by his enemies to a level probably unprecedented in Europe since the defeat of Napoleon, and was much caricatured, his moustache lending itself to lampoons. Three months after this photograph he abdicated and went into exile in Holland, having been advised that suicide was the only other course of action open to him. Here he wears the stiff-sided grey kepi restricted to Austrian general staff personnel, worn in preference to the soft field-cap of the rest of the army, bearing the Austrian cockade on the front, gold with black centre.

68. King Ferdinand of Bulgaria, who according to the constitution of that country wielded absolute military power, being commander-in-chief with power of dismissal or promotion over the army, which he extended to control over subservient ministers. Upon the collapse of the Bulgarian military effort he abdicated in favour of his son Boris (4 October 1918). Here he wears German field uniform, showing the fabric *Pickelhaube-*

cover to good effect; the red collar-patches bore a gold-embroidered ornament representing a tassel-ended loop, the distinctive device for general officers. He wears a number of decorations awarded by friendly nations, including low on the left side the Prussian Iron Cross and immediately above it the distinctive breast-star of the Austrian Order of Maria Theresa.

69. Bulgarian infantry advancing into shell-fire near Monastir. Their uniform is of Russian style with peaked cap, officially the 1908–pattern grey-green type, but shortages during the war led to the use of the previous brown uniform, and considerable quantities of German supplies, upon which Bulgaria depended for its war effort. The large German cash subsidy was withdrawn in January 1918, and no further munitions were sent after March, which hastened Bulgaria's exit from the war. There was considerable internal unrest within the country, order having to be restored by some of the German troops used to bolster the Bulgarian Army.

70. The Serbian Army was re-equipped by the Allied nations following its re-location in the Salonika area. This photograph shows clearly the adaptation of French uniform for Serbian service: the French Adrian helmet has the Serbian coat of arms applied in pressed metal on the front. The cap worn under the helmet, and the sheepskin poncho-like garment tied with string, were common additions to combat the winter weather.

69▲ 70▼

▲71

▲72 ▼73

Salonika region. This typical group illustrates the use of Allied *matériel* with which the reconstituted Serbian Army was equipped, most obviously the French Adrian helmet. The man in the foreground with a blanket or greatcoat worn bandolier-fashion carries at his waist the semi-circular drum-magazines for the French Modèle 1915 Automatic rifle or Chauchat gun.

73. Entertainments for the troops were an important method of maintaining morale, to which end unit concert-parties were given official sanction. The British 26th Division maintained a concert-party called 'The Splints', whose writer and producer was Sergeant Weston Drury of the Royal Army Medical Corps, seen here wearing a general's uniform and George Robey-style eyebrows (right). The 26th Division arrived in the Macedonian theatre in late 1915 and served there for the remainder of the war: the RAMC units (Drury's corps) were the 78th, 79th and 80th Field Ambulances.

74. The prevarication of the Greek administration led to a long delay before official Greek Army units saw action in the war. Mobilization was only completed in April 1918, and by July some ten Greek divisions, about a quarter of a million

71. This Serbian infantryman on the Salonika Front is armed with the French Modèle 1915 Automatic Rifle, known as the Chauchat gun after the designer of the 1907 pattern upon which the 1915 was based. The semi-circular drum magazine held twenty 8mm cartridges; it was capable of a rate of fire of 240 rounds per minute. The gun was air-cooled by means of an aluminium radiator over the barrel, as shown here. It was mounted with a shoulder-stock but was not held like a rifle but by two pistol-grips, mounted forward and behind the trigger. Note here the protective shield, and the fabric cover worn over the Adrian helmet.

72. Serbian infantry forming part of the Allied forces in the

men, were at the disposal of the Allied command, for the first time giving the Allies a definite numerical superiority on the Macedonian Front. Greek troops first saw action on 30 May at Skra di Legen, and on 22 September fought well alongside the British in the assault on the Doiran heights. This Greek pack-train was photographed before mobilization was completed; the Greek Army adopted a greenish-khaki field uniform from 1912, worn here with the ubiquitous Adrian helmet, apparently with fabric covers.

75. The collapse of the Russian war effort following the 1917 Revolution led to Roumania's exit from the war, further resistance being impossible without Russian assistance. Relations with the new Russian government deteriorated so severely that in January 1918 Roumanian troops marched into Bessarabia and some conflict occurred against the Bolsheviks. The intended Roumanian union with Bessarabia was thwarted by a threat of renewed hostilities by the Central Powers, and

74 ▲   75 ▼

◀76

Roumania was forced to sign a humiliating peace by the Treaty of Bucharest (May 1918). In this photograph, Roumanian officers (probably wearing the French horizon-blue uniform introduced to replace the grey-green in 1916, but which was only common among officers) receive direction from a French instructor (second from front) in the use of the Chauchat gun.

76. The service uniform of the Turkish Army remained unchanged throughout the war, but shortages of clothing and equipment were endemic. This

man wears a mixture of regulation dress and the improvisations which were common during the whole period: the khaki tunic of a somewhat German style is an item of regulation dress, but the 'native' sandals and strips of cloth in place of stockings are worn to compensate a shortage of the proper boots and khaki puttees. The cloth skull-cap was a common feature in place of the so-called 'Enver Pasha helmet'; when the latter was unavailable, some Turkish troops improvised loose turbans as a protection against the sun.

▲77

77. General Sir Edmund Allenby (1861–1936, later Field Marshal and 1st Viscount) was one of the most capable commanders of the war, whose presence was of major significance in the Palestine theatre. Nicknamed 'the bull' from his physique and short temper, his reputation concealed a sensitive side to his nature which included a great interest in literature and ornithology. His influence upon the Arabs was profound: they rendered his name *al-Nabi* ('prophet'), and so his entry into Jerusalem in December 1917 was seen as fulfilling the ancient prophecy of the coming of a messiah to free the Arabs from Ottoman domination. Here he poses by a captured German Albatros aircraft.

▲78 ▼79

78. The technology of modern war spread to even the most distant theatres of campaign: here, members of the King's African Rifles receive instruction from British officers in the use of the Lewis gun. The East African campaign lasted until the very end of hostilities despite the small number of German troops employed: virtually a guerrilla war, it was largely a matter of raid and pursuit, in which the KAR formed a most valuable part of the Allied effort.

79. An offshoot of the main Mesopotamian campaign was the expedition to Baku in Russian Transcaucasia (now Azerbaidzhjan), intended to deny that region's oil-fields to the Turks. Part of the Allied forces sent on the expedition was the British 39 Brigade of the 13th Division; the British formed the backbone of the defence against Turkish attack, as the Russian and Armenian troops also involved were of limited value. This photograph shows the 7th (Service) Battalion, North Staffordshire Regiment during the expedition; they wear tropical uniform as used in India, including shorts and topees. Note the Lewis gun in the foreground. (The other battalions involved were the 9th

Royal Warwickshires, 7th Gloucestershires and 9th Worcestershires).

80. The Russian Revolution and the ending of hostilities between Russia and the Central Powers did not bring peace to that country, but instead heralded further extensive conflict between the Bolsheviks and their 'White' opponents, a civil war which dragged on until 1920 and involved contingents from several of the Allied nations in support of the 'Whites'. This heavily armed armoured train formed part of the anti-Bolshevik forces in eastern Siberia, where Colonel Semenov and a force of loyal Cossacks maintained the fight against the 'Reds'.

81, 82. German baggage-wagons retreating through Belgium in November 1918. The vehicles halted in this small town-square represent a typical selection of army transport, a few motor vehicles but the majority horse-drawn; the crews mostly wear the comfortable soft cap (*Mütze*) in preference to the helmet. The smoke rises from a portable field-kitchen, a wheeled vehicle with a fire which could be kept burning on the march. From its chimney, which was stowed horizontally for transportation and which gave the appearance of a gun-barrel, the vehicle was commonly styled a *Gulasch-kanone* ('stew-gun').

80▲

81▲   82▼

▲83

▲84 ▼85

83. Architects of victory: a visit by Allied leaders to Cambrai, shortly after its recovery from the Germans in 1918. Sir Douglas (later Earl) Haig (1861–1928), commander-in-chief of the British armies on the Western Front, is shown at left; sometimes castigated as a slaughterer of his own forces, Haig was no worse a general than many in the war, and performed his duties earnestly. In the centre is Georges Clemenceau (1841–1929), President of France from late 1917, whose implacable determination to win the war at all costs sustained French resistance at a time of great difficulty. The unit presenting arms appears to be French *gendarmerie*, wearing that formation's black collar-patch bearing a white grenade, and carrying pistols on the left side of the waist-belt.

84. The symbol of victory: French Moroccan troops dip their *fanions* in the Rhine shortly after the Armistice. These company marker-flags were coloured to identify both battalion and company. For example, the *ler RTA* (*Régiment de Tirailleurs algériens*) had fanions blue, red, yellow and green respectively for the 1st-4th battalions, with the border, a crescent in each corner and central device of an open hand in sky-blue, pink, light-yellow and light-green for the 1st-4th company of each battalion. The *fanions* of the 5th-8th battalions were like those of the 1st-4th but with a vertical white stripe down the centre. (Not all were so simple in design: the 156th Infantry's 10th Company flag depicted a bunch of holly and the motto *Qui s'y frotte s'y pique!*). The officers in the foreground wear the amended and less-conspicuous rank-markings on the lower sleeve, one to three metallic lace bars for company officers and four or five for field ranks.

85. The multi-national aspect of the French Army is illustrated by this parade at the headquarters of Général Charles

Mangin (1866–1925) at Mainz: the band (centre) wear the ordinary greatcoat and Adrian helmet, the North African corps of drums in the foreground wear the *chéchia* or zouave cap, and in the left background are Spahis with voluminous cloaks. The detachment in the background with a flag is a unit of British seamen. Mangin was restored to the Tenth Army after a hiatus in his career caused by the disasters of the 'Nivelle offensive'; a great supporter of the employment of colonial troops, his beliefs are evident from the title of one of his books: *La Force Noire*.

86. A symbol of defeat: the headquarters of the German delegation to the Armistice Commision at Spa, the site of the German General Headquarters. Despite the presence of an armed German sentry, the white flag on the car emphasizes the defeat of the Central Powers, as does the notice-board written in English, 'International Armistice Commission'.

87. The German war effort collapsed amid internal conflict and mutiny among elements of the armed forces, culminating in a brief but violent insurrection by the Spartacist movement of revolutionary socialists who attempted to establish a new regime in Germany akin to that of the Bolsheviks in Russia. Led by Karl Liebknecht (1871–1919) and Rosa Luxemburg (1870–1919), the Spartacists began an armed revolt which was crushed by troops loyal to the government. Liebknecht was shot after capture, ostensibly while attempting to escape, and 'Red Rosa' was murdered in custody. This detachment of loyal troops has occupied a Spartacist position in Berlin; note the use of brassards, a return to the seventeenth-century practice of 'field-signs' to distinguish members of opposing factions whose costume was similar.

86 ▲ 87 ▼

▲88

▲89 ▼90

88. German infantry deploy in a Berlin street in opposition to the Spartacist revolutionaries. The troops wear a mixture of uniforms, including the 1915 *Bluse* with fly-front, the 1915 modification of the 1910 *Waffenrock* with turned-up cuffs, and the original 1910 tunic, some with three strips of *Litzen* (the lace loops indicative of Guard status) on the 'Brandenburg'-style cuff-flaps.

89. A measure of the collapse of Germany at the end of the war is the deployment of flamethrower teams in Berlin: that such measures would be necessary in the capital of the German Empire would have been thought preposterous even months before. The detachment is led by an NCO wearing a peaked cap, and includes a medical orderly wearing the peakless cloth *Mütze* and red cross brassard. The flamethrowers are the lightest pattern, the Wex introduced in 1917, of circular construction with a spherical gas container in the centre. Unlike the earlier patterns of *Flammenwerfer*, it was ignited automatically and did not require a naked flame to be applied to the nozzle.

90. The homecoming: a scene repeated throughout Europe and American with varying degrees of celebration. The London Scottish (14th County of London) was the first Territorial unit to see combat during the war, and here marches through London after the end of hostilities. They retain their Elcho-grey kilts (some here with khaki aprons), tunics cut away at the front to resemble a Scottish doublet, and Tam o'Shanters; the officers wear glengarries. Sixty-three of the unit's officers were killed in the war, a heavy toll for a single battalion.

91. Military hospitals had to treat an unprecedented number of casualties, so that numerous small establishments were opened as convalescent hospitals in addition to the main medical centres. This scene depicts one, where three convalescents have had their beds moved outside to take advantage of the fresh air. The fully dressed soldier lying on the bed at right wears 'hospital blues', the blue jacket and trousers which was the distinctive uniform of British and Empire convalescent servicemen.

91▲ 92▼

92. For countless families, the only mementoes of a lost relative were posthumous medals and a photograph such as this, showing the final resting-place of a loved one, here with its temporary marker. Although the inscription (in metal tape) is not visible on the two central markers, the more elaborate, painted cross at the left commemorates Major James Wightman, DSO, MC, East Surrey Regiment, who died of wounds on 9 April 1918. The inscription on the cross records the description of the Seigneur de Bayard: 'Without fear and without reproach'. Major Wightman was aged 26.

Ferdinand Foch (1851-1929)

Ferdinand Foch was arguably the most notable commander of the war, but he was distinguished initially as a military theorist and only later as a field commander.

Born at Tarbes, the son of a civil servant and grandson of an officer of Napoleon's army, he interrupted his studies to enlist as a private soldier during the Franco-Prussian War, but saw no active service. Graduating from the *Ecole Polytechnique* in 1873, he was commissioned into the artillery. As a captain, he trained at the *Ecole de Guerre* (the French staff college) 1885-7, graduating in fourth place. After employment with the general staff he returned there in 1895 as assistant professor, and from 1898 professor, of military history and tactics. There he developed the theories published as *Principes de la Guerre* (1903), a work extremely influential on French military thought, emphasising the importance of psychological superiority over an enemy, the idea that a general was not beaten until he believed he was, and the importance of offensive warfare.

In 1900, Foch returned to regimental duty, his progress probably blocked (at a time of some turmoil in the French military establishment) by his Roman Catholicism (he had been educated at two Jesuit colleges and his brother was a Jesuit priest), and not until 1903 was he promoted to colonel. In 1908, after promotion to general of brigade and a period as deputy chief of general staff, he was personally selected by Clemenceau as commandant of the *Ecole de Guerre*; in 1911 he was promoted to general of division and in 1913 was given command of XX Corps.

Foch performed well in the first campaign of the World War (his first experience of combat), and on 28 August 1914 assumed command of the newly-formed Ninth Army. In the Battle of the Marne he acted with the optimism and aggression demonstrated in his writings, never expressed better than by his famous statement, 'My centre is giving way, my right is in retreat; situation excellent: I shall attack'. On 4 October 1914 Joffre appointed him his deputy, and gave him control of the Northern Army Group in January 1915.

The experience of warfare on the western front caused a change in Foch's attitudes, an appreciation that the attrition of limited attacks in different areas could be equally effective as a concentration upon offence and the will to win. In 1916 he participated in the Battle of the Somme, but without a clear success on his own account he was too closely associated with Joffre to avoid the results of the latter's fall. Consequently, Foch was transferred from field command to a comparatively unimportant planning role, and sent to discuss with Italian general headquarters how France could react in the event of Italy requiring support.

The failure of the 'Nivelle offensive' and the dismissal of General Robert Nivelle caused Foch to be appointed chief of general staff (15 May 1917), but the real power in the French Army still resided with Nivelle's successor, Henri-Philippe Pétain. Following serious reverses on the Italian front, Foch returned to Italy to arrange the Franco-British support for the shaken Italian army, which demonstrated his capacity for coordinating various Allied forces; but the event which had most bearing upon his career was the appointment on 16 November 1917 of Georges Clemenceau as French prime minister.

Consequently, Foch now possessed the most powerful political ally, whose influenced extended far beyond France.

The Rapallo Conference in November 1917 established the concept of a Supreme War Council, to coordinate Allied strategy on all fronts. At the crucial time of the 'Ludendorff offensive', Foch was appointed coordinator of the Anglo-French forces on the western front, to which the British prime minister, David Lloyd George, acceded with alacrity, as it gave him greater control over the British commander-in-chief, Sir Douglas Haig. Foch's responsibilities increased from the right to give directions to both armies until on 14 April 1918 he was named as Allied commander-in-chief, over the head of his erstwhile superior, Pétain. This gave Foch almost complete jurisdiction over the western front (including the Americans, but not until September 1918 did his authority extend to the Belgian Army), and in June 1918 his command was extended to include Italy.

In the spring and early summer of 1918, Foch coordinated the Allied defence against the German assault, and then organised the counter-attack which won the war in the west. While maintaining his natural optimism and offensive spirit, he was cautious when necessary and his well-planned advances featured a number of thrusts in preference to concentration upon a single breakthrough. He described himself in terms of the conductor of an orchestra who beat time well, which has some truth in it: a coordinator of allies who succeeded not only through his own strategic skill but also by his personality, treating his allies as he would his own countrymen. He was as conscious, he remarked, of serving Britain as he was of serving France.

In the immediate post-war period Foch advocated that even more severe terms be imposed upon Germany, which brought him into conflict with Clemenceau; but he chose not to enter the world of politics to pursue his case. Foch was justifiably loaded with honours after the war; having been appointed a Marshal of France on 6 August 1918, he became a Field-Marshal of Great Britain on 19 July 1919, the first Frenchman so honoured since Jean Louis, Earl Ligonier (appointed 30 November 1757), but an even more singular honour in that Foch had never served in the British Army. The awards were fully merited: not only had Foch commanded one of the largest forces in history, he was one of the truly great military figures of the twentieth century.

References

Foch, Marshal F. *Memoirs of Marshal Foch*, London 1931.

Foch, Marshal F. *Principles of War*, London 1918.

Herwig, H.H., & Heyman, N.M. *Biographical Dictionary of World War I*, Westport, Connecticut, 1982.

Hunter, T.M. *Marshal Foch: a Study in Leadership*, Ottawa 1961.

Liddell Hart, Sir Basil *Foch: the Man of Orleans*, London 1931.

Liddell Hart, Sir Basil *Reputations*, London 1928.

Marshal Cornwall, General Sir James *Foch as Military Commander*, London 1972.